EVERYDAY DRINKING

THE DISTILLED
Kingsley Amis

BLOOMSBURY

New York • Berlin • London

Published by Bloomsbury USA, New York

All papers used by Bloomsbury USA are natural, recyclable products made from wood grown in well-managed forests. The manufacturing processes conform to the environmental regulations of the country of origin.

LIBRARY OF CONGRESS CATALOGING-IN-PUBLICATION DATA HAS BEEN APPLIED FOR.

ISBN-10: 1-59691-528-5 (hardcover)
ISBN-13: 978-1-59691-528-2 (hardcover)

First published by Bloomsbury USA in 2008
This paperback edition published in 2010

Paperback ISBN: 978-1-59691-628-9

1 2 3 4 5 6 7 8 9 10

Design by Sara Stemen

Typeset by Westchester Book Group
Printed in the United States of America by Worldcolor Fairfield

CONTENTS

THE MUSE OF BOOZE

IT'S REASONABLY WELL known that the arts of brewing and fermenting arose in nice time for the dawn of human civilization (there are ancient poems and mosaics and that sort of thing, dedicated to the celebration of the fact), but it's at least as notorious that an opened flask of alcohol is a mouth that can lead to hell as well as heaven. This being the case—and one day we shall work out the etymology that leads us to use the simple Italian word for a bottle, *fiasco*, in the way that we do—then it is as well to have a true Virgil to be our guide through the regions infernal as well as paradisiac.

The late Sir Kingsley Amis (who wrote these slender but thoughtful volumes before receiving his knighthood and who was also the expert to consult on things like the derivation of *fiasco*) was what the Irish call "your man" when it came to the subject of drink. More perhaps even than of Graham Greene, of whom he once wrote a short biography, it could be said that the booze was his muse. I cannot think of any of his fictional work in which it does not play a role, and in several of his novels that role is dominant. (The famous hangover scene in *Lucky Jim*, not equaled for alcoholic comedy in our literature even by Shakespeare's night porter or portly knight, has only one rival that I can call to mind, and that is Peter Fallow's appalling waking moment in Tom Wolfe's *The Bonfire of the Vanities*.) Fiascos apart, other Amis books like *One Fat Englishman* and *The Green Man* contain some incidentally sapient advice about how to keep drinking and yet remain functional.

It has been said that alcohol is a good servant and a bad master. Nice try. The plain fact is that it makes other people, and indeed life itself, a good deal less boring. Kingsley grasped this essential fact very early in life, and (so to speak) never let go of the insight. This does not mean that there are not wine bores, single-malt bores, and people who become even more boring when they themselves have a tipple. You will meet them, and learn how to recognize them (and also how to deal with them) in these pages.

In my opinion Kingers—which I was allowed to call him—was himself a very slight cocktail bore. Or, at least, he had to affect to be such in order to bang out a regular column on drinks for the pages of a magazine aimed at the male population. In "real" life, Amis was a no-nonsense drinker with little inclination to waste a good barman's time with fussy instructions. However, there was an exception which I think I can diagnose in retrospect, and it is related to his strong admiration for the novels of Ian Fleming. What is James Bond really doing when he specifies the kind of martini he wants and how he wants it? He is telling the barman (or bartender if you must) that he knows what he is talking about and is not to be messed around. I learned the same lesson when I was a restaurant and bar critic for the *City Paper* in Washington, D.C. Having long been annoyed by people who called knowingly for, say, "a Dewar's and water" instead of a scotch and water, I decided to ask a trusted barman what I got if I didn't specify a brand or label. The answer was a confidential jerk of the thumb in the direction of a villainous-looking tartan-shaded jug under the bar. The situation was even grimmer with gin and vodka and became abysmal with "white wine," a thing I still can't bear to hear being ordered. If you don't state a clear preference, then your drink is like a bad game of poker or a hasty drug transaction: It is whatever the dealer says it is. Please do try to bear this in mind.

A tremendous thing about the King—some of us were even allowed to call him that, too—was his abhorrence of meanness. From him I learned the gruff rule of his own house, which was more warm if less polite than his civil "How's Your Glass?" It ran: "I'll pour you the first one and after that, if you don't have one, it's your own f***ing fault. You know where it is." (I have ever since told this to all my guests.) From these pages you will learn—see the Mean Sods and Mean Slags section—of the stern attitude he took to any parsimony. With alcoholic ritual, the whole point is generosity. If you open a bottle of wine, for heaven's sake have the grace to throw away the damn cork. If you are a guest and not a host, don't find yourself having to drop your glass and then exclaim (as Amis once did in my hearing) "Oh—thank heavens it was empty." The sort of host who requires that hint is the sort of host you should have avoided in the first place.

On the sometimes-penitential consequences of generosity, do by all means consult the brilliant chapter on the physical and metaphysical hangover. It is a piece of selfless research, undertaken by a pioneer. It can save much avoidable pain and, to my certain knowledge, has done so. Thanks to Zachary Leader's excellent biography, the world now knows what Kingsley's innumerable friends had come to realize, which is that the booze got to him in the end, and robbed him of his wit and charm as well as of his health. But not everybody can take their own advice, or not forever, and the cheerful and wise counsel offered here will not lead you, dear reader, far astray. Winston Churchill once boasted that he himself had got more out of drink than it had taken out of him and, life being the wager that it is, was quite probably not wrong in that. In these pages, we meet another man who made it work for him, and for others, too.

—CHRISTOPHER HITCHENS

Christopher Hitchens is a columnist for Vanity Fair *and a visiting professor of liberal studies at the New School in New York City.*

EDITOR'S NOTE AND GLOSSARY

THE BOOKS THAT make up this collection—*On Drink*, *Every Day Drinking* (from which we've borrowed a title), and *How's Your Glass*—were written by Amis between 1971 and 1984, a busy period that produced eight other books and a handful of edited volumes. They represent the work of a man whose interest in alcohol somewhat transcended the merely casual. Indeed, Amis was a drinker—even a drink-ist—a scholar and practitioner and, perhaps above all, a connoisseur.

Despite his occasional claims of ignorance, his knowledge of drink was stunning, even encyclopedic. And being encyclopedic, these volumes seem best presented in their unabridged state. This creates a certain amount of overlap in spots; like all drinking companions, Amis occasionally repeats himself. But like the very best of them, he is unfailingly entertaining, and to miss his second hilarious dissertation on Albanian wine, or Speyside scotch, or the affront of lager and lime, merely because there had been another one elsewhere in the book would be as self-denying as passing up a Laphroig simply because you'd had a Glenfiddich earlier in the evening.

So here is the complete, unexpurgated shelf of Amis's musings on drink, taking in history, etiquette, social mores, trade secrets, arcana, and, of course, the practical aspects of the convivial life. It is, like its author, gloriously, unremittingly British, so we've included here a short glossary to translate a few less familiar terms for American lovers of drink. Otherwise, this is the complete vintage Amis: uncut, unfiltered, and made only better by age. Bottoms up.

—ED.

best bitter: a middleweight division of the pale ales, which also include the weaker "session" or "ordinary" bitter (at up to 4.1 percent alcohol) and the more forceful "premium" or "strong" bitter (at a serious-minded 4.8 percent or more)

bibber: see *sod*

Black Velvet: a cocktail made from stout and sparkling white wine, traditionally Guinness and champagne

blower: telephone

bob: a shilling; that is, twelve pence, or one twentieth of a pound

Bovril: a traditional British beef-flavored concentrated yeast extract, served spread on toast or mixed with hot water as a beverage

brace cold snipe: one pair of room-temperature cooked birds

castor sugar: very finely granulated sugar

Chambéry: a raspberry (framboise) liqueur; substitute Chambord

champagne cider: an effervescent fermented cider produced using a method similar to the one used for champagne

chaptalization: a method of fortifying wine by adding sugar to the unfermented grapes

claret: Any of the wines of Bordeaux. The British affinity for these wines may be traced to the Middle Ages, when the area containing the region was held by the Norman crown. After King John granted the region tax exemptions in hopes of shoring up shaky loyalties, Bordeaux became a main source of wines (including its typical *clairet*) for England.

cobbler: a tall drink involving lemon, soda, sugar, and some kind of alcohol, notably gin, bourbon, or sherry

crown-cork opener: Neither cork nor crown, the crown cork is what we think of as the ordinary top of a glass beer bottle. The opener, originally manufactured by the Crown Cork & Seal Company, is the typical piece of bar apparatus.

Darby and Joan Club: a senior citizens' social club

dipsography: writing about drinking (typically refers to literary writing, not bar tabs, public-indecency citations, and the like)

Double Diamond: a bitters-style beer brewed by Carlsberg UK, reviled by some and fiercely loved by others

elevenses: a small midmorning meal, much like afternoon tea but typically eaten around 11:00 AM

extract spread and tablets: Marmite and its hideous kin of yeast extracts, unaccountably enjoyed by the British and Australians as a spread on toast

fruit machine: a slot machine

GLC: Greater London Council, the administrative body that served the city area from 1965 to 1986

hock: Any of the white wines produced along the German Rhine. The name derives from the Rheingau village of Hochheim. Think Riesling, if it's for you, or liebfraumilch, if you're serving company.

Husband's Scotch: a whiskey (like J & B) whose light color makes it appear more watered down than it is

local: neighborhood pub

look a charley: appear foolish or tasteless

long drink: a highball; opposed to *short drink*

Malvern water: English spring water, a traditional favorite of royalty and the ideal accompaniment to good scotch

mean: stingy; ungenerous; cheap; sensible

Montilla: a fino sherry, named after the Spanish town of Montilla-Morales, where it is produced

Moselle: a wine from the Mosel-Saar-Ruwer area of Germany

off-license: a shop licensed to sell liquor to be consumed off the premises; the term may be applied to ordinary liquor stores, areas within supermarkets, or (praise God) spirits shops attached to a pub

old stager: a veteran or old hand; in this context, presumably a longtime *bibber*, *sod*, *toper*, or *slag*

peach wine: Typically chardonnay wine with peach flavoring, this is still widely available and a favorite of avowed non-connoisseurs. Once described as "the perfect wine for sitting in front of the TV with."

Pimm's: a maker of alcohol, known for Pimm's No. 1, a gin-based drink

piss-up: a drinking bender

plonk: cheap alcohol

poteen: An aggressive species of Irish moonshine made from potatoes or, less often, from barley and yeast. It was outlawed by the English in 1670, with much the same effect that prohibition had in the United States. Despite the fact that doctors through the years have suggested it may lead to alcohol poisoning and even mental illness, and that commercial (presumably nonblinding) brands of poteen were made legal in 1997, many traditionalists still prefer the rough-hewn authenticity of the homebrewed stuff.

sack: A strong Spanish wine, the antecedent of sherry. The term may also apply to sweet wines from Madeira, Malaga, and the Canary Islands. Favored by Shakespeare's Falstaff, likely for its assertive alcohol content, as high as 16 percent.

Sassenach: a term (a bit derogatory) used by Scots to describe the English

SDP: Social Democratic Party

short drink: a lowball

slag: a drunken slattern; alternatively, a thrifty connoisseuress of drink

slivovitz: a colorless, brandy-like, and extremely dangerous alcohol made from fermented plum juice

sod: see *toper*

spanking: new and delightful

squash: a concentrated syrup made of filtered fruit juice, most commonly orange, lime, or blackcurrant, served in cocktails with water, seltzer, spirits, or a combination thereof

stand-up party: as opposed to a dinner party, a gathering at which food is served buffet-style

stroppy: impertinent

stune: in Irish slang, a college's student union

toper: drunkard; sot; convivial person

tot: one-thirtieth of a bottle of liquor; 25 ml

VAT: value-added tax

Worthington: English brewery noted for its Worthington's White Shield ale, a traditional IPA-style brew. Now owned by Coors, which still sells White Shield as a specialty ale.

yobbo: according to the OED, "a rude and loutish young man"

On Drink

INTRODUCTION

ANTHROPOLOGISTS ASSURE US that wherever we find man he speaks. Chimpanzee lovers notwithstanding, no animal other than man is capable of laughter. And, although some undiscovered tribe in the Brazilian jungle might conceivably prove an exception tomorrow, every present-day society uses alcohol, as have the majority of those of the past. I am not denying that we share other important pleasures with the brute creation, merely stating the basic fact that conversation, hilarity and drink are connected in a profoundly human, peculiarly intimate way.

There is a choice of conclusions from this. One would be that no such healthy linkage exists in the case of other drugs: a major reason for being on guard against them. More to the point, the collective social benefits of drinking altogether (on this evidence) outweigh the individual disasters it may precipitate. A team of American investigators concluded recently that, without the underpinning provided by alcohol and the relaxation it affords, Western society would have collapsed irretrievably at about the time of the First World War. Not only is drink here to stay; the moral seems to be that when it goes, we go too.

It has certainly increased its hold on our lives with the world-wide move to the towns and the general increase in prosperity. Wine and beer are—in origin, in the countries that produce them—drinks of the village and the poorer classes; gin and whisky belong to the city and, these days at any rate, the rather better off. In other words, our drinks are getting stronger as well as more numerous.

The strains and stresses of urban living, to coin a phrase, are usually held accountable for these increases. I should not dissent from this exactly, but I should single out one stress (or strain) as distinctly more burdensome, and also more wide-spread, than most: sudden confrontation with complete or comparative strangers in circumstances requiring a show of relaxation and amiability—an experience that I, for one, never look forward to without misgiving, even though I nearly always turn out to enjoy it in the event. While the village remained the social unit, strangers appeared seldom, and when they did were heavily outnumbered by your family, your friends, people you had known all your life. Nowadays, in the era of the business lunch, the dinner party, the office party, the anything-and-everything party, strangers pour over the horizon all the time.

The reason why I, and most others, usually turn out to enjoy meeting such creatures is simply and obviously the co-presence of drink. The human race has not devised any way of dissolving barriers, getting to know the other chap fast, breaking the ice, that is one-tenth as handy and efficient as letting you and the other chap, or chaps, cease to be totally sober at about the same rate in agreeable surroundings. Well and good, the serious student of the effects of drink will retort in the grim, curmudgeonly tone peculiar to serious students of the effects of drink; well and good, but what about what happens later? What about those who drink, not to cease to be totally sober, but to get drunk? What about the man who drinks *on his own*?

Well, what about it and them and him? I have nothing to offer, nothing more to add to serious sociological speculation about the whys and wherefores of indulgence in alcohol. Or only this: leaving aside dipsomaniacs, most or many of whom are born, not made, I feel that there is very little we can safely add, in discussing our motives for drinking, to the verdict of the poet who said we do it because "we are dry, or lest we may be by and by, or any other reason why."

Where and what and how we drink, or should drink, are different and more interesting questions. As to where, this is so much a matter of individual preference and geographical opportunity that I should drop it right away, except that it gives me a long-sought chance to deliver a short, grouchy blast against what has been done, and what is still being done, to that deeply, traditionally British drinking centre, the pub.

With some shining exceptions, of which my own local is one, the pub is fast becoming uninhabitable. Fifteen or twenty years ago, the brewing companies began to wake up to the fact that their pubs badly needed a face-lift, and started spending millions of pounds to bring them up to date. Some of the results of their refurbishings have been admirable: more and more comfortable seating, improved hygiene, chilled beers, snack lunches that in general have reached such a standard that, when in quest of a midday meal in unfamiliar territory, you will usually find quicker service and much better value for money in the pub than in the near-by trattoria.

But that is about as far as it goes. The interior of today's pub has got to look like a television commercial, with all the glossy horror that implies. Repulsive "themes" are introduced: the British-battles pub, ocean-liner pub, Gay Nineties pub. The draught beer is no longer true draught, but keg, that hybrid substance that comes out of what is in effect a giant metal bottle, engineered so as to be the same everywhere, no matter how lazy or incompetent the licensee, and, in the cases of at least two well-known, lavishly advertised brews, pretty nasty everywhere. But all this could be put up with cheerfully enough if it were not for the bloody *music*—or that kind of uproar having certain connections with a primitive style of music and known as pop. It is not really the pop as such that I object to, even though pop is very much the sort of thing that I, in common with most of the thirty- or thirty-five-plus age-group, would have expected to go to the pub to get away from. For partly different reasons, I should also object to having Beethoven's Choral Symphony blaring away while I tried to enjoy a quiet pint with friends. If you dislike what is being played, you use up energy and patience in the attempt to ignore it; if you like it, you will want to listen to it and not to talk or be talked to, not to do what you came to the pub largely to do.

I have always understood that pop and popular music came to pubs because the brewers hoped thereby to reverse the falling-off in the recruitment of younger patrons noticeable in the post-war period. If I am right in that assumption, then they were wrong in theirs. Pop not only tends to drive the older customer out; it fails to attract, and even keeps away, large sections of the young, including some who welcome pop *on its own ground*. (I wonder very much what would be the effect on the trade of a publican who put up a notice at his door saying, "No Music Inside." Will someone try it?) Anyway, we pay the pipers; we ought to be able to call the absence of tunes.

Until we can, many of us will prefer to drink in our own or our friends' homes. But here too, certainly in the homes of more than one or two friends of mine, the fairly serious, reasonably discriminating drinker can find plenty to offend him without having to look at all far. What most often springs to his eye is not being given enough. Those of us who are poor or mean cannot or will not do much about this. But for the benefit of those who are neither, who have merely got their priorities wrong, let me enunciate

> G.P. (General Principle) 1: *Up to a point (i.e. short of offering your guests one of those Balkan plonks marketed as wine, Cyprus sherry, poteen and the like), go for quantity rather than quality. Most people would rather have two glasses of ordinary decent port than one of a rare vintage. On the same reasoning, give them big drinks rather than small—with exceptions to be noted later. Serious drinkers will be pleased and reassured, unserious ones will not be offended, and you will use up less chatting-time going round to recharge glasses.*

My final observation, before getting down to details, is that serving good drinks, like producing anything worth while, from a poem to a motor-car, is troublesome and expensive. (If you are interested, a worthwhile poem is expensive to the poet in the sense that he could almost always earn more money by spending the time on some other activity.) But I undertake, in what follows, to keep a sharp eye on both points, to show where and how trouble can be minimized and to what degree you can legitimately cut down costs.

> It is the unbroken testimony of all history that alcoholic liquors have been used by the strongest, wisest, handsomest, and in every way best races of all times.
> —GEORGE SAINTSBURY

"If I had a thousand sons, the first human principle I would teach them should be, to forswear thin potations."

—WILLIAM SHAKESPEARE
(Falstaff, *Henry IV, Part 2*)

There's nought, no doubt, so much the spirit calms
    As rum and true religion.

—LORD BYRON

DRINKING LITERATURE

ONE INFALLIBLE MARK of your true drink-man is that he reads everything on the subject that comes his way, from full-dress books to those tiny recipe-leaflets the makers tend to hang round the necks of their bottles. Never, by the way, despise the latter sort of thing as a mere commercial handout; on the contrary, the manufacturer knows more about his product than anybody else and, never mind from what base motives, will have tested out his recommendations with the utmost care. These days, too, off-licence pricelists can offer a lot of straight information.

This policy of unsleeping vigilance will bring you useful tips outside the common run: I have forgotten where I read that you can get much more juice out of a lemon you have dumped in a bowl of warm water for a few minutes than out of one straight from the fruit-bowl, let alone from anywhere cold, but it is true, and I always follow this advice myself when making a Bloody Mary (for instance) and have the time and patience. On the other hand, the books are full of lore that you will only very rarely, if ever, have the chance of translating into practice. I think of such attractive fantasies as the recipe given in *The Art of Mixing Drinks* (based on *Esquire Drink*

Book) for Admiral Russell's Punch. This starts off by inviting the mixer to get hold of four hogsheads of brandy, and explains that a hogshead is 63 gallons—U.S. gallons: the equivalent is something over 50 British gallons, or 300-plus bottles. Included, along with such items as five pounds of grated nutmeg, is the juice of 2,500 lemons, warmth or coldness not specified. My calculation is that the totality (a lot of wine goes into it too) will serve 2,000 guests for a more-intensive-than-average evening party, or alternatively six people for a year-round piss-up. Try the latter some time and let me know how you get on, if you can. Pick your company with care.

More practically, you will waste a lot of time—unless of course you are simply using your drinks manual as dipsography, the alcoholic equivalent of pornography—reading about concoctions that call for stuff you simply have not got to hand. You may like the sound of a Grand Slam as prescribed in *The Diners' Club Drink Book*, with its jigger of Carioca rum, whatever that is, its half-jiggers of brandy and Curaçao, its dash of Kirschwasser and the rest, but, professional bartenders and fanatical booze-collectors apart, you are likely to have to read on in search of something you can make from stock. (A way of reducing this problem is outlined in my note on The Store Cupboard.)

Most drink-men, however, will like to feel they have on their shelves an authoritative and reasonably comprehensive encyclopedia of liquor, and the present little book, although needless to say frighteningly authoritative, is, for reasons explained elsewhere, not comprehensive, at least so far as its recipes are concerned. *The Fine Art of Mixing Drinks*, by David A. Embury (Faber), scores high from this point of view, and is written in a pleasantly companionable style. It is also—inevitably—American, which slightly diminishes its usefulness in the British context, and the author is what I shall venture to call *wrong* here and there, but his book is without doubt your Best Buy. Of shorter guides of this kind, I would recommend *3 Bottle Bar*, by H.i.—Yes, i. No, I don't know— Williams (Faber). Both are in paperback.

Neither Embury nor Williams has much to say about wine, except as regards its role in hot or cold punches and the like. Their business is with cocktails, coolers, cobblers, cups; with mixed drinks, in fact. Very few people who are proficient in this field know or care anything about wine as such, and the same applies in reverse to wine men. As the reader will see, I am not much of a wine man, but some of my best friends are, and I have called in expert assistance to guide me here.

The *Easy Guide to Wine*, issued free by the Wine Development Board (6 Snow Hill, London ECI), will tell the beginner most of what he wants to know in its couple of dozen pages of sound, well-chosen information and advice. For the more advanced, or more inquisitive, Alexis Lichine's *Encyclopedia of Wines and Spirits* and all other alcoholic drinks too (Cassell) is very solidly professional and factual, laying much greater stress on wines than on spirits: it devotes more space to Gevrey-Chambertin, one of thirty wine-producing districts in part of Burgundy, than to gin. *Wines and Spirits of the World*, edited by Alec H. Gold (Virtue), is similarly comprehensive and equally wine-oriented, but with a lot of splendid photographs thrown in. A real dipsographic debauch, so much so that I had to struggle with my better nature for quite a few seconds before deciding to add, lifemanfully, that I did note one or two omissions: no mention is made of the wines of New York State, with their annual yield comparable to that of Cyprus . . . But those who, like me, have tasted some of the wines of New York State will find it hard to care. Lastly, *The Penguin Book of Wines*, by Allan Sichel, is an excellent cheap guide: unpretentious, thorough (300 pages) and very practical, quoting plenty of names and up-to-date (1971) prices.

With all these books, as with any on the subject, do not expect to turn yourself into an expert via the printed word alone. You can commit to memory everything Lichine has to say about Gevrey-Chambertin and still have no idea whether you would like the wine. Reading must be combined with as much drinking experience as pocket and liver will allow.

One final recommendation. You need not take the slightest interest in any of these matters to get a lot out of *Cocktail Party Secrets*, by Vernon Heaton (Elliot Right Way Books). The title set me off on fantasies about martinis based on industrial alcohol, whisky sours spiked with LSD, etc. And I was hooked by the bold opening statement, offered by way of answer to the equally challenging question, "Why a Cocktail Party?" that serves as title of the first chapter:

> Everybody, on occasion,
> (*a*) wants to,
> (*b*) feels they [*sic*] ought to,
> (c) or have [*sic*] reason to
> entertain their [*sic*] friends in their [*sic*] own homes [*sic*].

The author goes on to suggest reasons why people should get these ideas, such as that they enjoy parties, or want to return a party given by someone else at *his* home. In the same ground-covering style, he points out that parties can be small or large; that they require preparation but that bottles can be lined up in advance; that you must decide (*a*) who you *want* to invite, (*b*) who you *think* should come, (*c*) who you feel you *must* invite, (*d*) who you think it is *politic* to invite; that, where possible, cloakroom facilities should be available; and much, much more. My word, if these are secrets, what can be the like of the publicly available information on the topic that has been lying about unregarded all these years?

I must get hold of the same writer's *Wedding Etiquette Properly Explained* and *The Best Man's Duties*. I can see it now—"People get married because (*a*) they *want* to, (*b*) they feel they *ought* to, (*c*) somebody is *pointing a shotgun* at them . . ."

To make cock ale: Take ten gallons of ale and a large cock, the older the better; Parboil the cock, flay him, and stamp him in a stone mortar till his bones are broken (you must craw and gut him when you flay him), then put the cock into two quarts of sack [sweet or sweetish white wine], and put it to three pounds of raisins of the sun stoned, some blades of mace and a few cloves; put all these into a canvas bag, and a little before you find the ale has done working, put the ale and bag together into a vessel; in a week or nine days bottle it up, fill the bottles but just above the neck, and give it the same time to ripen as other ale.

— Old recipe given in F. C. Lloyd's
Art and Technique of Wine

To sweeten musty casks: Take some dung of a milking cow when it is fresh, and mix it with a quantity of warm water, so as to make it sufficiently liquid to pass through a funnel, but previously dissolve two pounds of bay salt and one pound of alum; then put the whole in a pot on the fire, stir it with a stick and when nearly boiling, pour it into the cask, bung it up tight, shake it about, and let it remain in for two hours, then give it another stirring and after two hours more it may be rinsed out with cold water.

— Prescription quoted in F. C. Lloyd's
Art and Technique of Wine

ACTUAL DRINKS

I PROVIDE HERE only a selection. A complete account of all known drinks, from absinthe to the Zoom cocktail (brandy, honey and cream—not today, thank you) would be deadening to write and read. Completeness would also involve the rehearsal of a good deal of common knowledge. It would be rather shabby to take money for explaining that, for instance, a gin and tonic consists of gin and tonic, plus ice and a slice of lemon. However, this gives me occasion to remark that that admittedly excellent and refreshing drink gains an extra thirst-quenching tang from a good squeeze of lemon juice in addition to the lemon slice, and so to propound

> G.P. 2: *Any drink traditionally accompanied by a bit of fruit or vegetable is worth trying with a spot of the juice thrown in as well.*

I confine myself, then, to giving recipes intended to offer something of my own, whether it be a modest tip like the one exemplified above, an attack on some received notion, or, as in some cases, a whole new formula—if there is any such thing in a field so extensively and intensively studied.

What follows is the fruit of some dozen years' research; I started drinking much longer ago, be in no doubt of that, but had to reach a certain stage of affluence before I could risk spoiling even a mouthful of liquor by foolhardy experiment. My three categories are the Short and the Long and the Hot, an illogical but, there being no short hot drinks, practical mode of division.

SHORT DRINKS

If, as Philip Larkin observed not so long ago, the age of jazz (not the same thing as the Jazz Age) ran roughly from 1925 to 1945, the age of the cocktail covered the same sort of period, perhaps starting a little earlier and taking longer to die away finally. The two were certainly associated at their inception. Under Prohibition in the United States, the customer at the speakeasy drank concoctions of terrible liquor and other substances added in order to render the result just about endurable, while the New Orleans Rhythm Kings or the Original Memphis Five tried to take his mind further off what he was swallowing. The demise of jazz cannot have had much to do with that of the cocktail, which probably faded away along with the disappearance of servants from all but the richest private houses. Nearly every cocktail needs to be freshly made for each round, so that you either have to employ a barman or find yourself constantly having to quit the scene so as to load the jug. Straight drinks are quicker, and guests can—indeed, often do—help themselves to them.

The Dry Martini and its variants have hung on longer than most. In this case it is possible to make up a large quantity beforehand and keep it chilled; but there are several snags to this procedure. The main part of the standard refrigerator is not cold enough to keep the drink cold enough for more

than half an hour at the outside, and the ice-making compart-
ment of such a refrigerator is not tall enough to hold any
decent-sized jug. (You can muck about with teacups and such
if you like, but this will take you about as long as mixing fresh.)
A deep freeze will keep the drinks cold enough as long as anybody could want, but, again, you must put your jug back in it
the moment you have finished pouring each new round, and
this will probably involve you in a good deal of walking to and
fro. And most experts will tell you that the bloom begins to
fade from a martini as soon as it is first mixed, which may be
pure subjectivism, but, in any drinking context, subjectivism is
very important. No, I am sorry, but the only way to give your
guests first-rate martinis without trouble to yourself is to take
them to a first-rate cocktail bar. At home, you will just have to
grit your teeth and get down to it, as follows:

The Dry Martini
12 to 15 parts gin
1 part dry vermouth
Lemon rind or cocktail onions
Ice cubes

A couple of hours before the party, get your glasses together.
These should be on the small side—the second half of a too-
large martini will have become too warm by the time the average drinker gets to it—and have some sort of stem or base to
prevent the hand imparting warmth. (Like Glass No. 2 in
Tools of the Trade, page 41.) Fill each with water and put it in
the refrigerator.

With, say, fifteen minutes to go, make an honest attempt
at the fiendish task of cutting off some little strips of lemon
rind so thinly that you take off none of the white pith underneath. Fill—and I mean fill—your jug with ice and pour in

the gin and the vermouth, enough for one round, i.e. about one bottle of gin for every ten guests. (You will soon learn to judge the proportion of vermouth by eye.) Stir vigorously for about a minute. Leave to stand for two to three minutes. The books are against this, remarking truly that you will be allowing the ice to melt further and so dilute the mixture, but it does make the result appreciably colder; which leads me straight to

G.P. 3: *It is more important that a cold drink should be as cold as possible than that it should be as concentrated as possible.*

While the jug is standing, empty the water out of the glasses and drop a bit of lemon rind in each. If you can face it, try squeezing the rind over the glass first to liberate the pungent oil within. There is a knack to this which I have never mastered. Partly for this reason, I prefer to substitute a cocktail onion for the rind.

Stir again for a few seconds and pour. If there is any liquor left over, you have my permission to put it in the refrigerator for use in the next round, provided you remove every particle of ice beforehand.

Notes. (i) Use Booth's dry gin, the yellow sort. White gin is for long drinks—with tonic, bitter lemon, etc.

(ii) Use Martini e Rossi dry vermouth. Noilly Prat darkens the drink, making it look less dry than it is, and is too strongly flavoured. (However, it is probably the best dry vermouth for drinking on its own.)

(iii) In pursuit of G.P. 3, stand by with ice cubes, to rechill the partly drunk drinks of any rotters or slackers who may opt out of later rounds.

(iv) Experts will say that I have described, not a dry martini, but its drier derivative, the Gibson, which does substitute an onion for the true martini's lemon rind. Well, yes, but few people, I think, who have sampled the formula I give, by which the vermouth flavour disappears as such and yet the total flavour is still not at all that of straight gin, will want to return to the 4:1 or 3:1 ratios prescribed by convention. And my version is stronger.

The Lucky Jim

12 to 15 parts vodka
1 part dry vermouth
2 parts cucumber juice
Cucumber slices
Ice cubes

For this derivative of the Vodka Gibson, proceed as for the Dry Martini where appropriate. The cucumber juice can be made quite simply, though not without some effort, by cutting off a chunk, or series of chunks, about two inches long and applying first one end, then the other, to an ordinary manual lemon-squeezer. Sieve the result through a coffee-strainer into your mixing-jug on top of the liquor and ice, give an extra thorough stirring, and serve. What you serve should be treated with respect, not because it is specially strong but because it tastes specially mild and bland. It looks unusual, rather mysterious in fact: faintly coloured and faintly cloudy, the green wine of the Chinese emperors come to vigorous life. For visual reasons, the cucumber slice you float on top of each glass should have its peel left on.

Notes. (i) Use a British vodka, the cheapest you can find, in pursuance of

G.P. 4: *For any liquor that is going to be mixed with fruit juices, vegetable juices, etc., sweetening, strongly flavoured cordials and the like, go for the cheapest reliable article. Do not waste your Russian or Polish vodka, etc.*

(ii) The character after whom I have named this drink would probably make his Clement Freud face if offered one, but he would be among the first to appreciate that its apparent mildness might make it an excellent love-philtre to press on shy young ladies, if there are any of these left anywhere in the land.

The Copenhagen
4 or 5 parts vodka
1 part Danish akvavit
Blanched almonds
Ice cubes

Proceed as before, dropping an almond into each glass as you serve. Wondering what the almond is doing there (I believe it is a Scandinavian good-luck token) will keep your guests' tongues wagging until the liquor sets them wagging about anything under the sun. Distilled out at 79° proof, akvavit is a strong drink, so much so that it seems to extend its power over the whole.

The following short drinks are best prepared by the glass, not in quantity.

The Pink Gin

Yes, yes, gin and half a dozen drops—no more—of Angostura bitters and some ice. But see that the gin is Booth's (my choice) or Plymouth (preferred by most other authorities), and, for a quick kick, dilute with Perrier or Apollinaris if you can afford it, soda water if not, rather than plain water. This takes account of

> G.P. 5: *The alcohol in any bubbly drink will reach you faster than in its still version. Hence, or partly hence, the popularity of champagne at weddings and other festivities.*

Drop a cocktail onion in each glass, and, acting on G.P. 2, try adding a few drops of the solution the onions have been pickled in. The Pink Gin is a rather démodé drink well worth reviving. It is also, of course, a long drink if you add a lot of soda. Better not.

The Gin (or Vodka) and
Orange or Peach Bitters
2 parts gin (or vodka)
1 part orange or peach bitters
Ice cubes

I include this not because I can claim to have invented it, but because not many people seem to know that orange and peach bitters exist. They are not, these days, very easy to come by, but your supplier should be able to order them for you. They are bitters in the dilute, Campari sense, not in the concentrated, Angostura sense. Mixing them with gin (or vodka) gives a pleasing alternative to the standard short gin (or vodka) drinks.

The Salty Dog
1 part gin
2 parts fresh grapefruit juice
Salt
Ice cubes

Take two saucers and fill one with plain water, the other with table salt. Moisten the rim of each glass and then twirl it about in the salt, so that it picks up a thickish coating about a quarter of an inch deep. Carefully add the gin and juice, stir, add ice, stir, and drink through the band of salt. You either like it or not.

The MacCossack

Equal parts of vodka and green ginger wine poured over ice. Very good if you like ginger wine (and vodka). I do.

The Kingers
2 parts montilla
1 part fresh orange juice
1 small shake Angostura bitters
Ice cubes

Montilla is a lightly fortified wine from Spain, similar to sherry (as the sherry-growers, a couple of hundred miles down the road, have often taken advantage of noticing in an unproductive year), but nuttier: well worth drinking, chilled, on its own. The present drink is a sort of cobbler—if you think that means it will mend your shoes, you are wrong. Just mix everything together, stir with ice, remove the ice and serve.

The Dizzy Lizzy
4 oz. Chambéry
1 teaspoon framboise
1 teaspoon cognac
1 small shake Angostura bitters
Ice cubes

Chambéry is the classiest French vermouth, and framboise a
fine raspberry liqueur. Both are very drinkable on their own,
framboise with caution. Mix with ice, remove ice and serve.
Named, not *all that* inappropriately, after its deviser, my
wife.

Queen Victoria's Tipple
½ tumbler red wine
Scotch

I have it on the authority of Colm Brogan that the Great Queen
was "violently opposed to teetotalism, consenting to have one
cleric promoted to a deanery only if he promised to stop advo-
cating the pernicious heresy," and that the above was her
dinner-table drink, "a concoction that startled Gladstone"—as I
can well believe.

The original recipe calls for claret, but anything better
than the merely tolerable will be wasted. The quantity of
Scotch is up to you, but I recommend stopping a good deal
short of the top of the tumbler. Worth trying once.

Scholars will visualize, pouring in the whisky, the hand of
John Brown, the Queen's Highland servant, confidant and
possibly more besides; and I for one, if I listen carefully, can
hear him muttering, "Och, Your Majesty, dinna mak' yoursel'
unweel wi' a' yon parleyvoo moothwash—ha'e a wee dram o'
guid malt forbye." Or words to that effect.

The Old-Fashioned

Theoretically, one should be able to make up a lot of this
in advance, but I have never done so successfully. For each
drink, then, take

1 huge slug bourbon whiskey (say 4 fl. oz.)
1 level teaspoon castor sugar
As little hot water as will dissolve the
sugar completely
3 dashes Angostura bitters
1 hefty squeeze of fresh orange juice
1 teaspoon maraschino-cherry juice
1 slice orange
1 maraschino cherry
3 ice cubes

This is far less complicated and bothersome than it may look, and the result is the only cocktail really to rival the martini and its variants. Put the dissolved sugar into a glass, add the bitters, the juices and the whiskey, and stir furiously. Add the ice cubes and stir again. Lastly, push the orange slice down alongside the ice, drop in the cherry, and serve. You may supply drinking-straws if it is that sort of party.

Note. You really have to use bourbon. The Rye Old-Fashioned is not too bad; the Irish version just tolerable; the Scotch one not worth while.

The (Whiskey) Manhattan
4 parts bourbon whiskey
1 part Italian (red) vermouth
1 dash or so Angostura bitters
1 maraschino cherry
Ice cubes

As above, stir the fluids together very hard before adding the ice and fruit. Whatever the pundits may say, this is in practice the not very energetic man's Old-Fashioned, and is an excellent drink, though never, I think, as good as a properly made Old-Fashioned, As above, again, or even more so, you really have to use bourbon.

The Iberian
1 part Bittall
1 part very dry sherry
1 orange slice
Ice cubes

You can surely see how to make this. Bittall is a Portuguese wine apéritif consisting in effect of light (i.e. non-heavy) port flavoured with orange-peel. I myself find it delicious on its own—serve well chilled—but some will find it a little on the sweet side for a pre-meal drink: mixing it with the sherry off-sets this. (See also under Hot Drinks, below.) It is not on general sale, but your wine merchant can get it for you.

I can hardly stop you if you decide to make your guests seem more interesting to you and to one another by mixing in a shot of vodka.

The Normandy
1 slug calvados (2 fl. oz.)
1 dose champagne cider (about 3 fl. oz.)
1 dash Angostura bitters
1 level teaspoon castor sugar
As little hot water as will dissolve the sugar completely
1 apple slice
Ice cubes

Put the dissolved sugar, the bitters and the calvados into a glass and stir furiously. Add ice and stir furiously. Remove ice, add chilled cider, drop in apple slice, and serve.

Note. Connoisseurs will already have sussed that this longish short drink is a translation of the orthodox champagne cocktail, based on brandy and champagne, out of grape into apple. They should also have sussed that it is substantially cheaper: calvados is a few shillings dearer than a three-star cognac, but champagne cider is a quarter the price of even the very cheapest champagne. This cocktail tends to go down rather faster than its strength warrants; I have had heads in the soup when offering it as an apéritif.

The Tigne Rose
1 tot gin
1 tot whisky
1 tot rum
1 tot vodka
1 tot brandy

Even if you keep the tots small, which is strongly advisable, this short drink is not very short. It owes its name to Tigne Barracks, Malta, where it was offered as a Saturday lunchtime apéritif in the Sergeants' Mess of the 36th Heavy A.A. Regt., R.A., to all newly joined subalterns. The sometime 2nd Lieut. T. G. Rosenthal, R.A., from whom I had the recipe, says he put down three of them before walking unaided back to his room and falling into a reverie that lasted until Monday-morning parade. A drink to dream of, not to drink.

LONG DRINKS
There is no need to wax sociological over these. You must, however, try to observe

G.P. 6: *With drinks containing fruit (other than the decorative or olfactory slice of lemon, orange, etc.) it is really worth while to soak the fruit in some of the liquor for at least three hours beforehand.*

Everything else is *ad libitum*, as can be seen from this recipe for

Generic Cold Punch
A lot of cheap medium-dry wine, white, red or rosé— your wine merchant will help you choose
Some vodka—the quantity depending on your pocket and how drunk you intend your guests to become, but not more than one-quarter of the quantity of wine
A glass or two of some relatively non-sticky liqueur— optional
A load of any fresh fruit that happens to be about—peaches and strawberries are best
Ice cubes

Cut up the fruit and put it in some sort of bowl—anything from a tureen to a baby's bath will do. Pour some of the wine over it and leave to stand as under G.P. 6. When the party approaches, add the rest of the drink and stir thoroughly. The best method of serving is via your jug—with luck you will be able to fill this by submerging it bodily in the bowl, though it is worth taking out and throwing back any chunks of fruit that have got into the jug. Soaked fruit looks nasty. (If you want to do the thing in style, you will have a fresh supply of fruit to go in the individual glasses.) Now, no sooner, is the time to introduce ice. Stir the punch and the ice *in the jug* and start pouring, keeping ice out of the glasses.

Stern application of G.P. 4 makes any such potion inexpensive, but the best value for money of the lot, and a very pleasant medium-strength long drink, is provided by

The Careful Man's Peachy Punch
5 bottles medium-dry white wine
4 bottles champagne cider (dry if possible)
2 bottles British peach wine
1 bottle vodka
2 lb. fresh peaches (more if possible,
and tinned if really necessary)
Ice cubes

Stone, cut up and soak the peaches as above. Put the cider in the refrigerator for a couple of hours beforehand. When the time comes, mix in the white wine, the peach wine and the vodka. Fill your jug, add ice, stir and pour, adding the chilled cider to each glass in the proportion of two from the jug to one from the bottle. Serve immediately.

Notes. (i) This will give you about sixty generous glasses at an outlay of about 15p each. If you can undercut me with anything similar, as strong and non-poisonous, I shall be interested to hear from you.

(ii) These British fruit wines are fortified up to a strength approaching that of sherry or vermouth—and sell at about 70p a bottle, which makes them, strength against price, an excellent buy. One would not perhaps want to drink more than, even as much as, one glass straight, but they are satisfactory in combination, as here. Besides peach there are apricot, redcurrant, damson and cherry versions, so that even quite stupid and unimaginative careful men will not find much difficulty in improvising variations on the theme I have provided.

Jo Bartley's Christmas Punch
3 bottles dry or medium-dry white wine
2 bottles gin

1 bottle brandy
1 bottle sherry
1 bottle dry vermouth
5 quarts medium-sweet cider
Ice cubes

(If you feel like throwing in the unfinished drinks from last night, nobody will notice.) Mix everything together and serve from jugs that have some ice in them. Remember G.P. 4 and cut all the corners you can: Spanish wine, cocktail gin, non-cognac (but *not* non-French) brandy, British sherry and British vermouth; the cider will cover them and blend them into a new and splendid whole. Despite the potency that lurks behind its seeming mildness, I have never known anybody to suffer while or after drinking it.

I have named it after its creator, the scholar, wit and dear friend of mine who died in 1967.

Paul Fussell's Milk Punch
1 part brandy
1 part bourbon whiskey
4 parts fresh milk
Nutmeg
Frozen milk cubes

The previous evening (this is the hardest part) put milk instead of water into enough ice-trays in your refrigerator. On the day, mix the fresh milk and the spirits thoroughly together—in an electric blender, the deviser of the recipe says, and by all means do that if there is one lying about and not wanted by someone else and clean and with no bits missing and in working order. For me, stirring in a jug will do just as well. Pour into biggish glasses, drop in milk cubes, dust with nutmeg and serve.

This punch is to be drunk immediately on rising, in lieu of eating breakfast. It is an excellent heartener and sustainer at the outset of a hard day: not only before an air trip or an interview, but when you have in prospect one of those gruelling nominal festivities like Christmas morning, the wedding of an old friend of your wife's or taking the family over to Gran's for Sunday dinner.

Note. Do not, of course, use an expensive bourbon or a brandy that is anything more than just French. And taste each bottle of milk before pouring it in. There is a risk that sour-milk punch would not be as good.

Reginald Bosanquet's Golden Elixir
Champagne
Fresh peaches

The proportion is three biggish or four smallish peaches to one bottle; it is not critical. Put the stoned fruit through an electric blender—I hate the things, but I cannot think of a manual method that will do the job effectively. Pour the chilled champagne into wine glasses and top up with the strained peach-juice. "The best drink in the world," says its creator with conviction. Very good, to be sure—and *healthy*.

Jittersauce
1 part Scotch
1 part gin
2 parts champagne
Ice cubes

Mix the Scotch and the gin, add ice, stir, pour champagne on top. This smooth-tasting drink, Robert Conquest tells me, was popular in some circles at Oxford in the late Thirties. It is a translation into action of the words of Cab Calloway, who at that time was in the habit of singing:

> If you want to be a jitterbug,
> First thing you do is git a mug;
> Pour whisky, gin and wine within,
> And then begin.

But try not to go on too long.

Evelyn Waugh's Noonday Reviver
1 hefty shot gin
1 (½-pint) bottle Guinness
Ginger beer

Put the gin and Guinness into a pint silver tankard and fill to the brim with ginger beer. I cannot vouch for the authenticity of the attribution, which I heard in talk, but the mixture will certainly revive you, or something. I should think two doses is the limit.

Woodrow Wyatt's Instant Whiskey Collins
As much bourbon whiskey as you fancy
½ standard split-size bitter lemon drink
1 maraschino cherry
Ice cubes

You can work this one out for yourself. For once, you can use rye or Irish whiskey or Scotch whisky* if you feel like it.

---

* Fact for the factually-minded: only Scotch may legally be spelt without the "e."

Whatever the purists may say, this is a good drink; it pays to remember

> G.P. 7: *Never despise a drink because it is easy to make and/or uses commercial mixes. Unquestioning devotion to authenticity is, in any department of life, a mark of the naïve—or worse.*

The Bloody Mary
½ bottle vodka
2 pints tomato juice
2 tablespoons tomato ketchup
4 tablespoons lemon juice
4 tablespoons orange juice
1 tablespoon (at least) Worcester sauce
1 level teaspoon celery salt
Ice cubes

You will want to make up a lot of this before the party starts, or before the last breakfasters have finished. Put into some smallish container the vodka, ketchup, sauce and celery salt. Stir furiously until the ketchup is fully emulsified and the lumps in the celery salt broken up. (The ketchup is the secret of the whole thing: I am not at all clear on what it does, but it does something considerable.) Mix the tomato juice and (strained) fruit juices into your usual jug, stir in the vodka-ketchup-sauce-salt mixture, add ice, stir again and serve in wine glasses or the equivalent; as with the Dry Martini, the bottom half of a too-large drink is warm when you get to it.

This delicious and sustaining potion is often thought to relieve hangovers, and certainly it will make you drunk again if you drink enough of it, but there is hardly anything distinctive about that. Some would argue that the tomato juice is

food smuggled into a stomach that would shrink from it un-
softened with alcohol, to which one might reply that there are
more digestible alternatives; further, that those whose stomachs are in fair shape, probably the majority, are having their
appetites for lunch spoiled to no end. And yet, on the
principle—very nearly worth erecting into a G.P.—that in all
alcoholic matters subjectivism plays a big part, a lot of people
will feel better after one or two Bloody Marys simply because
they expect to.

La Tequila con Sangrita

$1/4$ pint plus (i.e. equal to the mixture that follows) tequila
$1/4$ pint tomato juice
1 tablespoon fresh lime juice (or 2 tablespoons fresh lemon
juice)
$1/2$ teaspoon tabasco
1 small pinch cayenne pepper

An exotic short-long drink to round off this section. I have
never seen it served outside Mexico, though since drinking a
good deal of it there I may not have looked very hard, I admit. Tequila is distilled from the juice of a cactus, and tastes
like it, too. "Sangrita" means "little blood" or "blood-ikins" (and
"con" means "with," if you must know). The drink is a sort of
Bloody Maria, very hot, and unique in being kept in two
halves: the tomato concoction and the tequila do not meet
until they arrive to start a joint operation on your stomach.
Each partaker gets a small glass of neat, unchilled tequila and
a twin glass of the stirred, also unchilled red stuff, and sips at
each in alternation.

I have had to specify $1/4$ pint because any smaller quantity makes the measurement of the other ingredients difficult;
I am not suggesting that this is one round for one chap. The

formula will serve three or so. You will find it a splendid pick-me-up, and throw-me-down, and jump-on-me. Strongly dis-recommended for mornings after.

HOT DRINKS

There is not much to be said in general about these either. They will warm you up, and they will make you drunk if you drink enough of them. Remember that their alcohol will affect you sooner than if you drank the same drink cold, chilled, iced. In those conditions the stomach must warm the stuff up to body temperature before absorption can take place; taken hot, it will start getting to you (or your girl-friend) at once. Ingredients, proportions and so on are not much more critical than with cold punches, as can be seen from this recipe for a

Generic Hot Punch

A lot of cheap red wine and/or cheap port-type wine

A glass or two or more of cheap (but French) brandy

Some oranges and lemons

Sugar

Spices—cinnamon, nutmeg, cloves, etc.

Water.

Put the sliced fruit into a saucepan (preferably one with a pouring beak), add and mix the wine and brandy and put on a slow gas. Stir in powdered spices if you feel like it, though about as much as these do in my experience is contribute a sediment. As the mixture warms, stir in castor sugar. Here you must use your judgment and keep tasting the result, which you will enjoy doing unless you are the wrong person to be giving the party.

Put a kettle on, get ready some expendable wine glasses or any sizeable glasses with a handle or, if you have them, those tumblers that fit inside raffia holders, and stand a dessertspoon in each. The moment the mixture in the saucepan has started to smoke, pour it into a pitcher (a stout enough one not to crack) and at once fill each glass half full. Add half as much boiling water to each drink, so that glasses are now three-quarters full. The presence of the spoon will prevent the glasses cracking very nearly but not absolutely always; hence the "expendable" proviso. Remove spoons and serve, bearing in mind that they should go back in momentarily whenever you top up drinks that are more than half drunk. Keep the remains in the saucepan on the stove, perhaps on an asbestos mat if you can handle the bloody things, remembering that as soon as the mixture starts to bubble, even slightly, you are boiling off alcohol.

Notes. (i) As always, "cheap" wine, etc., does not mean any old plonk. Steer clear of Moroccan claret, Venezuelan tawny-port-style and such dubieties. As always, consult your wine merchant. On the other hand, never use good wine or real (Portuguese) port for a hot brew. They will be utterly wasted in that state. On yet another hand, if you ever find yourself saddled with a batch of non-lethal but unpalatable red wine, keep it by you for use in a hot punch, where its unpalatability will disappear.

(ii) Pundits will try to get you on to the fearful chore of roasting in the oven an orange stuck with real cloves, rubbing lemon rind off on lumps of sugar and all that. Pay no attention.

If, however, you want to offer something a little more than run-of-the-mill—and also rather less trouble—try

Portuguese Hot Punch
Bittall
Water

Proceed as above where appropriate, keeping the proportions of two wine and one hot water. The orange flavour of the Bittall comes through, rendering unnecessary any antics with fruit and the rest. You may need to stir in a little sugar, but I doubt it. I heartily recommend this simple drink.

The Polish Bison
1 generous teaspoon Bovril
1 (adjustable) tot vodka
Water
A squeeze of lemon juice (optional)
A shake of pepper

Make the Bovril as if you were merely making Bovril and stir the other stuff in. Named in salute to the nation that makes the best vodka, but its product will be wasted in this mixture: use a British version. This is a very cheering concoction, especially in cold and/or hungover conditions.

Hot Buttered Rum
Rum (any sort, but an expensive sort will be wasted)
Maple syrup
Butter
Water
Cinnamon

Put a generous tot of rum and a teaspoonful of maple syrup (or sugar syrup) in a mug, fill with hot water and stir till blended. Drop in a small knob of butter and dust with cinnamon. Not my discovery, but less well known, as warmer and nightcap, than it should be.

David Embury disagrees. He admits a version into his book for completeness' sake, but concludes sternly: "How anyone can possibly consume [it] for pleasure is utterly beyond me . . . I believe that the drinking of Hot Buttered Rum should be permitted only in the Northwest Passage, and, even there, only by highly imaginative and over-enthusiastic novelists." Dear dear.

Serbian Tea
Slivovitz (plum brandy)
Honey (the runny sort)

Heat the slivovitz in a saucepan and stir in honey to taste. Serve in small mugs. Much esteemed in the Balkans as a cold-cure. It does seem to help, but, in the words of one user, "after a pint or so you can feel the lining of your stomach wearing thin." So watch it.

Woe unto them that rise up early in the morning, that they may follow strong drink.

—ISAIAH

He is not deserving the name of Englishman who speaketh against ale, that is, good ale.

—GEORGE BORROW

ALFRED, LORD TENNYSON, Poet Laureate, on the occasion of his visit to the International Exhibition, 1862, having written an ode to be sung by a choir of four thousand at its opening: "Is there anywhere in this damned place where we can get a decent bottle of Bass?"

What two ideas are more inseparable than Beer and Britannia?

—SYDNEY SMITH

"I rather like bad wine," said Mr. Mountchesney; "one gets
so bored with good wine."

— BENJAMIN DISRAELI

There is nothing which has yet been contrived by man by
which so much happiness is produced as by a good tavern
or inn.

— SAMUEL JOHNSON

"Champagne certainly gives one werry gentlemanly ideas,
but for a continuance, I don't know but I should prefer mild
hale."

— ROBERT SMITH SURTEES

TOOLS OF THE TRADE

THE AIM HERE is to keep everything as simple as possible. Resist being led astray by any Compleat Barman's Presentation Wherewithal, which will be incompleat and largely unnecessary and badly designed, and accumulate your equipment only after personal inspection and careful thought. If you can rely on yourself not to be carried away, and I am far from sure I can rely on me when I have money to burn, you may visit the relevant departments of your local emporium. First as to your essential

BAR KIT

1. A refrigerator. All to yourself, I mean. There is really no way round this. Wives and such are constantly filling up any refrigerator they have a claim on, even its ice-compartment, with irrelevant rubbish like food. Get one of your own and have it fitted with racks the thickness of a bottle apart. This is not expensive and, adapted on these lines, even a small refrigerator will hold a lot of bottles and tins in an easy-to-get-at way. Use rubber or rubberoid icetrays. The metal and the plastic ones have a longer life, but it is hell getting out the three or four

cubes that are often all you need at a time; no problem with the rubber version.

2. A measuring-jug. The 1 pint/20 fl. oz. size is best.

3. A mixing-jug. This should be of glass, tall and narrow, with a lipped beak to hold in the ice when pouring. But check that it holds enough, not less than a quart. With a party of any size you will, when making a martini, say, want to use a bottle of spirits at a time and still leave plenty of room for ice and enthusiastic stirring.

4. An ice-container. With a Thermos lining and room for 30 or 40 cubes.

5. A bar spoon, i.e. with a long shank and a tiny bowl.

6. A lemon-squeezer. This should be of the acoustic sort, i.e. non-electrical, manual, and so always in working order. Plastic is better than glass, because the flutes on the central dome are usually sharper.

7. A strainer.

8. A really very sharp knife. (If you want to finish the evening with your usual number of fingers, do any cutting-up, peel-slicing and the like before you have had more than a couple of drinks, preferably before your first.)

9. A corkscrew. Go for the butterfly type or the sort that involves turning instead of pulling.

10. A crown-cork opener.

That is the lot. Keep them in a place only you have the key to, or they will not be there when you want them, I can assure you. (Locking up your refrigerator calls for some ingenuity, but good luck if you can get it fitted with a padlock.) Similarly, it will save you time in the end, as well as earning you domestic popularity, to do your own washing-up.

Half the point of the above list is what it leaves out. The most important and controversial of your non-needs is a cocktail-shaker. With all respect to James Bond, a martini should be stirred, not shaken. The case is a little different with drinks that include the heavier fruit-juices and liqueurs, but I have always found that an extra minute's stirring does the trick well enough. The only mixture that does genuinely need shaking is one containing eggs, and if that is your sort of thing, then clear off and buy yourself a shaker any time you fancy. The trouble with the things is that they are messy pourers and, much more important, they are far too small, holding half a dozen drinks at the outside. A shaker about the size of a hatbox might be worth pondering, but I have never seen or heard of such.

An electric blender is also unnecessary, though by all means use one if you are quite confident of not having to clean it afterwards. Those little battery-powered whirlers are fun to play with, but in my experience they do nothing that a vigorously rotated spoon will not do.

Ice-tongs have become acceptably replaced by the human hand. Thanks to the ring-and-tab arrangement, beer-tin openers are no longer required, and, thanks to the innovation of the screw cap, item 10 of the kit will be droppable any day.

The same policy of sticking to essentials has been followed in selecting your

GLASSES

1. A wine glass holding about eight ounces when full, though it's a sensible general rule not to fill it more than about two-thirds of the way up. (Same goes for sherry, port, etc.) It will do for all wines, including champagne. The only essentials are that the bowl should be the right shape to be cupped in the palm for warming a chilly red wine, and that there should be some sort of stem to prevent your fingers warming a white wine.

Those hock and moselle glasses with the brown and green stems respectively are pretty and practical enough, but they break easily, and you may earn cries of horror and contempt if you try to serve anything but hock or moselle in them, so they are an extra, or an extravagance.

A third characteristic of the decent wine glass is one it shares with all other decent glasses: the part containing the drink, indeed the whole thing in the case of tumblers, etc., *must* be of plain glass so that you can see and appreciate the colour of the wine (though a light floral or similar pattern on a basic plain-glass ground is acceptable).

There are plenty of coloured drinking glasses about, and not quite all of them are horrible to look at, but the exceptions belong on your display shelf, not on your table. If somebody you are really very anxious to outdo should ever try to give you black burgundy, or bottle-green beer, ask politely if you can have it out of a white plastic tooth-mug instead, explaining that that at least allows you to see the true colour of the drink from above.

2. A sherry glass. This, filled to the brim, should hold about six ounces. It should have a stem to avoid hand-heating, like the wine glass, but that stem need only be long enough to be held comfortably between thumb and forefinger. The shape is up to you. I favour a sort of small wine glass with a U-shaped bowl. In this you can, with perfect propriety, serve not only sherry, but port, vermouth, liqueurs and brandy. Yes, brandy. If you notice any foreheads beginning to pucker at this, say you have always thought the traditional brandy snifter looked frightfully pompous and silly, and add carelessly that only inferior brandies are worth sniffing anyway. If you object that the amount of liqueur you feel like dispensing to your guests appears rather mean in a six-ounce glass, then you are just a mean sod.

3. An Old-Fashioned glass. In other words, a short broad tumbler holding about eight ounces when full. The point of it

is not just that it looks pretty—though it does, very—but that in it you can get a lot of ice cubes into a short drink without piling them up above the surface and so numbing the drinker's nose. It is an ideal vessel not only for the Old-Fashioned cocktail but for anything drunk on the rocks: spirits, vermouths, wine apéritifs like Dubonnet, Punt e Mes, etc.

4. A Highball or Collins glass. In other words, a tall thin tumbler holding 11 or 12 ounces or something over half a pint. This will do for all long drinks from gin and tonic onwards. You can serve beer in it if pushed, but at the cost of hand-heating, and on this and other grounds I favour

5. A beer glass. The familiar pub tankard with handle. The half-pint size is the more generally useful, but a few pint ones will come in handy, not only for pints, but for Pimm's* (the presence of ice and all that vegetation makes the half-pint Pimm's a rather short-weight affair) and long drinks that froth up a lot, like Black Velvet. (It goes against the grain to have to spell out such common knowledge in a treatise on the present level, but this "sour and invigorating draught," as Evelyn Waugh called it, consists of equal parts of chilled Guinness and chilled champagne, with the latter put in first. Try it with a sweeter stout if the champagne, or your stomach, is on the acid side.) These glasses are not always easy to come by. Inquire from your wine merchant or at your off-licence.

> No, Sir, claret is the liquor for boys; port for men; but he who aspires to be a hero [smiling] must drink brandy . . . Brandy will do soonest for a man what drinking *can* do for him.
>
> — SAMUEL JOHNSON

---

* Few such things are more worth the trouble than adding a little cucumber juice and lemon juice to each portion of Pimm's.

THE STORE CUPBOARD

. . . IS NOT THE same place as the cellar or the larder or wherever you keep your stock for daily use. In other words, I am not insulting your (in many respects) considerable intelligence by letting you know that to lay in some gin, wine, beer, etc., is a good idea if you want to get a spot of drinking done; I am taking up an earlier point of mine about the relatively uncommon liquors called for in some cocktail and other recipes, and will go on to suggest a basic set that will enable you to try your hand at some of the more out-of-the-way mixtures. A small basic set: to be in a position to make every drink in David Embury's book, for instance, would call for a store cupboard, or room, holding something like four hundred different bottles, not to speak of a small greengrocer-fruiterer's shop and a miniature dairy.

The liquors referred to are mostly liqueurs. (I know the latter are primarily intended to be drunk separately; I know too how it feels next day to have drunk a lot of one or more of them separately—see The Hangover.) A general word on these fatal Cleopatras of the world of booze comes in quite handily here. They are not really worth individual notice, except for *kitró*, little known and so justifying a brief digression.

Kitró is little known because you have to go to the Greek island of Naxos to get it—the neighbouring island of Ios produces another and slightly less nectarean version. They do not
export it even to the Greek mainland; at any rate, I have never
found it there after plenty of looking. It is based on the lemon,
but seemingly on the rind as well as the juice, hence its peculiar tang. Should you find yourself in Athens, you seriously
should make the trip to Naxos, or Ios, and come away with as
many bottles as you can carry. They are nice islands anyhow,
even when not seen through a *kitró*-haze.

To resume, then: a liqueur can be defined as a strong
drink with a fruity or herbal flavour. There are two main fam-
ilies: a thinner kind made by distilling the fermented juices of
fruits other than the grape, such as pears, strawberries, ap-
ples, plums, and a thicker kind made by mingling brandy,
sugar, and fruit juice or herbal infusions. The first kind is little
used in mixed drinks and need not concern us here. The second kind subdivides, the largest group consisting of liqueurs
with an orange flavour. These may be dark in colour—
Curaçao, Grand Marnier, Van der Hum: the last is flavoured
with a fruit that is not exactly an orange, but I have shoved it
in here—or white, like Cointreau and Triple Sec. (The latter
name, for one of the sweetest drinks ever made, must be a
joke.) All have their own individual flavour, but the difference will hardly show in a mixture, especially when lemon
juice is also present, as it often is; so pick from this group the
one you like best straight and use it whenever any of them
comes up in a recipe. Adopt the same principle with the
cherry group—Maraschino, Cherry Heering and the Dutch
version made by Bols.

There are other necessary liqueurs which are not interchangeable, which I include below, together with one or two
miscellaneous items. Your store cupboard, then, should contain:

1. An orange liqueur.
2. A cherry liqueur.
3. Bénédictine—which needs no introduction.
4. Crème de Menthe—ditto. Pundits say the white sort is better than the green, but I cannot tell the difference in flavour, and the green is much prettier, and you can never find the white anyway.
5. Crème de Cacao. A very thick drink supposedly tasting of cocoa. Gives mixtures an individual twist, but not recommended for drinking straight. The least indispensable on this list.
6. A pseudo-absinthe such as Pernod or Ricard. True absinthe (the name is from a Greek word meaning "undrinkable") has been illegal in most places for a long time. It is, or was, flavoured with the herb wormwood, which, as the French authorities noticed after years of using absinthe in their army to combat fever, "acts powerfully on the nerve-centres, and causes delirium and hallucinations, followed in some cases by idiocy" (*Encyclopaedia Britannica*). The perfectly wholesome successors to absinthe are flavoured with anis, or aniseed. The result always reminds me, not unpleasantly, of those paregoric cough-sweets children ate before the war, and I see that paregoric does contain aniseed, but throws in opium, camphor and benzoic acid as well, so I am probably just being nostalgic. Anyway, when recipes call for absinthe, as they can still do if their compilers and revisers have been too ignorant or lazy to make the change, use Pernod or Ricard instead.

Incidentally, what happened about vermouth, which is or was also flavoured with wormwood?—"vermouth" being a French or German attempt to say "wormwood." Could the idiocy, or bloody foolishness, which comes to afflict the multi-martini-man be the result of the wormwood in the vermouth? No. It is the alcohol, you see. (And I suspect it was the alcohol in the absinthe, too, that caused the trouble all along, when the stuff was taken to excess.)

7. A bottle of orange bitters, a decent-sized one. Avoid the little shakers got up to look like the Angostura article.

8. A bottle of grenadine. A non-alcoholic, sweetened sort of pomegranate juice, nice to look at, odd in flavour—I am never sure whether I like it or not. But quite a few recipes include it.

9. A bottle of sugar syrup, a preparation continually called for in mixed-drink books. To have a supply of it will save you a lot of time when making up, for instance, my Old-Fashioned and Normandy recipes. Concoct it yourself by the following simple method:

Down a stiff drink and keep another by you to see you through the ordeal. Put a pound of castor or cube sugar in a saucepan with half a pint of water and bring the dissolving mixture to the boil. Keep it there for five minutes. Let it cool and pour into an old (clean) spirits bottle. *The Constance Spry Cookery Book* recommends adding a teaspoon of liquid glucose to the sugar and water, as a guard against later crystallization.

Remember you are dealing with one of the stickiest substances known, so select with forethought the surface where you will do the pouring, and cover it with a month's old newspapers. For the same reason, bind some flannel or something round your bottle to absorb stray dribbles from its mouth—so see that its neck is long enough—or make a collar for it from one of those plastic sponges that harden when dry.

Your bottleful will last for months, and you will have been constantly patting yourself on the back for your wisdom and far-sightedness.

Slimmers can save both time and weight by using a liquid artificial sweetener and establishing the quantities needed by trial and error. There is a flavour problem here, but remember that the sweetener will generally be sweetening a mixture of flavours much more powerful on the palate than tea or coffee. Up to you.

Note. I have assumed you realize that the above are not the only extras you need to supplement your fundamental gin, vodka, whisky, rum, brandy, etc. You will also, of course, have to have French and Italian vermouths, Campari, Angostura bitters, tonic water and all that lot. But I take these to form part of your daily stock.

Freedom and Whisky gang thegither!

—ROBERT BURNS

Wine snob—a man or woman who drinks the label and the price.

—OLOF WIJK

Porter. . . . drink, sir, is a great provoker of three things. *Macduff*. What three things does drink especially provoke? *Porter*. Marry, sir, nose-painting, sleep, and urine. Lechery, sir, it provokes, and unprovokes: it provokes the desire, but it takes away the performance: Therefore much drink may be said to be an equivocator with lechery; it makes him, and it mars him; it sets him on, and it takes him off; it persuades him, and disheartens him; makes him stand to, and not stand to: in conclusion, equivocates him in a sleep, and, giving him the lie, leaves him.

—WILLIAM SHAKESPEARE, *Macbeth*

They who drink beer will think beer.

—WASHINGTON IRVING

FIRST THOUGHTS ON WINE

> Deep colour and big shaggy nose. Rather a jumbly, untidy sort of wine, with fruitiness shooting off one way, firmness another and body pushing about underneath. It will be as comfortable and as comforting as the 1961 Nuits-St-Georges once it has pulled its ends in and settled down.

That genuine extract from a wine journal is the sort of thing that gets the stuff a bad name with a lot of people who would enjoy wine if they could face trying it seriously. Let it be said at once that talking about big shaggy noses and so forth receives a deeper and more educated contempt from real wine-drinkers than from the average man in the pub. But, before I get to a more positive approach, let me describe, in careful stages, not what you should do when serving wine to your guests, but what you nearly always do (if you are anything like me):

1. Realize that They will be arriving in less than an hour and you have done damn-all about it.

2. Realize, on your way to the cellar or wherever you keep the stuff, that the red wine to go with the roast beef will be nowhere near the required room temperature if left to warm up unassisted.

3. Realize, on reaching the stuff, that it has not had time to "settle" after being delivered, and that you should have realized six weeks—or, if you had wanted to give Them a treat, ten years—ago exactly what wine you were going to need tonight.

4. Decide that They can bloody well take what They are given, grab some bottles and take them to the kitchen.

5. Take the foil off the necks of the bottles. (Now that the bottlers have mostly decided they can cut costs by leaving the lead out of this, your present task is like removing nailpolish with a fish-knife.)

6. Look for the corkscrew.

7. Having (we will assume) found the corkscrew, unscrew the cork that somebody has left screwed on it and open the bottles.

8. Find something to take the gunk or crap off the bottle-necks and take it off.

9. Decide that, while any fool can tell when wine is cold, and nearly any fool knows nowadays that a red wine is not supposed to be cold, hardly anyone knows a decent glass of it from a bad one, and stick the bottles in a saucepan of warm water.

10. Spend parts of the next hour-and-a-half wondering whether old Shagbag, who is reputed to know one wine from another, will denounce you for boiling out whatever quality tonight's stuff might have had, or will suffer in silence. Also wonder whether the others will think 1971 a rather insultingly recent year for a Médoc, whether to get up another bottle on the off-chance that They can force down what you have "prepared" for the table, whether to boil that too or to bank on Their being too drunk to notice or too polite to mention its coldness, and kindred questions.

11. Do not enjoy the wine much yourself when you come to drink it.

Now let me contrast the procedure when serving beer:

1. Do nothing at all before you get to table, beyond ensuring you have enough.

2. At table, inquire, "Anyone not for beer?"

3. Subtract the number so signifying from the total sitting down.

4. From larder or refrigerator bring one tin of beer for each person concerned, tear off the tabs and start pouring, in the total certainty that the stuff will be all right.

5. Say, "If anyone wants any more he's only got to shout." Streamlined version of the above:

1. Five minutes before everybody goes "in," put one tin of beer at each place.

2. Let the sods open and pour themselves.

The point is that wine is *a lot of trouble*, requiring energy and forethought. I would agree without hesitation that (if the comparison can properly be made at all) the best wine is much better than the best beer, though many would not, at least in private, and many more will bless you under their breath for giving them a decent Worthington or Double Diamond instead of what they too often get, Algerian red ink under a French label. And this is the other half of the wine/beer comparison: a lot of beer is probably better than a lot of wine, in this country at any rate.

Those who take this view are in a difficult position. The pro-wine pressure on everybody who can afford to drink at all is immense and still growing. To offer your guests beer instead of wine (unless you are serving a curry, a Scandinavian cold table, eggs and bacon, etc.) is to fly in the face of trend as well as of established custom. It looks—and in some cases it no doubt is—neglectful and mean. Worse, it may seem affected, bogusly no-nonsensical, as who should say, "Tek thi ale and be glad on it, lad; it wor good enough for mi dad home from pit and mi mam home from mill"—an attitude common enough among wealthy socialists, but hardly the thing for you and me. Lastly, for every secret beer-drinker you may please by your policy, you will displease at least one open wine-drinker. The latter may not be able to tell a Chablis from a Château d'Yquem, be entirely motivated by snobbery, but, under that old basic rule, if he thinks he likes wine, he likes wine. What is to be done?

I said right at the beginning that you cannot give your guests good drinks without taking a lot of trouble, and even though the trouble you have to take about wine is extra troublesome, and differs from the kind of trouble you take with (say) a dry martini, in that sufficient trouble over a dry martini guarantees a good dry martini, whereas a hell of a lot of trouble over wine is in itself no such guarantee—even so, we have to soldier on with the stuff, relieving our feelings every now and then with such things as the not very balanced or temperate outburst near the start of this section. I have therefore devised

THE WINE-RESENTER'S SHORT HANDY GUIDE

1. Keep saying to yourself (what is true) that really good and properly served clarets and red burgundies are the best drinks yet devised by man. (I have admittedly never had the chance of tasting, among other things, kumiss, the drink made by the nomadic Tatars out of fermented mares' or camels' milk, but I doubt if it is even as good, let alone better.)

2. Always drink wine, except with curry and so on, when you eat out in restaurants and especially at your friends' houses. You may learn something: see (4) below.

3. At least serve *white* wine at home whenever the food permits. It needs only to be served cold, though not too cold

(an hour in the refrigerator is about right), and you are exempted from those horrible moments of discovering that you ought to have opened it three hours earlier. My advice would be to stick to hocks and moselles, which everybody likes, and avoid white burgundies, which some people prefer to almost anything, but which others will find too dry, whatever the depth of their superstition about the okayness of dryness. "Closely resembling a blend of cold chalk soup and alum cordial with an additive or two to bring it to the colour of children's pee" was how a character in a novel of mine described, perhaps opinionatedly, the generic white burgundy.

4. Get yourself a first-rate wine merchant. I do not just mean a reputable one who will invariably sell you wholesome drinks at not-excessive prices; they will all do this; I have never yet come across a disreputable wine merchant. What you want is a learned, experienced, energetic man who himself drinks not only good wine but a lot of wine, in other words a *first-rate* wine merchant. How you find him is another question. Go for a small or smallish firm, who have the chance of getting to know the individual customer and his tastes. Ask your friends. Grab a fellow wine-resenter and make a start on the classified directory.

5. Having found your man, trust him. Ask him for a decent drinkable red you will enjoy yourself and can offer to guests without shame. These days this will cost you £1 a bottle. Resign yourself to that. Also ask for a treat wine for anniversaries and when old Shagbag comes to dinner. This will cost £3 a bottle. Resign yourself to *that*. There are also, of course, wines at £2, and listen carefully to what your chap says about them. Also take his advice on hocks and moselles, shutting your ears when he rhapsodizes about white burgundies.

6. Grit your teeth and do as much as you can bear of the let-it-settle, bring-it-up-ahead-of-time, open-it-well-before-

drinking routine. It really will make a difference. But bear in mind

> G.P. 8: *Careful preparation will render a poor wine just tolerable and a very nice wine excellent. Skimping it will diminish a pretty fair wine to all right and a superb wine to merely bloody good. That is about as much difference as it will make. Much more important is price, which is normally a very reliable indicator of quality. Nevertheless*

You will find that, when you are confident of serving something at least reasonably drinkable, you will be the more anxious to improve it by taking trouble beforehand.

7. Hit your wine merchant across the mouth when, innocently trying to put you on to a good thing, or what he sees as one, he recommends you to "buy for laying down." It is true that wine improves and increases in value with age, broadly speaking, and that you can save a lot of money (and worry) by seeing to it that the ageing takes place after, rather than before, you buy it. But "Pay now, drink in 1984" strikes me—perhaps me more than most, but indubitably me—as a dreadfully depressing slogan. (It is this consideration, by the way, that hurls out of court any scheme for making your own beer, mead, elderflower wine, etc., though stand ready to drink *other people's* home-made brews like mad: they are often amazingly good. "Cork tightly and keep for eighteen months" the books will gaily enjoin, when continuing in suspense for eighteen minutes is rather more than most respectable drink-men would be justified to endure.) Fork out your £1–3 and look and feel pleasant. Life is too short.

8. Keep at hand a good supply of beer, stout and cider, not to speak of stronger waters, to console you when the whole business gets too much for you.

If all be true that I do think
There are five reasons we should drink;
Good wine—a friend—or being dry—
Or lest we should be by and by—
Or any other reason why.

—HENRY ALDRICH (1648–1710)

Ale, man, ale's the stuff to drink
For fellows whom it hurts to think:
Look into the pewter pot
To see the world as the world's not.

—A. E. HOUSMAN

If ever I marry a wife,
    I'll marry a landlord's daughter,
For then I may sit in the bar,
    And drink cold brandy and water.

—CHARLES LAMB

I would to God that I were so much clay
    As I am blood, bone, matter, passion, feeling;
For then at least the past were past away,
    And for the future—but I write this reeling,
Having got drunk exceedingly today,
    So that I seem to stand upon the ceiling:
I say, the future is a serious matter;
But now, for God's sake, hock and soda-water!

—LORD BYRON

FURTHER THOUGHTS
ON WINE*

FOR THE MAN whose curiosity on the subject has not been totally assuaged by the foregoing.

1. Make up your mind to drink wine *in quantity*. I am not exactly advising you to add three bottles of vintage claret to your normal daily intake, but even when drunk to excess, wine has less severe short-term and long-term effects on your condition than an excess of spirits or fortified wines (sherry, port). Unless you are uncontrollably rich, in which case you are probably not deigning to read this, try the cheap table wines from France, Spain, Portugal or Austria that are sold under brand names in every off-licence. They are carefully blended to ensure that their taste and general standard remain constant, and are an excellent basis from which to start your more ambitious forays into the vintages. Shop around until you find one you really go for, but carry on shopping around after that.

2. Also shop around under your wine merchant's auspices. Ask him to make up an assorted case for you—two bottles each

---

* This and the two following sections were compiled with the aid of my friend Christopher Leaver.

of six different wines is better than one each of a dozen—and tell him whether you prefer dry or sweet, light or heavy, cheap or not so cheap. Repeat the treatment *ad libitum*.

3. Join a wine club. There are plenty of these springing up; there might be one in your area; your wine merchant might be able to recommend one. You may even find a course on wine being given by your local night school, especially in London under the G.L.C.

4. On the principle of not barking yourself if you keep a dog, test out the wine waiter whenever you eat in a restaurant, as follows. If he wears a little silver badge in his lapel, he is a member of the Guild of Sommeliers (cellarmen), and you stand a chance. If, asked what he recommends, he shows no interest in what you are eating, or refers to a wine merely by its number on the list, consign him to hell either silently or aloud, according to taste. If, requested to fetch a Pommard 1966 domaine-bottled, he leans over to see where you are pointing and says, "Ah yes, a bottle of Number 65—that is very good," he is no less of a villain, for he has shown he does not even know his way round his cellar, let alone have any idea of what is good or not so good in it. If he passes so far, and if you are in a tolerant, unexacting frame of mind, you may let him guide you. But if he then brings you something that you think is either ordinary at a high price or nasty at any, tell him so and *make him sample it himself*. This will take him down a satisfying peg, however hotly he may protest on tasting that the wine is first-rate, and he might even—who knows?—try a little harder next time. If you want to cut out all fuss and argument, simply ask for a carafe of the house hock, claret or whatever. This, without necessarily being very good to drink, will always be good value, because the management must both keep its price down and see to it that it remains at a consistent not-bad level. And if, of course, you want to put the wine

waiter down, study the wine list long and carefully before handing it back with a smiling shake of the head and ordering your carafe: a hefty implication that either they have nothing up to the standard you and your guests expect, which is conceivable, or they are charging too much for their listed wines, which is quite likely.

5. Follow the advice of wine merchants, wine clubs, wine waiters, even wine journalists, but never forget that your own taste is the final judge. Like the solicitor who keeps his clientèle safely under sedation by the use of fanciful legal jargon—did you know that any fool can do his own conveyancing, i.e. legally transfer property between himself and another?—so the wine snob, the so-called expert and the jealous wine merchant (there are a few) will conspire to persuade you that the subject is too mysterious for the plain man to penetrate without continuous assistance. This is, to put it politely, disingenuous flummery. It is up to you to drink what you like and can afford. You would not let a tailor tell you that a pair of trousers finishing a couple of inches below the knee actually fitted you perfectly; so, with wine, do not be told what is correct or what you are sure to like or what suits you. Specifically:

(*a*) Drink any wine you like with any dish. You will, in practice, perhaps find that a heavy red burgundy drowns the taste of oysters (though my wife likes claret with them), or that a light flowery hock is overpowered by a steak *au poivre*. But what is wrong with red wine and chicken, a light claret accompanying a Dover sole? The no-reds-with-fish superstition is widespread and ingrained, so much so that, in the film of *From Russia, With Love*, James Bond was able to say, in jest but without further explanation, that he ought to have spotted one of the opposition when the man broke that "rule" in the dining-car of the Orient Express. All he should reasonably have inferred was that the chap was rather independent-minded. I myself will happily drink red with any fish, and the fact that I will even more happily drink a hock, a moselle or an Alsatian wine with my fish stems from the other fact that I am particularly fond of hocks, moselles and Alsatian wines. The North of England couple I once read about who shared a bottle of crème de menthe (I hope it was a half-bottle) to go with their grilled turbot should be an inspiration, if not a literal example, to us all. Anyway, why not start by choosing a wine you know you like and then build your meal round it?

(*b*) Vintages—aargh! Most of the crap talked about wine centres on these. "The older the better" is another popular pseudo-rule. It does apply up to a point to château-bottled clarets, especially those known as classed growths. This is a precise technical term, not a piece of wine-snobs' jargon, but I cannot expound it here; consult your wine merchant or wine encyclopedia. There are rich men who will drink nothing but old first-growth clarets to show their friends how well they know their wines (and how rich they are). These are likely to be wonderful wines, true, but such men are missing a lot—see below. And old wines as such are not necessarily good; they may well have gone off or always have been bad, whatever that bloody vintage chart or card may have said. Throw it away, or keep it in a drawer until you know the subject a bit and can pick up cheap the good wines of a "bad" year.

6. A couple of warnings. Beware of curiously shaped or oddly-got-up bottles: you are likely to be paying for the parcel rather than what is wrapped up in it. I would not want to decry Mateus Rosé, a pleasant enough drink which has been many a youngster's introduction to wine, but its allure, and its price, owe a lot to the work of the glassmaker. Also, beware of those imitation champagnes called sparkling burgundies. They are forms of bottled death. (Leaver's phrase and view; Amis is

defiantly rather fond of red sparkling burgundy. He admits he has never found any food it can be drunk with, but a half-bottle of it makes a—shall we say?—interesting apéritif and, if you handle the situation properly, ordering it, let alone appearing to enjoy it, can be a splendid knock-down to any companion who fancies himself as a bit of an expert on wine. It is without doubt the most vulgar drink known to man.)

> A bumper of good liquor
> Will end a contest quicker
> Than justice, judge, or vicar.
> — RICHARD BRINSLEY SHERIDAN

> The horse and mule live 30 years
> And nothing know of wines and beers.
> The goat and sheep at 20 die
> And never taste of Scotch or Rye.
> The cow drinks water by the ton
> And at 18 is mostly done.
> The dog at 15 cashes in
> Without the aid of rum and gin.
> The cat in milk and water soaks
> And then in 12 short years it croaks.
> The modest, sober, bone-dry hen
> Lay eggs for nogs, then dies at 10.
> All animals are strictly dry:
> They sinless live and swiftly die;
> But sinful, ginful, rum-soaked men
> Survive for three score years and ten.
> And some of them, a very few,
> Stay pickled till they're 92.
> — ANON, quoted in Arnold Silcock's
> *Verse and Worse*

WINE SHOPPER'S GUIDE

IN CHOOSING YOUR wine, whether from a supplier's price-list or in a restaurant, the obvious temptation is to go for a name you recognize. You would not recognize it unless it had a long reputation for quality; but such reputations set prices rising, and unfamiliar names may well bring you better value for money. As regards home drinking, faith in your wine merchant's recommendations will bring you that value and also provide you with interesting variety. In the restaurant, a good policy is to forget names, labels and vintages and go for a wine imported by a shipper whose wares you have enjoyed in the past. This brings up a general point of some importance.

Two bottles of a wine of the same year and from the same district will not necessarily taste the same. Soils can vary from one side of the road to the other; the vines on a southern slope will get more sun than those on a northern; M. Crapaud's processes may differ from M. Grenouille's. This becomes particularly noticeable in a large area like Beaune in Burgundy.°

° Point for pedants. The established rule is a capital for the place and a small letter for the wine, so you drink burgundy in Burgundy (if you have the luck), see that your champagne comes from one of the best

Shippers' methods differ too. One well-known firm matures its Meursault (a—usually—white burgundy from a sub-district within Beaune) in cask for three years before bottling; others bottle after two or even one. This is where your wine merchant comes in: he will know how individual shippers handle their wine, and will guide you to the one(s) who suit(s) your taste. (Shop salesmen are rarely much good for this kind of help, though their knowledge is, by and large, increasing.) Finally, have no fear of non-vintage "house" *vins ordinaires* labelled simply Red Bordeaux (etc.). They are nearly always better than all right, and excellent value.

Now to the wines of individual regions.

1. BORDEAUX. Reds (clarets). Here you have a couple of hundred different names to cope with, if you feel you must cope. One you recognize does carry with it a sort of guarantee: nowadays, the well-known châteaux can, by blending, offer a vintage every year regardless, and are too careful of their reputation to produce any bad wine under their label. But, as suggested earlier, you will to some extent be paying for the name. For better value for money, look for wines from these three districts: Côtes de Bourg, Côtes de Blaye and Côtes de Fronsac. They will be of a recent year, but never mind: they mature fast. 75p to £1 retail.* You will almost certainly have to pay much more than that for something good under more familiar names like Médoc or St Emilion.

Whites—specifically sweet whites. These can be first-rate value. Non-vintage Sauternes and Barsacs at 80–90p are

---

spots in Champagne. This breaks down when we come to districts within a wine-producing region. I have yet to read of anybody calling for a nice médoc or knocking back a glass of pouilly fuissé.

* What with the floating of the pound, the coming of V.A.T., etc., drink prices are on the rise. All the ones I quote are approximate.

delicious with fruit (or cheese) and for lingering over at the end of a meal. If you have more to spend and fancy something really luscious and fruity, you can get château-bottled° wines like Château Climens or Château Rieussec for £1.50 or less.

2. BURGUNDY. Wines with Burgundian village names, such as Pommard, Gevrey-Chambertin, Chambolle Musigny or Vosne Romanée, are becoming dearer and dearer and less and less value for money. It is even hard to find genuine examples of them, unless they are bottled by a highly reputable shipper, by your own wine merchant, or, best of all, at the *domaine*—which is to burgundy as château is to Bordeaux wines. The better-known names, like Nuits St Georges, are starting to disappear from merchants' lists; supply cannot meet demand, prices have shot up, and the "stretching" (=adulterating) of wines in the recent past has led to a virtual insistence on the growers' part that their product be bottled on the spot: more lowering of supply and increase in price. The answer is to look for less famous names, such as Givry, Fixin, Mercurey and Monthélie. These are ready to drink within four years of the vintage. In general, drink neither reds nor whites too old—ten years old is too old—and, as before, remember shippers' names.

Whatever I may have said elsewhere, the dry white wines of Burgundy are very good value, probably the best of their type in France. Go for Pouilly Fuissé, which can be drunk young at something under £1. Chablis, Meursault, Puligny Montrachet will cost you a little more.

2a. BEAUJOLAIS. (This is strictly a sub-region of Burgundy, but it is usually spoken and thought of as a region in its own right.) It was said, not very comfortably long ago, that the

° Bottled at the place of origin. A château in the wine sense is not literally a castle; it is much more likely to be a straggle of sheds.

French and the British between them drank every year five times the amount of beaujolais that Beaujolais annually produced, I believe, or perhaps merely hope, that since this became fairly common knowledge, and since the French had to get out of Algeria, we have returned to drinking real beaujolais. Anyway, what we now get under that name will cost about £1, and should be attacked in quantity, like beer, and, like beer, slightly chilled, and, like beer, as soon after bottling as you like—so, at any rate, with anything labelled just beaujolais or Beaujolais Villages. Moulin-à-Vent and Morgon need a couple of years in bottle. Fleurie, Brouilly and Chiroubles are good too.

Pink or rosé wines are sometimes looked down on as ladies' or non-drinkers' wines, but Beaujolais Rosé has more to it than most, being dry and—an oddity—servable either slightly chilled or at room temperature and with either hot or cold meals. One shipper claims you can drink it with curry, but I have not tested this. Good value at about 90p.

3. RHONE. The full, strong reds of these southern vineyards deserve to be better known. Everybody has heard of Châteauneuf du Pape (the white is good, too), but less famous names can be better value: Lirac, St Joseph, Crozes-Hermitage, Cornas, Gigondas. Being comparatively obscure, they are not shipped for chain distribution and hence there is no need to stretch them. They are well worth buying English-bottled whenever they can be found on a wine merchant's list, but you should not go above £1 or so.

With an exception or two, the whites are not really up to much. Tavel Rosé from the Rhône is always considered one of the best French rosés, but I find it rather dull. You may like it, though.

4. LOIRE. As the Rhône produces some of the best value in French reds, so the Loire for dry whites, but these are nearly always better when French-bottled. Muscadet, Touraine

Blanc and Vouvray are each about £1. Sancerre and Pouilly Fumé are better and pricier. All are excellent with sea-food or as an apéritif.

Reds: Chinon and St Nicholas de Bourgeuil really are fruity, often with a raspberryish flavour, but will run you into money: £1.50 or more. Rosé: Anjou Rosé, medium sweet. Sweet dessert white: Quarts de Chaume. Sparkling: Saumur, made in the champagne manner, but cheaper, and far from being bottled death. Good for summer mornings, weddings, etc.

5. ALSACE. Until recently, the Alsace whites (no reds are made) were very good value for money, but they have become popular and dearer. Each is named after the type of grape it is made from. Sylvaner and Riesling are good and not expensive at 90p or so. Traminer and Gewurtztraminer will take you up to £1.50, but have an extraordinary herby flavour all their own. Tokay d'Alsace is a toothsome dry wine at £1.25 or so. I like them all, but my favourite is Muscat, made, clearly enough, from the muscatel grape but without a trace of sweetness; about £1.25. Do try it—but leave some for me.

6. CHAMPAGNE. Any wine from France under this name will be good. By and large, you need not pay the extra 50p or so for vintage champagne. Bollinger N.V., one of the driest of all, is often as good as other people's vintage quality. Some pink champagne is made, but if you are with somebody who knows about these things, have a counter-attack ready when you order it. Some sweet champagne is made, and very horrible it is.

7. GERMAN WINES. These divide broadly into moselles or mosels, from the valley of the river of that name, and hocks or Rhine wines, from the valley of the guess-which. All, or all you will ever see unless you go there, are white. Generally, and in the cheaper range especially, moselles are drier and thinner than hocks, which are more varied. At under £1, look for such

moselles as Piesporter and Zeltinger, and, at perhaps a little more, for Bernkasteler—Deinhard's Bernkasteler "Green Label" is splendid value. With hocks, start with the wines of Niersteiner, find one you like, note the shipper and proceed from there.

Whatever the men in the know may say, a German wine label is a fearful thing to decipher. It tells you (starting at the top of the bottle) the vintage, the name of the village, the vineyard, the type of grape—moselles are always made from the Riesling type, and in their case this information is usually omitted, which makes things even more straightforward— the state of maturity of the grape when picked, in effect whether or not the wine was German-bottled, and the name of the grower or shipper. All very conscientious, but more than I want to know. However: note, as always, the shipper's name, and you can learn something from the state-of-maturity bit, the word invariably ending in *-lese. Spaetlese*, or "late picked," means a higher quality and often a good buy. *Beerenauslese* and *Trockenbeerenauslese* signify respectively selected grapes and selected overripe grapes, and produce the great sweet wines of Germany. I have never found one of these to beat a Château d'Yquem, the finest and most expensive of the Sauternes, but then I have never drunk a 1959 *Trockenbeerenauslese*. You can, if you can find one and can lay out £20 *a bottle*.

There are sparkling hocks and moselles. I can hear Leaver muttering about bottled death, and some people find them a little headachy, but I never have. They are considerably cheaper than champagne, can usually be passed off as it with the aid of a napkin round the bottle (a good tip for the mean man), and will certainly enliven a wine punch.

8. OTHERS. In general, these are best approached under merchants' advice or via your off-licence as described in the

first paragraph of my Further Thoughts on Wine, but here are a few notes.

Italy. Remember that chianti is not the only Italian wine; some people will find some of the reds a little heavy (cut them with Pellegrino mineral water). Barolo is a good solid red, and Soave a nice lightish white.

Spain. Rioja is usually spoken of as the best Spanish red. Avoid all sweet whites, and according to some (me included) the dry whites are not very nice either.

Portugal. Dão, both red and white. Mateus Rosé for student-age types.

Switzerland. If you are flush, try the full but soft red Dôle and the light white wines of Neuchâtel and Fendant.

Algeria. There are plenty of sound full-blooded reds at about 75p.

Yugoslavia. The Lutomer wines are usually good value and quite cheap.

Hungary. Bull's Blood is a fine strong red. You must try Tokay, the famous sweet desert and after-dinner wine.

FINAL NOTE

If you can afford the initial outlay (about £150 for something drinkable, £190 for something really good), buy a hogshead and bottle it yourself. You will end up with something like 300 bottles and save about a third on what the same wine would have cost you ready-bottled. Your wine merchant will arrange a preliminary tasting for you and give you the necessary advice and aid. A crew of three can cope easily. Remember that you may well find yourself "trying" the stuff while bottling, so take care not to invite too many neighbours in to "help," or that 300 will diminish sharply.

WHAT TO DRINK WITH WHAT

What
Simply-flavoured dishes,
hot or cold. Mild cheeses
of the English variety

Beef, lamb, pork, game,
poultry, any full-blooded
stuff. Stronger cheeses.
Pâté. Stews

Eggs and bacon, eggs and
chips, baked beans and
sausages

Hot and cold meats, picnic
meals, or nothing at all

What to drink with it
Inexpensive clarets like
Côtes de Bourg, Côtes de
Blaye, Côtes de Fronsac

Givry, Fixin, Dôle,
Monthélie, Old Algerian,
Mercurey, Morgon,
Moulin-à-Vent, Cornas, Lirac,
Gigondas, Châteauneuf du
Pape, Hermitage, Côte Rôtie,
Crozes-Hermitage, St Joseph

Any of the above, also beer,
cider, Guinness, Scotch and
water without ice (first-rate)

Any of the wines listed as
going with beef, lamb, pork,
etc., plus beaujolais, Beaujolais Villages, Fleurie, Brouilly,
Chiroubles

Soups	Sherry, Madeira if you're feeling fancy, or the end of your apéritif provided it doesn't contain hard liquor
Oysters	Chablis, Muscadet, Guinness, Black Velvet
Fish and chips	Guinness
Curry	Beer, cider, or try a tough red chianti
Cold dishes, fish, shellfish, salads, picnics	Puligny Montrachet, Meursault, Alsace Riesling or Sylvaner, Tokay d'Alsace, Tavel Rosé (if you must), Sancerre, Pouilly Fumé, Pouilly Fuissé, a non-pricey hock or moselle
Shellfish, jellied eels, cold meats	Gewurtztraminer, Traminer
Vichyssoise, melon, before lunch	Muscat d'Alsace, Piesporter, Zeltinger
Salads, shellfish, cold buffet	Beaujolais Rosé chilled
Hot dishes not heavily spiced	Beaujolais Rosé at room temperature

Desserts, fresh fruit, especially peaches	Quarts de Chaumes, Châteaux Rieusses and Climens, Sauternes, Barsac
Fondue	Neuchâtel will help you to force it down
Anything, everything or nothing	Champagne N.V.

ABROAD

I AM NOT referring to places like Paris, where you can drink as safely as anywhere in the world, and as enjoyably too if you have £25 per day to spend on drink alone and are slow to react to insolence and cheating; nor do I mean the wine-producing areas of France or Germany, where all you need is a couple of spare livers; I mean places more apparently un-civilized, off the more remorselessly beaten-up sections of the track.

1. The presence of a labelled bottle surrounding a wine guarantees nothing. You will do as well, or as ill, and more cheaply, with the stuff out of the barrel. If you can find out what the locals go for, choose that. (A sound general rule for eats as well.)

2. Faced with a choice between bad or untrustworthy red wine on the one hand, and ditto white on the other, pick the red. In Greece, where what red there is is often sweet, pick the resinated rather than the unresinated white.

3. Smell the stuff carefully before drinking. This is not empty winemanship; the object is merely to make sure it smells of wine, and not of decaying cabbages, damp blankets,

musty corks or vinegar. Not all these non-winey danger signals are unpleasant in themselves; also be on your guard against a whiff of almond or pear-drops.

4. If the red strikes you as thick, dark and heavy, feel no shame in cutting it with the local bubbly mineral water; worth trying in parts of Italy and Spain. And/or add ice. Nay, stare not so; we are not talking about vintage burgundy. The cheaper Portuguese reds are better iced, as the locals know.

5. If you still quail, try the beer. It will arrive too cold, and will often not be very nice, but I have never heard of positive harm being done by it.

6. Those with upset guts should avoid both wine and beer. Even at their best, they irritate the large intestine. No spirit does, but stick to brands you know. Spirits made abroad are suspect, apart from brandies, fruit brandies like slivovitz and calvados, and one or two oddities like Lisbon gin. I remember, not very well, an encounter with Yugoslav Scotch . . .

7. The cautious should look narrowly at all sparkling wines, except genuine French champagne, and at all sweet drinks. Still, one small glass cannot do you much harm; indeed, with some of those sparklers one sip is enough—so be even warier of ordering a whole bottle.

8. Gin men should slip a small bottle of Angostura into their luggage. You can knock together some sort of drink with it—and gin—under almost any conditions, and you can never find it abroad; well, yes, Gibraltar and Malta, perhaps.

Wine cheers the sad, revives the old, inspires the young,
makes weariness forget his toil, and fear her danger, opens a
new world when this, the present, palls.

—LORD BYRON

The dipsomaniac and the abstainer are not only both mistaken, but they both make the same mistake. They both regard wine as a drug and not as a drink.

— G. K. CHESTERTON

MEAN SOD'S GUIDE

THE POINT HERE is not simply to stint your guests on quality and quantity—any fool can pre pour Moroccan red into burgundy bottles, or behave as if all knowledge of the existence of drink has been suddenly excised from his brain at 10 p.m.—but to screw them *while seeming, at any rate to their wives, to have done them rather well*. Note the limitation: your ideal objective is a quarrel on the way home between each husband and wife, he disparaging your hospitality, she saying you were very sweet and thoughtful and he is just a frustrated drunk. Points contributing to this end are marked •.

• 1. Strike at once by, on their arrival, presenting each lady with a rose and each gent with bugger-all. Rub this in by complimenting each lady on her appearance and saying in a stentorian undertone to the odd gent, "I heard you hadn't been so well" (=pissed as a lizard every day) or "You're looking much better than when I saw you last" (i.e. with that emperor-sized hangover).

2. Vital requirement: prepare pre- and post-dinner drinks in some undiscoverable pantry or broom-cupboard well away from the main scene. This will not only screen your niggardlinesses; it will also make the fetching of each successive round look like a slight burden, and •will cast an unfavourable

limelight on any individual determined to wrest additional drinks out of you. Sit in a specially deep easy-chair, and practise getting out of it with a mild effort and, later in the evening, a just-audible groan, though beware of overdoing this.

3. As regards the pre-dinner period, procedures vary. The obvious one is to offer only one sort of drink, a "cup" or "punch" made of cheap red wine, soda water, a glass of cooking sherry if you can plunge that far, and a lot of fresh fruit to give an illusion of lavishness. Say you invented it, and add menacingly that it has more of a kick than might be expected. Serve in small glasses.

The cold-weather variant of this—same sort of wine, water, small glass of cooking brandy heated in a saucepan, pinch of nutmeg on top of each glass or mug—is more trouble, but it has two great advantages. One is that you can turn the trouble to positive account by spending nearly all your time either at the cooker, conscientiously making sure the stuff goes on being hot enough, or walking to and from the cooker—much more time than you spend actually giving people drinks. The other gain is that after a couple of doses your guests will be pouring with sweat and largely unable to take any more. (Bank up the fire or turn up the heating to aid this effect, remembering to reduce the temperature well before the kicking-out stage approaches.)

If, faced with either of these, any old-stager insists on, say, Scotch, go to your pantry and read the paper for a few minutes before filling the order. •Hand the glass over with plenty of emphasis, perhaps bawling as you do so, "One large Scotch whisky delivered as ordered, *sah!*"

Should you feel, as you would have reason to, that this approach is getting a little shiny with use, set your teeth and give everybody a more or less proper first drink. You can salve your pocket, however, by adding a tremendous lot of ice to fill up the glass (troublesome, but cheaper than alcohol), or, in the case of martinis, by dropping in an olive the size of a baby's fist (see *Thunderball*, by Ian Fleming, chapter 14). Cheat on later drinks as follows: in preparing a gin and tonic, for instance, put the tonic and ice and thick slice of lemon in first and pour on them a thimbleful of gin *over the back of a spoon*, so that it will linger near the surface and give a strong-tasting first sip, which is the one that counts. A friend of mine, whose mother-in-law gets a little excited after a couple of drinks, goes one better in preparing her third by pouring tonic on ice, wetting a fingertip with gin and passing it round the rim of the glass, but victims of this procedure must be se-lected with extreme care. Martinis should be as cold as before, but with plenty of melted ice. Whiskies are more difficult. Use the back-of-the-spoon technique with coloured glasses, or use the darkest brand you can find. Water the sherries.

4. Arrange dinner early, and see that the food is plentiful, however cheap it is. You can get away with not serving wine with the first course, no matter what it may be. When the main course is on the table, "suddenly realize" you have not opened the wine, and proceed to do so now with a lot of cork-popping. The wine itself will not, of course, be French or German; let us call it Ruritanian Gold Label. Pour it with cer-emony, explaining that you and your wife (•especially she) "fell in love with it" on holiday there and will be "interested" in people's reactions. When these turn out to consist of polite, or barely polite, silence, *either* say nostalgically that to appre-ciate it perhaps you have to have drunk a lot of it with that marvellous local food under that sun, etc., *or* announce bluffly, "Doesn't travel, does it? Doesn't travel." Judge your audience.

5. Sit over the remains of dinner as long as you dare or can bear to, then take the company off to the drawing-room and make great play with doling out coffee. By this stage (a vague, prolonged one anyhow), a good half-hour of abrupt

and total forgetfulness about the very idea of drink can profitably be risked. At its end, "suddenly realize" you have imposed a drought and offer brandy, explaining a good deal less than half apologetically that you have no cognac, only a "rather exceptional" Armagnac. This, of course, produced with due slowness from your pantry, is a watered-down cooking brandy from remote parts of France or from South Africa—a just-potable that will already, did they but know it, be familiar to those of your guests who have drunk "Armagnac" at the average London restaurant.* • Ask the ladies if they would care to try a glass of Strelsauvada, a "rather obscure" Ruritanian liqueur made from rotten figs with almond-skin flavouring which admittedly can "play you up" if you are not used to it. They will all say no and think highly of you for the offer.

6. Play out time with groan-preceded, tardily produced, ice-crammed Scotches, remembering the recourse of saying loudly, • "I find *myself* that a glass of cold *beer* [out of the cheapest quart bottles from the pub] is the best thing *at this time of night*."

7. Along the lines of sticking more fruit than any sane person could want in the pre-dinner "punch" or "cup," put out a lot of pseudo-luxuries like flood-damaged truncheon-sized cigars, bulk-bought •after-dinner mints, bankrupt-stock • vari-coloured cigarettes, etc.

8. Your own drinks. These must obviously not be allowed to fall below any kind of accustomed level, however cruel the deprivations you force on your guests. You will naturally

* The more sophisticated, and troublesome, method, much used in restaurants, is to take a couple of handfuls of raisins, split them open, put them in a basin, pour some lousy brandy over them and leave for twenty-four hours. Strain and serve as, probably, a little-known cognac rather than Armagnac.

refresh yourself with periodic nips in your pantry, but going thither at all often may make undesirable shags think, even say, that you ought to be bringing thence a drink for them. So *either* choose between a darkly tinted glass ("an old friend of mine in Venice gave it me—apparently it's rather valuable, ha ha ha") and a silver cup of some sort ("actually it's my christening-mug from T. S. Eliot—believe it or not, ha ha ha,") which you stick inseparably to and can undetectably fill with neat whisky, *or* boldly use a plain glass containing one of those light-coloured blends known, at any rate in the U.S.A., as a "husband's Scotch"—"Why, hell, Mamie, just take a look; you can see it's near as a damn pure water," and hell, Jim, Jack, Joe and the rest of the crowd.

9. If you think that all or most of the above is mere satirical fantasy, you cannot have been around much yet.

MEAN SLAG'S GUIDE

The following menu is intended only as an example. Remember that there must be plenty of everything, and that the hot dishes must be hot, so as to forestall a couple of obvious complaints. •The mean sod can help by making faces and vague noises at a couple of wives to suggest that the mean slag is at a difficult time of the month.

> *Petits pains et beurre*
> *Pouding de Yorkshire*
> *Spaghetti poco bolognese*
> *Boeuf à bon marché*
> *Pommes bouillies*
> *Navets vieux*
> *Salade de fruits sans sucre*
> *Café*

Notes. (i) A good ten minutes with no food in sight but rolls and butter will, as restaurants know, take the edge off most appetites.

(ii) Explain that in your native Wales they often start a meal with plain Yorkshire pudding, and hint that it is a particularly working-class dish in order to appease, or at least silence, any lefties in the company.

(iii) This is just spaghetti with not nearly enough sauce.

(iv) If, after this broadside of almost unrelieved starch, any of your guests are still afloat, roast stewing beef with boiled potatoes and old turnips (new ones are very nice if properly done) should finish them off. The no doubt considerable unconsumed portion of the beef can be curried next day.

(v) Leaving all sugar out of a fruit salad built mainly on fresh pineapple and oranges will make it virtually uneatable. You cannot actually refuse to provide sugar if asked, but there is a good chance that, in their beaten state, your guests will not raise the matter. As before, the leftovers can be rescued next day.

(vi) Must be fresh, and the process of making should be the most elaborate and lengthy and hitch-prone that can be found, with as much of it as possible taking place in front of the guests. It is a job for sod rather than slag, for while he is fiddling with the coffee he obviously cannot be pouring drinks, and there is • value there too.

A little-known Central American liquor: "Cassiri . . . the local drink made of fermented cassava [a root vegetable]." He drank some and handed the bowl to Tony. It contained a thick, purplish fluid. When Tony had drunk a little, Dr. Messinger explained, "It is made in an interesting way. The women chew the root up and spit it into a hollow tree-trunk."

— EVELYN WAUGH

THE HANGOVER

WHAT A SUBJECT! And, in very truth, for once, a "strangely neglected" one. Oh, I know you can hardly open a newspaper or magazine without coming across a set of instructions—most of them unoriginal, some of them quite unhelpful and one or two of them actually harmful—on how to cure this virtually pandemic ailment. But such discussions concentrate exclusively on physical manifestations, as if one were treating a mere illness. They omit altogether the psychological, moral, emotional, spiritual aspects: all that vast, vague, awful, shimmering metaphysical superstructure that makes the hangover a (fortunately) unique route to self-knowledge and self-realization.

Imaginative literature is not much better. There are poems and songs about drinking, of course, but none to speak of about getting drunk, let alone having been drunk. Novelists go into the subject more deeply and extensively, but tend to straddle the target, either polishing off the hero's hangover in a few sentences or, so to speak, making it the whole of the novel. In the latter case, the hero will almost certainly be a dipsomaniac, who is not as most men are and never less so than on the morning after. This vital difference, together with much else, is firmly brought out in Charles Jackson's marvellous and horrifying *The Lost Weekend*, still the best fictional account of alcoholism I have read.

A few writers can be taken as metaphorically illuminating the world of the hangover while ostensibly dealing with something else. Parts of Dostoevsky can be read in this way. Some of Poe's Tales convey perfectly the prevailing gloomy uneasiness and sudden fits of outlandish dread so many of us could recognize, and Poe himself had a drink problem; contrary to popular belief, he was not a dipsomaniac, but his system was abnormally intolerant of alcohol, so that just a couple of slugs would lay him on his back, no doubt with a real premature-burial of a hangover to follow. Perhaps Kafka's story *The Metamorphosis*, which starts with the hero waking up one morning and finding he has turned into a man-sized cockroach, is the best literary treatment of all. The central image could hardly be better chosen, and there is a telling touch in the nasty way everybody goes on at the chap. (I can find no information about Kafka's drinking history.)

It is not my job, or anyway I absolutely decline, to attempt a full, direct description of the metaphysical hangover: no fun to write or read. But I hope something of this will emerge by implication from my list of countermeasures. Before I get on to that, however, I must deal with the physical hangover, which is in any case the logical one to tackle first, and the dispersal of which will notably alleviate the other—mind and body, as we have already seen, being nowhere more intimately connected than in the sphere of drink. Here, then, is how to cope with

THE PHYSICAL HANGOVER

1. Immediately on waking, start telling yourself how lucky you are to be feeling so bloody awful. This, known as George

Gale's Paradox, recognizes the truth that if you do *not* feel bloody awful after a hefty night then you are still drunk, and must sober up in a waking state before hangover dawns.

2. If your wife or other partner is beside you, and (of course) is willing, perform the sexual act as vigorously as you can. The exercise will do you good, and—on the assumption that you enjoy sex—you will feel toned up emotionally, thus delivering a hit-and-run raid on your metaphysical hangover (M.H.) before you formally declare war on it.

Warnings. (i) If you are in bed with somebody you should not be in bed with, and have *in the least degree* a bad conscience about this, abstain. Guilt and shame are prominent constituents of the M.H., and will certainly be sharpened by indulgence on such an occasion

(ii) For the same generic reason, do not take the matter into your own hands if you awake by yourself.

3. Having of course omitted to drink all that water before retiring, drink a lot of it now, more than you need to satisfy your immediate thirst. Alcohol is a notorious dehydrant, and a considerable part of your physical hangover (P.H.) comes from the lack of water in your cells.

At this point I must assume that you can devote at least a good part of the day to yourself and your condition. Those who inescapably have to get up and do something can only stay in bed as long as they dare, get up, shave, take a hot bath or shower (more of this later), breakfast off an unsweetened grapefruit (m.o.t.l.) and coffee, and clear off, with the intention of getting as drunk at lunchtime as they dare. Others can read on—but let me just observe in passing that the reason why so many professional artists drink a lot is not necessarily very much to do with the artistic temperament, etc. It is simply that they can afford to, because they can normally take a large part of a day off to deal with the ravages. So, then,

4. Stay in bed until you can stand it no longer. Simple fatigue is another great constituent of the P.H.

5. Refrain at all costs from taking a cold shower. It may bring temporary relief, but in my own and others' experience it will give your M.H. a tremendous boost after about half an hour, in extreme cases making you feel like a creature from another planet. Perhaps this is the result of having dealt another shock to your already shocked system. The ideal arrangement, very much worth the trouble and expense if you are anything of a serious drinker, is a shower fixed over the bath. Run a bath as hot as you can bear and lie in it as long as you can bear. When it becomes too much, stand up and have a hot shower, then lie down again and repeat the sequence. This is time well spent.

Warning. Do not do this unless you are quite sure your heart and the rest of you will stand it. I would find it most disagreeable to be accused of precipitating your death, especially in court.

6. Shave. A drag, true, and you may well cut yourself, but it is a calming exercise and will lift your morale (another sideswipe at your M.H.).

7. Whatever the state of your stomach, do not take an alkalizing agent such as bicarbonate of soda. There is some of this in most hangover remedies but not enough to do you any harm, and the bubbling is cheerful. Better to take unsweetened fruit juice or a grapefruit without sugar. The reasoning behind this, known as Philip Hope-Wallace's Syndrome, is that your stomach, on receiving a further dose of acid, will say to itself, "Oh, I see: we need more alkaline," and proceed to neutralize itself. Bicarbonate will make it say, "Oh, I see: we need more acid," and do you further damage.

If you find this unconvincing, take heed of what happened one morning when, with a kingly hangover, I took bicarbonate with a vodka chaser. My companion said "Let's see what's happening in your stomach," and poured the remnant of the vodka into the remnant of the bicarbonate solution. The mixture turned black and gave off smoke.

8. Eat nothing, or nothing else. Give your digestion the morning off. You may drink coffee, though do not expect this to do anything for you beyond making you feel more wide-awake.

9. Try not to smoke. That nicotine has contributed to your P.H. is a view held by many people, including myself.

10. By now you will have shot a good deal of the morning. Get through the rest of it somehow, avoiding the society of your fellows. Talk is tiring. Go for a walk, or sit or lie about in the fresh air. At eleven or so, see if you fancy the idea of a Polish Bison (hot Bovril and vodka). It is still worth while without the vodka. You can start working on your M.H. any time you like.

11. About 12:30, firmly take a hair (or better, in Cyril Connolly's phrase, a tuft) of the dog that bit you. The dog, by the way, is of no particular breed: there is no obligation to go for the same drink as the one you were mainly punishing the night before. Many will favour the Bloody Mary, though see my remarks on this in the Drinks section. Others swear by the Underburg. For the ignorant, this is a highly alcoholic bitters rather resembling Fernet Branca, but in my experience more usually effective. It comes in miniature bottles holding about a pub double, and should be put down in one. The effect on one's insides, after a few seconds, is rather like that of throwing a cricket-ball into an empty bath, and the resulting mild convulsions and cries of shock are well worth witnessing. But thereafter a comforting glow supervenes, and very often a marked turn for the better. By now, one way or another, you will be readier to face the rest of mankind and a convivial

lunchtime can well result. Eat what you like within reason, avoiding anything greasy or rich. If your P.H. is still with you afterwards, go to bed.

Before going on to the M.H., I will, for completeness' sake, mention three supposed hangover cures, all described as infallible by those who told me about them, though I have not tried any of the three. The first two are hard to come by.

12. Go down the mine on the early-morning shift at the coal-face.

13. Go up for half an hour in an open aeroplane, needless to say with a non-hungover person at the controls.

14. Known as Donald Watt's Jolt, this consists of a tumbler of some sweet liqueur, Bénédictine or Grand Marnier, taken in lieu of breakfast. Its inventor told me that with one of them inside him he once spent three-quarters of an hour at a freezing bus-stop "without turning a hair." It is true that the sugar in the drink will give you energy and the alcohol alcohol.

At this point, younger readers may relax the unremitting attention with which they have followed the above. They are mostly strangers to the M.H. But they will grin or jeer at their peril. Let them rest assured that, as they grow older, the M.H. will more and more come to fill the gap left by their progressively less severe P.H. And, of the two, incomparably the more dreadful is

THE METAPHYSICAL HANGOVER

1. Deal thoroughly with your P.H.

2. When that ineffable compound of depression, sadness (these two are not the same), anxiety, self-hatred, sense of failure and fear for the future begins to steal over you, start telling yourself that what you have is a hangover. You are not sickening for anything, you have not suffered a minor brain lesion,

you are not all that bad at your job, your family and friends are not leagued in a conspiracy of barely maintained silence about what a shit you are, you have not come at last to see life as it really is, and there is no use crying over spilt milk. If this works, if you can convince yourself, you need do no more, as provided in the markedly philosophical

G.P. 9: *He who truly believes he has a hangover has no hangover*.

3. If necessary, then, embark on *either* the M.H. Literature Course *or* the M.H. Music Course *or* both in succession (not simultaneously). Going off and gazing at some painting, building or bit of statuary might do you good too, but most people, I think, will find such things unimmediate for this—perhaps any—purpose. The structure of both Courses, HANG-OVER READING and HANGOVER LISTENING, rests on the principle that you must feel worse emotionally before you start to feel better. A good cry is the initial aim.

HANGOVER READING

Begin with verse, if you have any taste for it. Any really gloomy stuff that you admire will do. My own choice would tend to include the final scene of *Paradise Lost*, Book XII, lines 606 to the end, with what is probably the most poignant moment in all our literature coming at lines 624–6. The trouble here, though, is that today of all days you do not want to be reminded of how inferior you are to the man next door, let alone to a chap like Milton. Safer to pick somebody less horribly great. I would plump for the poems of A. E. Housman and/or R. S. Thomas, not that they are in the least interchangeable. Matthew Arnold's *Sohrab and Rustum* is good, too, if a little long for the purpose.

Switch to prose with the same principles of selection. I suggest Aleksandr Solzhenitsyn's *One Day in the Life of Ivan Denisovich*. It is not gloomy exactly, but its picture of life in a Russian labour camp will do you the important service of suggesting that there are plenty of people about who have a bloody sight more to put up with than you (or I) have or ever will have, and who put up with it, if not cheerfully, at any rate in no mood of self-pity.

Turn now to stuff that suggests there may be some point to living after all. Battle poems come in rather well here: Macaulay's *Horatius*, for instance. Or, should you feel that this selection is getting a bit British (for the Roman virtues Macaulay celebrates have very much that sort of flavour), try Chesterton's *Lepanto*. The naval victory in 1571 of the forces of the Papal League over the Turks and their allies was accomplished without the assistance of a single Anglo-Saxon (or Protestant). Try not to mind the way Chesterton makes some play with the fact that this was a victory of Christians over Moslems.

By this time you could well be finding it conceivable that you might smile again some day. However, defer funny stuff for the moment. Try a good thriller or action story, which will start to wean you from self-observation and the darker emotions: Ian Fleming, Eric Ambler, Gavin Lyall, Dick Francis, Geoffrey Household, C. S. Forester (perhaps the most useful of the lot). Turn to comedy only after that; but it must be white—i.e. not black—comedy: P. G. Wodehouse, Stephen Leacock, Captain Marryat, Anthony Powell (not Evelyn Waugh), Peter De Vries (not *The Blood of the Lamb*, which, though very funny, has its real place in the tearful category, and a distinguished one). I am not suggesting that these writers are comparable in other ways than that they make unwillingness to laugh seem a little pompous and absurd.

HANGOVER LISTENING

Here, the trap is to set your sights too high. On the argument tentatively advanced against unduly great literature, give a wide berth to anyone like Mozart. Go for someone who is merely a towering genius. Tchaikovsky would be my best buy in this department, and his Sixth Symphony (the *Pathétique*) my individual selection. After various false consolations have been set aside, its last movement really does what the composer intended and, in an amazingly non-dreary way, evokes total despair: sonic M.H. if ever I heard it.

Alternatively, or next, try Tchaikovsky's successor, Sibelius. *The Swan of Tuonela* comes to mind, often recommended though it curiously is (or was in my youth) as a seduction background-piece. (Scope for a little article there.) Better still for our purpose, I think, is the same composer's incidental music to Maeterlinck's play, *Pelléas and Mélisande:* not to be confused with Debussy's opera of that name. The last section of the Sibelius, in particular, carries the ever-so-slightly phoney and overdone pathos that is exactly what you want in your present state.

If you can stand vocal music, I strongly recommend Brahms's *Alto Rhapsody*—not an alto sax, you peasant, but a contralto voice, with men's choir and full orchestra. By what must be pure chance, the words sung, from a—between you and me, rather crappy—poem of Goethe's, *Harzreise im Winter*, sound like an only slightly metaphorical account of a hangover. They begin, *"Aber abseits wer ist's?"*—all right, I am only copying it off the record-sleeve; they begin, "But who is that (standing) apart? His path is lost in the undergrowth," and end with an appeal to God to "open the clouded vista over the thousand springs beside the thirsty one in the desert." That last phrase gets a lot in. You can restore some of your fallen dignity by telling yourself that you too are a

Duerstender in der Wueste. This is a piece that would fetch tears from a stone, especially a half-stoned stone, and nobody without a record of it in his possession should dare to say that he likes music. The Kathleen Ferrier version is still unequalled after twenty years.

Turn now to something lively and extrovert, but be careful. Quite a lot of stuff that appears to be so at first inspection has a nasty habit of sneaking in odd blows to the emotional solar plexus; ballet music (except Tchaikovsky) and overtures to light operas and such are safer—Suppé, if you have no objection to being reminded of school sports days here and there, is fine. Or better, Haydn's Trumpet Concerto, which would make a zombie dance.

Jazz is not much good for your M.H., and pop will probably worsen your P.H. But if you really feel that life could not possibly be gloomier, try any slow Miles Davis track. It will suggest to you that, however gloomy life may be, it cannot possibly be as gloomy as Davis makes it out to be. There is also the likely bonus to be gained from hearing some bystander refer to Davis as Miles instead of Davis. The surge of adrenalin at this piece of trendy pseudo-familiarity will buck up your system, and striking the offender to the ground will restore your belief in your own masculinity, rugged force, etc.
Warning: Make quite sure that Davis's sometime partner, John Coltrane, is not "playing" his saxophone on any track you choose. *He* will suggest to you, in the strongest terms, that life is exactly what you are at present taking it to be: cheap, futile and meaningless.

Wine maketh merry: but money answereth all things.
— ECCLESIASTES

THREE NOTABLE BREAKFASTS

Sir Winston Churchill's
1 brace cold snipe
1 pint port

Horatio Bottomley's
1 pair kippers
1 tumbler brandy and water

Samuel Taylor Coleridge's **(Sundays only)**
6 fried eggs
1 glass laudanum° and seltzer†

° Alcoholic tincture of opium.
† An effervescent mineral water.

I never tasted [whisky], except once for experiment at the
inn at Inverary . . . It was strong but not pungent . . . What
was the process I had no opportunity of inquiring, nor do
I wish to improve the art of making poison pleasant.
— SAMUEL JOHNSON

THE BOOZING MAN'S DIET

THE FIRST, INDEED the only, requirement of a diet is that it should lose you weight *without reducing your alcoholic intake by the smallest degree*. Well, and it should be simple: no charts, tables, menus, recipes. None of those pages of fusspottery which normally end—*end*, after you have wasted minutes ploughing your way through—"and, of course, no alcohol" in tones of fatuous apology for laying tongue to something so pikestaff-plain. Of *course*? No *alcohol*? What kind of people do they think we are?

This diet took over a stone off me in three months, or what would have been three months if I had not often backslid with a curry or a fruit pie. That is about as fast a rate of loss as is medically desirable, which reminds me to say that you will consult your physician before embarking on the regime. No one, including no one's widow, is going to be able to sue me for having brought about a case of scurvy, osteitis deformans, alcoholic poisoning, diabetes, beri-beri or any other illness, disease or malady of any kind or sort whatsoever.

The scheme rests on

G.P. 10: *Eating fattens you.*

Nearly all diets start with the exclusion of bread, potatoes and sugar. This one goes on to exclude vegetables and fruit as well, or nearly. But remember, remember that drink is in. Here is

YOUR DAY'S FOOD

Breakfast is a whole grapefruit eaten without sugar, or, if you must, with artificial sweetener. Tea or coffee with the same sweetener if required. One boiled egg if you honestly have a long morning to get through. No bread or toast—and that goes for that bit of crust off your wife's toast. Drop it this minute, I say!

Lunch and dinner consist of a selection of thin soup, eggs, fish of all kinds, meat, poultry, game, etc., and cheese, laced with mustard and Worcester sauce. No thick sauces or pickles. Tea or coffee as required. Eat as much salt as you like. Some diets disrecommend this, on the grounds that salt causes the body to retain fluids and so in effect makes you heavier. This is true but ludicrous, unless you are so titanic that an extra few ounces will kill you as you rise from your chair. As well lose weight by donating blood or having your hair cut.

Notes. (i) Pick a sweetener combining saccharine with a little sugar for palatability's sake. Consult your chemist.

(ii) The point of the mustard and Worcester sauce is partly that you must have something to eke out the bareness of what you are allowed, and partly that both of them irritate the large intestine, giving the laxative effect you will need with a reduced food intake. Onions (avoid fried ones) will assist here.

(iii) Another substantial advantage of the diet is that you can stick pretty closely to it even when eating out, a testing time for diets. But, unless you fancy spending most of the meal discussing your weight problem with the company, say that your new-found aversion to vegetables, fruit, thick sauces and the rest springs from psychiatric advice or a religious conversion, either of which you prefer not to go into now.

(iv) Another eating-out tip, applying to restaurants: order a dish you hate or one you know they do badly. After a few mouthfuls of the average chicken à la Kiev or boeuf Stroganoff—two of my own unfavourites—your appetite will be fully satisfied. Make the waiter leave your plate in front of you while your companions' gâteaux, crêpes suzette and so on are being ordered and consumed.

YOUR DAY'S DRINK

Is a much more cheerful topic. Although your intake of alcohol will, as promised, remain undiminished, there are kinds of drink you should do your best to cultivate and give the go-by to respectively, as follows:

1. Keep your wines and fortified wines as dry as you can. However much nicer it may be, a Sauternes is more fattening than a white burgundy. Similarly, stay off sweet liqueurs, a policy which will, as noted, also help your hangover problem.

2. Avoid non-alcoholic additives, apart from water and soda. Slimmers' tonic water may well be less damaging to your figure than the ordinary kind, but I have conducted no controlled experiments in this field. Juices, especially tomato juice, are great fatteners.

3. Drink diabetic or low-calorie beer; so much the better if you can substitute some for your apéritif or after-dinner drink. There is an excellent one called Diät Pils (short for Pilsner, not pills) obtainable through some off-licences and groceries or direct from Holsten Distributors Ltd, 63 Southwark

Park Road, London SE16. There are shags who would attack this brew as artificial, non-authentic, etc., on which point consult G.P. 7 and ignore them. Diät Pils is very adequately alcoholic, pleasant to the eye, at least as tasty as most ordinary beers, and totally wholesome: approved, indeed, by the British Diabetic Association. It is admittedly a bit pricey, but, to my mind, worth every penny.

4. Alcohol science is full of crap. It will tell you, for instance, that drink does not really warm you up, it only makes you feel warm—oh, I see; and it will go on about alcohol being not a stimulant but a depressant, which turns out to mean that it depresses qualities like shyness and self-criticism, and so makes you behave as if you had been stimulated—thanks. In the same style, the said science will maintain that alcohol does not really fatten you, it only sets in train a process at the end of which you weigh more. Nevertheless, strong drink does, more than anything else taken by mouth, apart from stuff like cement, cram on the poundage. If you can face it, if you really want to be shapelier faster, if you are dissatisfied with zipping up your trousers at 45 degrees instead of vertically, cut down on hard liquor. Doing so will carry the bonus of—dare I say it?—conducing to your general health.

> Such power hath Beer. The heart which grief hath
> > canker'd
> Hath one unfailing remedy—the Tankard.
> > — CHARLES STUART CALVERLEY

HOW NOT TO GET DRUNK

THIS IS STRICTLY two topics—how to keep sober (or at least relatively in control) at a drinking party, and what to avoid with the morning after in mind—but they overlap so much in practice that I will treat them under the same heading.

Staying away altogether is a stratagem sometimes facetiously put forward at the outset of such discussions as these. To move at once to the realm of the practical, *eating* has much to be said for it. As well as retarding (though not preventing) the absorption of alcohol, food will slow up your drinking rate, not just because most people put their glasses down while actually chewing, but because you are now satisfying your appetite by eating rather than drinking: hunger makes you drink more than you otherwise would. According to some, oily foods are the most effective soakers-up of the drink already in your stomach, but others point to the risk of upsetting a digestion already under alcoholic attack.

There is a great deal of folklore about *taking some olive oil or milk* before joining the party. This will indeed retard absorption of alcohol, but, as before, it will all get to you in the end. Do not, in any case, overdo the fatty prelude. An acquaintance of mine, led astray by quantitative thinking, once started the evening with a tumbler of olive oil, following this up with a dozen or so whiskies. These, after a couple of hours of nibbling at the film of mucilage supposedly lining his stomach, finally broke through in a body and laid him on the floor of the saloon bar of the Metropole Hotel, Swansea, fortunately after I had left. I would be chary of this tactic. The principle does, however, work well the other way round. In the middle of a greasy meal, a quick neat double brandy certainly seems to hose down your stomach wall and give you heart and strength to continue eating.

Diluting your drinks sounds a good idea to many, and will help to reverse the dehydration that all alcohol brings, so that you will be better off next day. But, again, the alcohol itself will get to you in full. Nor is it true (in my experience, at least) that a double Scotch, say, diluted with a lot of soda takes longer to put down than the same with a little, so reducing your effective intake. The opposite of all this is truer. Spirits distilled out at 70° British proof, which are what you will usually meet, are too strong in the neat state to be wholly absorbed by the system; a proportion is eventually passed without ever having reached you. Dilution with just less than an equal amount of water is the point at which all the alcohol will enter your bloodstream—a fact known, without benefit of science, to Scotch and Irish drinkers for two centuries. So, in fact, spirit-bibbers should try *drinking neat un-iced spirits*, a practice so gruelling that their actual intake is almost bound to drop too.

I pass over such unhelpful prescriptions as *being tall and fat*; it is nevertheless true that your degree of drunkenness depends on a proportion between how much you drink and how large a frame you have to spread it over, with the result that big men, other things being equal, can take more than small men. Other things, of course, never are equal, though there is not much that can be done about them either. *Not being tired, not being depressed, not being specially elated*—these and other negative states will also stiffen your resistance to alcohol, but I know they do not descend at will. It can be said, however, not very cheeringly, that you should watch your drinking rate when you are tired, depressed, etc., (in fact always, because x drinks drunk in y minutes are more potent than x drinks drunk in $2y$ minutes).

Fatigue is an important element in the hangover, too. Alcohol gives you energy, or, what is hard to distinguish from it, the illusion of energy, and under its influence you will stand for hours at a stretch, throw yourself about, do exhausting imitations, perhaps fight a bit, even, God help you, dance. This will burn up a little alcohol, true, but you will pay for it next morning. A researcher is supposed once to have measured out two identical doses of drink, put the first lot down at a full-scale party and the second, some evenings later, at home with a book, smoking the same number of cigarettes on each occasion and going to bed at the same time. Result, big hangover and no hangover respectively. *Sitting down whenever possible*, then, will help you, and so, *a fortiori*, will *resisting the temptation to dance*, should you be subject to such impulses.

An equally unsurprising way of avoiding fatigue is *going to bed in reasonable time*, easily said, I know, but more easily done, too, if you allow the soporific effects of drink to run their natural course. This means staying away from stimulants, and that means *avoiding coffee*, both on its own and with liquor poured into it: the latter, by holding you up with one hand while it pastes you at leisure with the other, is the most solidly dependable way I know of ensuring a fearful tomorrow. Hostesses, especially, should take note of this principle, and cut out those steaming midnight mugs which, intended to send the company cheerfully on its way, so often set the tongues wagging and the Scotch circulating again.

Avoiding things can hardly help coming up more than once in the present connection. To proceed, then: *avoiding very strong drinks* is more than the piece of padding it may seem. The alcoholic strength or proof of a wine, spirit, etc., is not a straightforward index of its power to intoxicate. The relationship is non-linear, or, if you must have everything spelt out, the graph plotting proof against kick is not straight. Above the standard strength of spirits it bends sharply upward, so that for instance green Chartreuse, which is distilled out at 96° proof, is not just a bit over a third as strong again as, say, a gin at 70°, but several times stronger in its effect.

I once shared a half-litre bottle of Polish Plain Spirit (140° proof) with two chums. I only spoke twice, first to say, "Cut out that laughing—it can't have got to you yet," and not all that much later to say, "I think I'll go to bed now."

Hand in hand with this warning comes one about *avoiding sweet drinks*. These play hell with you next day; I forget why, but I remember how. So go carefully, at least, with Southern Comfort, a delicious compound of old bourbon whiskey, oranges and peaches that tips the scales at 87.7° proof.

Avoiding unfamiliar drinks is my final interdiction. Here, again, I mean more than just steering clear of Malagasy malaga, St Peter Port port-type and such, at any rate when you are not in a mood of pure curiosity and cold sober. A friend reports seeing a Highland sergeant, weaned on a bottle of Scotch a day, pass out in his chair after his first-ever half-dozen glasses of table wine. I asked if he was shamming, and was told that his mates were kissing his girl over his recumbent form, which was felt to clinch matters. It is as if—and in the always subjective, idiosyncratic context of drink it need only be as if— body and mind together develop a tolerance to your usual potation, a kind of self-conferred immunity. Do not test this hypothesis too rigorously.

I suppose I cannot leave this topic without reciting the old one about *drinking a lot of water and taking aspirin and/or stomach powders before you finally retire*. It is a pretty useless one as well as an old one because, although the advice is perfectly sound, you will find next morning that you have not followed it. Alternatively, anyone who can summon the will and the energy and the powers of reflection called for has not reached the state in which he really needs the treatment.

After all these bans and discouragements I will throw in one crumb, or tot, of comfort. I am nearly (yes, nearly) sure that mixing your drinks neither makes you drunker nor gives you a worse time the following day than if you had taken the equivalent dosage in some single form of alcohol. After three dry martinis and two sherries and two glasses of hock and four of burgundy and one of Sauternes and two of claret and three of port and two brandies and three whiskies-and-soda and a beer, most men will be very drunk and will have a very bad hangover. But might not the quantity be at work here? An evening when you drink a great deal will also be one when you mix them.

Well—if you want to behave better and feel better, the only absolutely certain method is *drinking less*. But to find out how to do *that*, you will have to find a more expert expert than I shall ever be.

When a man commits a crime under what is miscalled the "influence" of drink, he should, where possible, be punished double—once for the bad act, and once for the misuse of the good thing, by forcing it to reveal his true nature.

— GEORGE SAINTSBURY

Every Day Drinking

THERE'S A CERTAIN satisfaction to be got from bringing out a book of collected journalism. Being paid twice for the same basic work is always agreeable, and in my case not as frequent as I should like. More than that, you have the chance of correcting your mistakes of fact and style, or some of them, putting in stuff you forgot or didn't know about the first time round, and righting the wrongs done you by the copyeditor and the printer. Some of the satisfaction given by the last of these is of the rather grim variety, because of damage already done. It would be nice if everybody who saw the newspaper columns were to buy and read this book, but no, and all over the place some people will continue to think that I think that "anymore" and "forever" are single words and (thanks in the first place to the copytaker on the telephone) that "alright in it's way" is all right in some way or other.

The most satisfying satisfaction of all, at least until the cheque comes, is afforded by restoring editorial cuts. There's no such thing as a non-cutting editor; it's not in the nature of the beast. The fellow prowls through your copy like an overzealous gardener with a pruning hook, on the watch for any phrase he senses you were rather pleased with, preferably one that also clinches your argument and if possible is essential to the general drift of the surrounding passage. Then— slash! Sending in exactly the number of words asked for only sharpens his eye and his cutting edge.

I have made no serious attempt to disguise or repair the Saturday-newspaper look and feel of these articles. To do so with any style would have involved transforming them entirely into longish essays on wine, spirits, beer, etc., implying a claim to a sort of completeness and authority I'm afraid I'm not up to. Let me rub in for a moment the fact that the pieces were written to be read one at a time at weekly intervals. This accounts for and perhaps excuses the occasional recurrence of favourite themes. It also suggests that readers of this book might do well to take it a bit at a time. A couple of dozen cocktails on the trot, some no doubt better made than others, can lead to a definite feeling of fullness.

My close personal involvement with drinks and drinking goes back all of forty years. In that time my experience has been varied and farflung. I have drunk cognac in Cognac, port in Oporto, raki in Turkey, tequila in Mexico City, moonshine in Kentucky, not to mention poteen in Fleet Street, bitter and industrial alcohol in Oxford, Yugoslav whisky in Yugoslavia, Japanese whisky in Glasgow and sweet Spanish wine and lemonade in Swansea. Also gin in England.

Drinks writers have got to put on a show of covering the whole subject, but I would never believe a man who claimed to be equally interested or qualified in all the kinds of booze. I am basically a beer-and-spirits man myself, at least I started off with beer. You virtually had to in those far-off days. I drink a good deal less of it now, partly because I can afford not to, partly because in this country beer is intimately associated with pubs and pub life, and something horrible has happened to pub life.

With spirits I feel I am on home ground. They are really my tipple. I have to face it. At the same time I have found out quite a lot about them. Quite recently they have started to become important in a new way with this cocktail revival, hard to believe in but apparently real enough.

Cocktails have always appealed to me because they involve mixtures, experiments, paraphernalia, testing, tasting, finally serving. For the same reason I enjoy cups and coolers, and punches both cold and hot with wines and spirits and all combinations.

Now we reach the point at which my credentials become slightly less than impeccable. With all those drinks I have got through, what I have not done is drink first-rate table wines at their place of origin, work my way through classic vintages and develop an educated palate. To do that, what you really need, shorn of the talk, is a rich father, and I missed it. No complaints, but my lack of erudition in this department is going to limit my remarks on wine to the short, the sharp and the practical, to what my own God-given taste will reach to.

While I was passing up the chance of finding out about the great Burgundies, I was at any rate learning something about the vital part played in the world of drink by finance. At its crudest, this involved a straight calculation of alcoholic potency against price, and there was a time I remember well when after some research it was established that three barley wines, a pint of rough cider and a small whisky gave you the best return on—can it have been five bob? Unhappily, there are no bargains above that sort of level—you tend to get what you pay for. Treat all alcoholic snips with the greatest reserve.

Apart from the occasional hint designed to protect you against being bullied by a wine waiter or poisoned by your host at a private party, my advice will be meant to help you to serve good drinks in your own home.

Gin was invented by the Dutch, but the English took it up about four hundred years ago and spread it round the world. It consists of an extremely pure spirit, flavoured with juniper berries and other ingredients, or "botanicals," such as coriander seed and cinnamon bark. There are no fine gins as there are fine brandies and fine whiskies, but there are some very good and popular ones. Always buy one or other of these, a nationally known brand, and avoid supermarket and off-licence gins.

Most gin in this country is drunk with tonic and ice and lemon. And, if you want to take trouble, a squeeze of fresh lemon juice. After many years of exposure, I find this a rather unworthy, mawkish drink, best left to women, youngsters and whisky distillers. Its history is suspect: in the days of the Empire, you were supposed to drink quinine water, the ancestor of tonic, to keep away fever. Someone noticed that the vile stuff went down a little better if you splashed gin into it. What an idea!

One large gin and tonic is acceptable as a thirst quencher. You will do better, even so, with gin and Schweppes ginger beer (and plenty of ice). I would name this one of the great long drinks of our time, almost worth playing a couple of hours' cricket before imbibing.

For further, serious, drinking I recommend gin and water—and ice and lemon. This combination is favoured by the understandably popular George Gale. My advice: make sure you don't overdo the water.

Gin and water is an all-round improvement on gin and tonic: cheaper, less fattening and less filling as well as not being sweet or gassy. Gin is a real and interesting drink, carefully prepared with those botanicals and all, and it deserves to be sampled with its flavour unimpaired. Try it un-iced, with a little Malvern water—and nothing else. Very comforting in cold weather. Do this persistently and you will find marked differences between brands.

The Singapore Sling is a famous old gin mix with many recipes, some of them elaborate. As served in the Long Bar of Raffles Hotel, Singapore, it has eleven ingredients. My corner-cutting, tasty, forceful version calls for two parts gin, one cherry brandy (Cherry Heering is the best) and two or three parts fresh fruit juice (orange will do very well).

Now, an unusual gin cocktail: the Salty Dog, which I picked up on a trip to Nashville, Tennessee. (No, nothing to do with the bloody music.) Moisten the rim of a glass and twirl it about in a saucer of table salt, so that it picks up a thickish coating about a quarter of an inch deep. Carefully add one part gin and two parts fresh grapefruit juice, stir thoroughly, add ice, stir again, and drink through the band of salt. Splendid for out of doors.

Just why the British pub has declined so disastrously in recent years is a matter for argument. The greed of the brewers, the rise of youthful affluence, changes in the wage structure and the new stay-at-home "culture" must all be something to do with it. But that there has been a disaster is beyond dispute.

Once, an evening in the pub was a joy, a social event unlike any other. Now, in most places it would be a severe ordeal for all sorts of people, people of widely varying ages and tastes. An ordeal in what ways? I may as well spell them out.

First, the first thing you notice is the music—to be heard in what proportion of pubs? Seventy per cent? More? And what music? Usually, the least imaginative, most predictable records in the Top Twenty, picked for their supposed catchiness, the musical equivalent of bubble gum. If not this, then country music, Irish records, whatever, as long as it's *loud*, loud enough to make conversation a strain.

Next, the decor, intended not to please the customer but to set trends, win prizes for interior design and look good in trade photographs. The effect is showy and obtrusive, with red walls, red carpets, even red furniture, not quiet and pleasantly restful as it should be. On the plus side: more places to sit down than formerly.

As regards drink itself, the decline is less marked. Various bland-tasting, weak and overpriced lagers, often with foreign names, are on draught, also many a sweet, gassy "best bitter," but nobody is forced to drink them in preference to real ale and higher-gravity bottled lagers. On spirits, no complaints. In fact you will be served a better gin and tonic today than you used to get. Only the wine is a scandal, particularly the red, nearly always poor to plain bad and again overpriced. Remember the shouts of victory when at last the pubs agreed to serve wine by the glass!

The food, though I suppose one should be glad to see it there at all, is frequently appalling, greasy lukewarm hamburgers and sausages with tinned veg and rehydrated potato.

The clientele is usually amiable enough, but some patrons regard the increasing presence of women, and even more that of children, as an encroachment and an attack on the pub's time-honoured function as a male refuge.

The staff, much more often than in the past, are inclined

to be indifferent or surly, lazy too, leaving glasses uncleared, ashtrays overflowing and litter piling up. Pride in the job seems to have gone.

And if, despite everything, you look like having a good time, there are Space Invaders machines to distract you and, lately, new improved fruit machines with more advanced lights and noises.

However it started, why does it still go on? Because we put up with it. In shops, in restaurants, in places of entertainment, in pubs, however bad it is, we troop back for more.

British people of all classes hate complaining and making a fuss. I suppose if they ever started to, it wouldn't be in the pub. But what a nice thought.

The Bloody Mary is a delicious and most sustaining concoction, universally popular, just the thing for a Sunday morning party or pre-brunch session—or indeed any time when the afternoon is vacant. When you're making up a large quantity of the mixture in advance for an occasion like this, you reckon on using a rather more elaborate formula than the simple double vodka, plus tomato cocktail, plus Worcester sauce you get in the pub, perfectly good as that is.

My recipe, perfected after years of experiment, goes like this (the proportions are not critical): ½ bottle vodka, 2 pints tomato juice, 2 tablespoons tomato ketchup, 4 tablespoons orange juice, 4 tablespoons lemon juice, 1 tablespoon (perhaps more) Worcester sauce, 1 flat teaspoon celery salt, and lots of ice. Other recipes include tabasco, cayenne pepper and similar heat-producing agents. Best avoided—it's all too easy to overspice this drink.

Mixing the ingredients together is no problem with a blender. In its absence, put the vodka in some smallish container and stir the ketchup into it till fully emulsified, add celery salt and stir till all lumps are broken up, then stir in the orange and lemon juice. Add this mixture to the tomato juice in large jug, stir vigorously with ice and remove ice before serving in wineglasses. Makes 12–15 drinks.

Doing all this is quite a lot of trouble, as making good drinks always is, but if you really want to be told you make marvellous Bloody Marys, as opposed to just being given a grunt of thanks at best, you will find it well worthwhile. What does the trick is the blandness of the orange juice, which seems to soften the acidity of the lemon juice, and even more the sugar in the ketchup. Although they don't much care for being told so, quite a lot of people in this country don't like dry drinks and often prefer a hint of sweetness. (Remember this when choosing wine for dinner parties.)

With mixed drinks you can sometimes cut corners, and with this one the cheapest supermarket vodka will do very well, but the tomato juice must be the most expensive you can reasonably find; make sure, though, that it's free of added flavouring. The fruit juices must, of course, be fresh and freshly squeezed.

This is a sustaining drink, as I said, which means among other things that it fills you up. Bear this in mind when you come to feed the fellows. Instead of any kind of full-dress lunch, give them cold cuts, salads, baked potatoes, cheese, that kind of thing. In winter you can probably rise to a soup. Keep beer and some light wine handy, but their lack of enthusiasm for this is likely to be quite noticeable as, clutching what may or may not be their last Bloody Mary, they slump down at the table.

The Bloody Mary is sometimes thought to be good for

hangovers. This seems odd to me. All those acid fruit juices, plus Worcester sauce, would be apt to go down rather badly on any sort of upset stomach. A whisky and dry ginger is far kinder.

The most popular summery or out-of-doorsy drink is undoubtedly Sangria, that old Spanish concoction with the three great advantages of being cheap, easy to make up and pretty harmless—so that you can drink a lot of it without falling down. The standard recipe calls for red wine and soda water in the proportion of two to one plus a spot of sugar, say four teaspoons per bottle of wine melted in a little hot water. Throw in any fresh fruit you have, but remember it starts looking tired after half an hour or so. Ice too, of course. The Spaniards float a bit of cinnamon stick on top.

One worthy variant is wine and fizzy lemonade, which means you can forget the sugar—perfectly okay. What is not okay is short-changing on the wine. It should be cheap but drinkable, good enough to be drinkable on its own, in fact. Although this is a Spanish tipple, the Spanish reds you get in this country are in my experience to be treated with reserve, and I would go for something modest from France or Italy.

When you next see fresh limes on offer, grab a couple of dozen and a couple of bottles of rum—the Jamaica is the best for this—and give a Planters Punch party. There are dozens of recipes. The traditional version, a kind of rhyme, specifies one part of sour (lime juice), two of sweet (sugar), three of strong (rum), four of weak (soda water and ice). Very good, but perhaps a little bland. I prefer the so-called American formula, one sweet, two sour, three weak, four strong. Serve in tall glasses, with sprigs of mint, a maraschino cherry and straws for the full treatment.

Here is a Victorian recipe for something called a Cool Cup, unusual but straightforward. Take a quarter of a pint of Amontillado sherry and stir in sweetened lemon juice, say one lemon and 6 teaspoons of sugar. Add ice cubes, stir and pour in a quart bottle of chilled dry cider. The book tells you to add a sprig of borage, thyme or mint but here you can afford to suit yourself. Makes 10 drinks.

If you have a bit of money to throw around, try what Cyril Ray calls his Swagger Sling. This is a bottle of champagne, a bottle of claret, a glass of brandy, a glass of Grand Marnier, lemon and sugar and nothing else. No ice, he says. Chill the ingredients beforehand. Calculated to put young ladies completely at their ease.

Shandy is an old hot-weather drink on which the great and thirsty Evelyn Waugh produced his own variation. Put into a silver tankard, or failing that a pint glass, some ice cubes, one or two double gins according to mood, and a bottle of Guinness. Fill up with ginger beer. One advantage of this is that you can get it run up for you in the pub. Or, of course, club.

Warning: when your host offers you anything called any sort of punch or cup, try to avoid it unless you trust him and/or have had a peep at the bottles the stuff has come out of. Some chaps seem to think that any old muck is good enough if you ice it and throw some fruit into it.

The Dry Martini is the most famous and the best cocktail in the world. It was probably invented in New York about 1910

and some say it was the favourite tipple of John D. Rockefeller, the original oil tycoon. (He died at the age of ninety-eight, a fact worth remembering when you find yourself under attack for excessive boozing.)

The basic ingredients are gin and dry vermouth. Any nationally known gin is suitable, but the vermouth must be Martini Rossi dry—the name is a coincidence, nothing to do with the name of the cocktail. The standard recipe tells you to pour four measures of gin and one of vermouth into a jug half full of ice, stir vigorously for at least half a minute, strain, and serve in small, stemmed glasses.

There are variations on this. Some authorities, including James Bond, recommend shaking rather than stirring the mixture, which looks good but which I regard as a bit flashy. Rockefeller and his chums probably drank equal parts of gin and vermouth. Since then, people have come to prefer their Martinis drier and drier, i.e. with less and less vermouth. Sixteen parts gin to one vermouth is nowadays considered quite normal. Anyway, that's about how I like it. Finding out by experiment the precise balance you favour is no great ordeal. Don't hurry it.

Such is the classical or "straight-up" Dry Martini, with ice used in the mixing jug but no ice in the glass. The problem is that it starts to lose its chill from the moment of serving. Far more than any other drink, it deteriorates as it warms up. Stirring with ice in the jug as before and then serving on the rocks is the solution, and quite trendy enough. Realize that it means fresh ice cubes not only for first drinks but for all subsequent ones too, that's if you want to do things properly.

I always try a Martini out of curiosity if offered one at a private house. I would never ask for one in a pub, as opposed to a cocktail bar. Even if I got it across that I didn't want a glass of plain dry vermouth (horrible muck on its own), I would be bound to be given a drink with too much vermouth in it. In an emergency I'd consider calling for a large gin and a small vermouth, dipping my finger in the vermouth and stirring the gin with it.

The best Dry Martini known to man is the one I make myself for myself. In the cold part of the refrigerator I have a bottle of gin and a small wineglass half full of water that has been allowed to freeze.

When the hour strikes I half fill the remaining space with gin, flick in a few drops of vermouth and add a couple of cocktail onions, the small, white, hard kind. Now that is a *drink*.

There was a man in New York one time who bet he could drink fifteen double Martinis in an hour. He got there all right and collected his money but within another minute fell dead off his bar stool. Knock that back and have another.

"Do you want to muck up your digestion good and proper?" asked a doctor friend over large gins. (Those were not his words but they will have to do.)

"Not particularly," I said.

"Well, if you ever change your mind, just go to a lot of wine and cheese parties, they'll do it for you."

"You mean, because I'd be drinking on a nearly empty stomach?" I asked intelligently.

"No," he said. "You're doing that now, but gin on an empty stomach won't hurt your digestion. Wine will, Think about it."

I have. Wine has a great deal to be said in its favour, but it has to be treated sensibly. It goes with food—meaning not just that it tastes better with food, though it does, but also that it stimulates the digestive juices. Give them nothing or too little to work on and the result is unlikely to be beneficial. So steer clear of your three or four unaccompanied glasses of rough red.

The other point is that, although wine goes with food, it doesn't go with all food, or even most food, not in the UK, which is not a wine-producing country. People know a lot of this just by common sense. Not much wine gets drunk with British lowbrow food, such as sausages and baked beans or fish and chips. Beer, stout, or (a favourite of mine) weak whisky and water are what to go for there. But pricey red wine is often drunk with the classier British dishes—extraordinary when you come to think of it. Why wash down roast beef served in the English style—which means accompanied by Yorkshire pudding, horseradish, mustard—with a good Burgundy, or waste a vintage claret on roast lamb with mint sauce and redcurrant jelly? A pint of real ale is a much better idea.

British drink with British food, then, seems right, and naturally when abroad you drink and eat as the locals do, or there seems not much point in going. Sure, but what about those foreign-inspired dishes, from humble spaghetti to elaborate French-type concoctions that you find on your plate from time to time? Well, if you can, you drink the appropriate wine, the wine that comes from the same place as the dish. But alas, it won't taste the same here as there.

The drinks and eats of a nation, or region, have grown up together over the centuries in a very close relationship, so that they set each other off perfectly. And clearly the eats include not only the basic materials, but everything from the herbs to the fuel in the stove, all of which will be different from place to place. Even, incidentally, the local sun, humidity, air, etc.

Now, of course, a bottle of fine wine is fine, if the accompanying food is intelligently chosen. And in summer a glass or two of chilled dry white wine is good, too. But, as I say, don't overdo it.

Scotch whisky is a great, an enormous subject. To expect me to cover all of it in one article would be like asking the dramatic critic to put down all his thoughts on Shakespeare in a couple of half-columns of print. So today I'll just offer a few bits of background.

The beginnings of Scotch are unknown. Perhaps originally it was the Irish who taught the Scots the process of distillation. The books say that while invading Ireland in the year 1170, Strongbow, Earl of Pembroke, noticed that the locals were drinking some sort of spirit as well as getting killed in large numbers. But who had taught them how to make the stuff? The idea of medieval Irishmen inventing a rather complicated technique like that of distilling, or anything at all for that matter, is hard to credit. And it was over three centuries before the Scots were recorded as producing spirits of their own, so they would have had plenty of time to learn how from the French or, being a clever lot, to find out for themselves. The art of distillation probably originated in more than one place, like the use of fire, another important step in human progress. My bet is that Scotch, or what became Scotch, started in Scotland.

That sixteenth-century liquor would have been pretty harsh by modern standards and so full of impurities that the hangovers it dealt out can only be imagined. I expect the boys were quite glad of it, though, to help them through a Scottish winter with nothing but a plaid to put round them and only porridge and an occasional bite of haggis to keep the wolf from the door. It went on like that for ages. Scotch stayed in Scotland, and the English only saw it when they went up there to shoot the jolly old grouse.

Then, about the middle of the last century, two things happened. A clever fellow invented a new method of making whisky with a gadget called the patent still, many times more efficient and faster and therefore cheaper than the pot still, the type that had been in use from the beginning. And the French vineyards were devastated by an insect plague, so quite suddenly there was no more brandy, the well-off Victorian Englishman's preferred tipple. Gin was much too lower class to fill the gap, but Scotch was acceptable and available. The consequent expansion of sales was followed by another lucky accident, the coming of Prohibition in the USA in 1919 and the establishment of a whole new market there. The biggest boom of all came in the sixties and seventies, with exports going up by over 400 per cent in twenty years. But recently, production has been cut back substantially. Is there too much Scotch about? Never, while I'm alive.

Scotch whisky is my desert-island drink. I mean not only that it's my favourite, but that for me it comes nearer than anything else to being a drink for all occasions and all times of day, even with meals. Not many people think of it as a table wine, but with water and no ice it suits a fry-up quite well, also cold food and other, unexpected, dishes. Try it as accompaniment to fish pâté and, after a decent interval, chocolate mousse.

Most people probably think of vodka as a version of gin, a refined or degenerate one according to taste. By manufacture, though, it's a straight (unblended) grain whisky and the makings are rye, barley and/or maize without artificial colouring.

So the books say. Things are different in Russia, where

they don't only drink to get drunk, they drink to stay drunk too, and no wonder. The demand for vodka is so enormous that any and every form of vegetable protein gets shoved into the distiller's pan, from potatoes and mangelwurzels to the nuts and dried fruit that a delinquent female keeper should have fed to the monkeys in the Moscow zoo, as in a famous case reported in *Pravda*.

Stolichnaya, Krepkaya and other Russian vodkas on sale in the West are another matter altogether—Kremlin tipple made by the rules, smooth, expensive, often stronger in alcohol than the British norm. They are well worth a try, especially in someone else's house, and should by rights be drunk chilled and neat with a bite of smoked salmon and, of course, caviar if there's any going. All the same I wonder very much if even an expert could infallibly tell the difference between one of them and a British vodka like Smirnoff or Cossack at a blind tasting.

These local vodkas have two basic jobs. One is to replace gin in established gin drinks for the benefit of those rather second-rate persons who don't like the taste of gin, or indeed that of drink in general. Anybody who calls for a vodka and tonic in my hearing runs the risk of that imputation. Other such gin-derived drinks are the Moscow Mule (vodka and ginger beer), and the Vodka Martini. This last is a softened version of the orthodox Dry Martini, the gin cocktail I described recently.

The other job for vodka of this sort is as a kick-imparter for Bloody Marys and summer coolers, which it does ideally well. Let me throw in here a recipe for a cooler I had no room for in my article on the subject last month. Take a bottle of good tough red wine, one with plenty of flavour, like something not too pricey from the Rhône or that Hungarian Bulls

Blood stuff, pour it and a bottle of vodka over some ice and drink the result. If you want to sweeten the mixture, the quickest way is to stir in a glass of some sticky liqueur. Will add interest to even the lousiest leg of the World Cup.

After being filtered through several yards of charcoal chippings, British vodka is a very pure spirit. What has been taken out of it is those substances which impart flavour and also give you hangovers. So the tastelessness of vodka is connected with its harmlessness. At the opposite extreme are impure drinks like cognac and malt whisky. And in the middle, with the best of both worlds, a pure spirit richly flavoured with innocuous or beneficial botanicals, stands gin.

This year, UK drinkers will probably get through about six million litres of champagne and just over twice as much sparkling wine of other sorts. It may be a bit down on that following general trends, but it may be a good deal up because of the incalculable amount of royal head-wetting going on this week (there was a big surge last 29 July).

The growth of sparkling wines, other than champagne, has been noticeable over the last few years. Today there are between eighty and ninety brands on the market. I have not tasted all, or even most of them. Before I mention any, I think it fitting to offer a small amount of science.

Most sparkling wine of any kind is the result of two successive fermentations. The first one produces ordinary still wine which could quite well be drunk as it stands; the second one puts the bubbles in. There are two main methods of doing this, the champagne method, in which the process goes on in the individual bottle, and the *cuve-close* method, in which it takes place in a huge sealed tank before final bottling. The champagne method is supposed to produce finer wines, and certainly the bubbles from it last longer after opening and pouring, a more important point than it sounds. The *cuve-close* method is cheaper.

Some non-champagne sparklers are made by the champagne method and others by comparatively expensive refinements of the *cuve-close* method. Nevertheless, champagne, the real thing, stands at the top end of a large price gap. You would have your work cut out to find a bottle of champagne at much under £6.50, whereas most sparkling wine retails in the £2–£3.30 range. In paying the extra you're paying for the quality, true enough, and you're paying for the name, fair enough. But you're also paying through the nose, as more and more people are beginning to feel.

Anyhow, among sparkling wines the brand leader is and has long been Veuve de Vernay, made by the *cuve-close* method from grapes from the Bordeaux area. I'm not the best judge of this sort of thing, but I doubt if anybody would find it less than perfectly drinkable and wholesome, and the fizz is always festive. And that, after all, is about as much as one wants from any sort of sparkling drink—a jolly blast-off to the party, and supplies for toasts and people's aunts. Any kind of serious drinker will soon look elsewhere.

The only one of these I really enjoy is Asti Spumante from northern Italy—unashamedly sweet, with the marvellous fruity tang of the muscatel grape, light in alcohol, and unique in being quite impossible to compare with champagne. Unlike the others, too, in going well with certain foods, ice cream, fruit salad and rich mild cheeses like Bel Paese. But good on its own, and nowhere better than at parties for two.

Champagne is only half a drink. The rest is a name on a label, an inflated price tag, a bit of tradition and a good deal of showing off. People probably enjoy it rather less for itself than because they feel it makes the occasion a special one—in other words, the host is spending a lot of money on them. No harm in any of that, and the wise host will play it up for all it's worth, shouting "Have some champagne" and "Bring more champagne" whenever he thinks of it.

He will ignore the pundits' killjoy advice to open the bottles silently and will let them pop as loudly as possible. The pundits also frown on the usual champagne glass with the wide bowl, complaining that it disperses the bubbles. Again, the sensible man will take no notice and stick to convention—though he will make as sure as he can that whatever glasses are used shall be absolutely clean, above all free from detergent.

The other point about serving is to see that the wine is properly chilled; not less than two hours in the refrigerator is my advice. That should be common knowledge, but the world is full of idiots who buy a bottle at the supermarket, let it kick around half the morning in the boot of the car, open it on arriving home and are amazed when the stuff goes all over the kitchen ceiling.

Now as to buying. The mark-up in restaurants is so ferocious that the fellow who's doing his own paying will get his champagne across the counter or off the shelf. Anything he comes across that's called "champagne" on the label will be the genuine article. Famous names like Moët et Chandon, Louis

Roederer, Mumm, Bollinger and Krug provide what's generally agreed to be the best and, of course, it costs extra. Supermarket and off-licence chains supply their own cheaper brands under less familiar names and they are perfectly good. The essential point is that, thanks to very detailed regulations rigorously enforced by French law, all champagne is a quality product.

This being so, the more expensive brands are best reserved for show-off occasions. The principle applies doubly to vintage champagne. It's a blend of the wines of a single outstanding year, whereas most champagne is a blend of wines of different years, and is priced accordingly. Can safely be left to connoisseurs and conspicuous consumers.

Champagne is said to go with any food and one can theoretically drink it right through a meal, though I've never known of anybody actually doing that. In practice it's supposed to be a splendid accompaniment to a cold summery lunch of smoked salmon and strawberries. Best of all on its own, I have heard its admirers say, about 11:30 a.m., with a dry biscuit. Which leaves plenty of time to sneak out to the bar for a real drink.

There is no better short drink in the world than malt whisky. Only the finest French brandy, a cognac or an Armagnac, could surpass it. As far as I know, no formal comparison or competition has ever been undertaken, but from my experience, and to my taste, the malt is the winner.

Historically, malt is the original Scotch whisky, made, indeed, from malted barley in the old pot still by a slow, cumbersome, expensive process that has not fundamentally changed for over four hundred years. Most of it goes for blending with what the new (nineteenth-century) patent still produces from a mixture of unmalted grains in a much faster, cheaper operation. The resulting blends comprise the Scotch we see around us all the time in shops and pubs—Long John, Haig, Teacher's, Bell's, Cutty Sark and about three thousand others.

They are all well enough, but they are not in the same league as the small proportion of malt whisky that does not go for blending and is matured in cask for eight or twelve or twenty years before bottling. The famous names here are Glenmorangie, Glenfiddich (the brand leader), the Glenlivet, Macallan, Glen Grant, Laphroaig, Isle of Jura and Talisker. Note that they are not the same sort of thing as the deluxe blends like Chivas Regal and Johnnie Walker Black Label. These are of some age and may be excellent whiskies but by definition they are not malts.

The manufacture of malt whisky has been simplified over the years, but the science of the thing is even now only broadly understood. The aroma and flavour of the finished product depend on a number of elements, starting with the local water, which, thanks to Scotland's peculiar geology, can change distinctly from one small stream to the next. Less obvious factors include the method of heating the still, the humidity of the warehouse and the size of the cask. Legend says that the proprietor of a famous Speyside malt once refused to have the spiders' webs cleaned out of his distillery, just in case.

Anyway, the variety to be met with among malt whiskies is very great. Glenmorangie, for example, a well-liked brand, has been called delicate and mild, even faintly sweet; Glenfiddich, fruity and well balanced; the Glenlivet, mellow, ripe and peaty; Macallan, my favourite, powerful and yet smooth. And so on. It's a marvellous field to browse in and in the last few years some pubs have taken to carrying a selection.

Malt whisky is a quality product if there ever was such a thing, all told only 2 per cent of the market in Scotch, nowhere near as widely known as it deserves to be. It should be drunk on its own, never with ice, perhaps with a little water—that's how I prefer it.

Yes, but what water? These days good water is harder to come by than good whisky. The head of a leading firm recommends Volvic. I think Highland Spring is very good.

Dealing with wine in a restaurant used to be quite a nervous business, and the chief generator of nervousness was, of course, the wine waiter himself. Although theoretically on hand to help you enjoy your meal, he often seemed set on spoiling it. He would frown or raise his eyebrows at your choice of wine, not serve it till after your food had arrived, shift to and fro with unconcealed impatience while you went through the ritual of tasting, and get stroppy if you presumed to do some pouring yourself when he was across the room. The only way of winning his approval was to be rich.

Then the trattoria–bistro–taverna revolution came along and broke his power, or at least reduced his territory. Finally the recession put the lid on things by ruling out forays into the wine list. The other day we took a vote at a wine merchant's lunch and, according to ten out of twelve of those present, ordering a carafe of the house red or the house white is what you do at any normal restaurant meal.

Just now and then, though, for one reason or another—a spirit of adventure is a good one, and so is someone else's money to spend—you may run into an old-fashioned wine waiter. To be old-fashioned he doesn't have to be old. In fact a really old wine waiter in a British city is apt to have had his spirit broken by generations of expense-account customers. Anyway, test him out by asking him what he recommends. If he shows no interest in what you're eating, or refers to a wine just by its number on the list, he's no good. Alternatively, order a wine on the list by name. If he has to lean over to see where you're pointing before he can identify it, he's also no good—he doesn't even know his way round his own cellar.

Do nothing with this information beyond letting it expand your files. It isn't worth antagonizing him at this stage. For the same reason, if the wine arrives in one of those cradle or basket affairs, just notice the fact as a handy sign of a suspect restaurant; don't do what is very tempting and take the bottle out and stand it on its end. On the other hand, if the chap has really annoyed you and if you're sure you won't be that way again, proceed as follows.

Having deviously asked for an extra glass ahead of time, say to him: "This wine is perfectly wholesome, but it's overpriced." (True in 99 per cent of UK restaurants.) When he disagrees, say: "Would you please try it yourself?" He can't refuse and will infallibly look a charley as he stands there pouring, sniffing and tasting. When he disagrees a second time, you can thank him for his trouble as man to man or politely insult him for saying what he's bound to say.

About the commonest causes of death in Mexico are murder and heart disease. The old bandit tradition may have something to do with the murder figures, and the high altitude of most of the country certainly encourages heart attacks. Although no figures are available, I can't help thinking that tequila makes a contribution in both departments.

Tequila is the national drink of Mexico, partly because the local beer and wine are indifferent or lousy, but more because it suits the national temperament. Evidently it suits others too, having done well in the USA and Canada over the last twenty years and more recently here. It's a white spirit made from a tropical plant that sometimes gets called a cactus, though the consensus seems to be that it isn't a cactus, just very like one. There we are, then. The manufacture is most carefully carried out by means of a pot still of the general type used for brandy and malt whisky. Export tequilas usually contain no colouring matter and are correspondingly light in flavour, occupying a similar part of the UK market to vodka and white rum at the pricier end.

The flavour of even a light tequila doesn't please all tastes. To me it's not so much disagreeable as strange, like the smoke of some exotic wood. Unlike other spirits, it's never advisedly drunk on its own. Even your humble peon will insist on his lime and salt. The stuff is quite often drunk like this in civilized places too, so I had better describe the procedure. Pour some table salt onto the back of your left hand round about the base of the thumb. Grip a slice of lime in your right hand. Have a tot of neat tequila standing by. As fast as possible, lick the salt, suck the lime, shut your eyes and drink up. (Some people do lime then salt.)

The Margarita cocktail is a kind of dude's version of this. Moisten the rim of a glass with a cut lime and twirl it in a saucer of salt. Shake or vigorously stir with ice, three parts tequila, two parts fresh lime juice and one part Cointreau and pour the result into your prepared glass. There's no point in denying that this is one of the most delicious drinks in the world, but *por Dios, Señor*, watch it! After three of the same I once had the most violent quarrel I have ever had with a female, and in Mexico City too—but luckily we were both unarmed at the time.

To repair the ravages, try a Tequila con Sangrita ("tequila with little blood"). My own recipe tells you to mix thoroughly and pour into a small glass 3 or 4 oz unchilled tomato juice, 2 teaspoons fresh lime juice and a dash of tabasco. Pour a similar quantity of unchilled tequila into a similar glass and sip at the two alternately. The two halves of this Bloody Maria, which I have never seen drunk outside Mexico except in my own house, don't meet until they arrive to start a joint operation on your stomach.

Every now and then there drifts across the Atlantic a rumour that the scientists in the USA are on the point of producing a hangover-free drink. Some day soon there'll be a bourbon whiskey or a gin which will satisfy all the connoisseurs, pack the same alcoholic punch as ever and yet leave us unharmed the next morning. Really? The idea strikes me as impossible in more than one way. Also undesirable—the abolition of the hangover would have far-reaching and perhaps dangerous effects on our civilization; a great restraining influence would be gone. Nevertheless, it's obviously important to go on battling against hangovers on a day-to-day basis as before. Here I have to say that most of the traditional ideas about the subject, the ones we were brought up with, are wrong.

Take the first part of the story, the business of hangover avoidance on the night of the party. The belief that mixing drinks upsets you is about as widespread and as mistaken as the one about bullies always being cowards. The confusion arises simply because the night you mix Dry Martinis and Burgundy and Sauternes and port and brandy and Scotch can't help also being the night you go over the top in sheer quantity.

Another superstition says you suffer less if you take a lot of water or other diluent with your booze. Obviously you'll get less dehydrated, but all the alcohol will reach you however you thin it out.

Although cutting smoking is good, it's easy to take a sip where before you would have taken a puff and so end up worse off.

Beware of coffee. It won't sober you up or neutralize alcohol. All it does is keep you awake, perhaps inducing you to stay up past your bedtime and drink more than you otherwise would. Much better to let the "downing" effect of alcohol have its way.

So what's the good advice?

1. *Avoid* all sweet drinks—dessert wine, port, liqueurs—or limit yourself to a single glass.

2. *Be* circumspect with a vintage claret, classy Burgundy and such. These wines are deceptively strong and also rich in congeners, the trace substances that give the flavour with one hand and the hangover with the other—Alcoholic Sod's Law. And remember, if it's red—which very much includes port as well—the better it is, the worse the hangover.

3. *Be* careful of pricey spirits like cognac and malt whisky. Congener territory again.

4. *Steer* clear of drinks you're not used to, even though they may be perfectly okay. The body doesn't like surprises—a good general rule.

5. *Insist* on eating but keep an eye on your menu. Stick to plain food. Avoid shellfish, greasy meat like pork, anything

cooked in butter. Again no surprises, so save that exciting new Ugandan restaurant for a quiet evening.

6. *Before* retiring, by all means drink a lot of water or milk and, if you must, take aspirins or stomach powders. But, of course, if you're in a condition to remember to do this or be bothered to, you don't really need to.

A hangover is the result of a shock to the system, chiefly from alcohol, sure, but also from fatigue—lack of sleep, burning up energy in ridiculous and shameful activities like dancing—and thirdly from other poisons contained in tobacco, unsuitable food and badly ventilated rooms. It's a mini-illness, worth taking and treating seriously. Alas, like the folklore about avoiding hangovers, most of the so-called cures are either useless or positively harmful.

Don't for heaven's sake risk a cold shower—it's just another physical shock. Take a warm shower or a warm bath, not too hot, and wash your hair elaborately, a calming, refreshing exercise and good for that shop-soiled feeling. Go easy with headache pills. Don't dose yourself with stomach medicines or antacid formulas. Try to let your digestion recover on its own. To help it, if you fancy breakfast at all don't eat much of anything, and let it be easy for your stomach to cope with: toast, cereal, milk, weakish coffee, not greasy fried food nor— what's more tempting—violent stuff like chilled fruit juice.

I remember from my youth a fearful thing called a Prairie Oyster that was supposed to pick you up. It consisted of a raw egg, brandy and Worcester sauce or cayenne pepper, and I suppose the idea was to give your digestion a kick to get it going. More often the poor old thing packed up for a couple

of hours of discomfort. There's a risk of the same sad result
with the concoction that's usually thought of as a magic hangover cure, the celebrated Bloody Mary. Well, it's undoubtedly
a most cheering drink, and its sheer reputation as a reviver
means that lots of people do actually feel better after a couple,
but in my experience it's too acid to be good for anyone who's
at all queasy or is suffering from heartburn. A Scotch and water or ginger ale is safer. That's if you must have a drink at all.
Certainly a bracer seems called for at the end of the morning,
but some would do better to avoid it, more senior types particularly. There you have it, of course. If the old grey cloud no
longer vanishes as if by magic at the first touch of alcohol, as it
once did, you know that middle age is upon you.

I have never come across a sure-fire cure for a hangover.
In my time I have been told of two: half an hour in an open
aeroplane and a stint at the coal face on the early shift. By all
means try them if you can get at them. Otherwise, rest is a
great healer. And—the one certainty—time works in the end.
That sounds obvious enough, but on really rough mornings it's
what you most need to remember.

Until almost the other day, 1970 or so, rum was hardly visible
in this country. It was dark, treacly stuff with vaguely medicinal and naval associations. Then quite suddenly there appeared
a new drink also called rum, but transparent, white, used in
mixed drinks and popular with the young. The usual brand
name—nobody remembered the others—was Bacardi. Last
year Bacardi outsold every other brand of spirit in the USA
and its success in the West generally has probably done more
than anything else to set going the trend for light-coloured,

light-flavoured drinks. Such drinks strike me as suitable for people who don't care a lot for drink or drinking, but then I'm a Scotch man.

Rum—here comes the statutory nugget of information— is a spirit made from the sugar cane, a type of giant grass not native to the Caribbean but brought there from the Azores by Columbus on his second voyage. White rum, like grain whisky and gin, is made by the patent or continuous still and emerges in a high state of purity.

The elaborate Bacardi process involves a unique strain of yeast in the fermentation of the sugar liquid. Founded and long situated in Cuba, the company moved out when Castro came and today operates in Puerto Rico, Mexico, Brazil and else-where. The Bacardi sold in the UK comes mainly from the Ba-hamas. Recently a tinted "gold" variety, a little fuller in flavour than the familiar colourless version, has become available.

The sign of what I call a serious spirit is that it's profitably or even preferably drinkable neat or with a little water. There's a rum, or *rhum*, from the French Caribbean island of Mar-tinique you can approach like that, and very satisfactorily drunk it'll make you, but Bacardi not really. It's a mixer, though a most agreeable one.

A lot of it goes into rum 'n' Coke, quite wasted in my view when teamed with that horrible stuff. I love America, but any nation that produces drive-in churches, Woody Allen and the cola drinks can't be all good. You can, of course, top up your Bacardi with tonic, bitter lemon, lemonade or any-thing else you fancy; it's a free country. But where Bacardi really comes into its own is as the basis of the Daiquiri (pro-nounced like "dikery," I think).

This world-famous cocktail, bland and powerful, requires you to have made up in advance some sugar syrup, which is no more than sugar dissolved in water. The cocktail consists of four parts Bacardi, one part fresh lime juice and sweetening to taste, shaken or vigorously stirred with ice.

Important note: if there's no fresh lime juice, substitute twice as much fresh lemon juice. And if there's none of either, forget it. Bottled juice kills the drink.

Some authorities recommend adding a dash of grenadine, which is a sweet reddish non-alcoholic syrup lightly flavoured with pomegranates. It looks quite nice.

Earlier this year I went off the booze for a few weeks, a purely voluntary move, let it be said. Among other things, I thought it might be interesting to look at life from the Other Side, so to speak.

It wasn't quite what I'd expected. Ex-topers, those warned off by the doc, will tell you emotionally that if only they'd known how much better they were going to feel without it, they'd have given it up years before they actually had to. This is a pathetic lie, designed to make you look like the one who's missing out and motivated by their hatred and envy of anybody who's still on it. In fact, not only is one's general level of health unaffected by the change, but daily ups and downs persist in the same way.

I discovered early on that you don't have to drink to build yourself a hangover. There were mornings when I groaned my way to consciousness, wondering dimly whether it was port or malt whisky that had polluted my mouth and dehydrated my eyes, until I remembered that it could only have been too much ginger beer and late-night snooker. Then, the next morning, I would feel fine, or at least all right, with the same mysterious lack of apparent reason.

My ability to sleep, which I had expected to suffer, didn't. The only department in which my health really took a turn for the better was the digestive one. The old organs have always (touch wood) served me reasonably well, but over the years I have had some mild trouble from wind, flatulence, belching, whatever word you like. Abstinence caused this to vanish at once and completely, and, of course, what did it was abstaining from wine, not from spirits, which don't directly affect the digestion. I've argued before in this column that wine can be a bad and acidity-producing idea in England with English food, and it was interesting to have the point confirmed, even if getting the confirmation this way was a bit of a drag.

As regards other parts of the system, my liver no doubt benefited from its sudden lay-off, but it didn't send me any cheering messages to say so. My mental powers seemed unaltered, certainly unimproved—I was no less forgetful, short on concentration, likely to lose the thread or generally unsatisfactory than I had been before. But now I had no excuse. That was the only big difference: when I was drinking I had the drink to blame for anything under the sun, but now it was all just me. A thought that must drive a lot of people to drink.

I hope I haven't discouraged anyone who might be thinking of taking a short or long holiday from grape and grain. The easiest part is the actual total not drinking, much easier than cutting it down or sticking to beer or anything like that. Very nearly the hardest part is putting up with the other fellow when he's drinking and you're just watching him. At such times you're probably not much fun yourself either. Fruit juice and company don't mix.

In practice, an aperitif is what a waiter calls a drink you drink before you eat. Theoretically it's supposed to stimulate your appetite, though in my experience all a drink stimulates your appetite for is another drink. I would allow just one possible exception, a single small glass of dry sherry—in this country the traditional prelude to a really serious gastronomic occasion, the sort where you talk about the wine for half an hour before you drink it and would as soon think of dancing on the table as of lighting a cigarette. At less momentous times a glass of chilled dry white wine seems generally acceptable and champagne is evidently always okay.

A development that's catching on, while not my kind of thing, is nevertheless worth a try. This is the mixture known as Kir (rhymes with beer)—about six parts dry white wine to one part crème de cassis or blackcurrant liqueur. The cunning French have recently brought out a pre-mixed version. Good for those who fancy a not-too-strong, not-too-dry refresher. Some people moisten the rims of the glasses and twirl them in castor sugar beforehand.

The various forms of vermouth started life as aperitif drinks. They consist of wine from inferior districts flavoured with herbs, spices, etc. (a very ancient practice), and lightly stiffened with grape alcohol, with sugar added to the sweet varieties. The Italian (sweet red) sort has a large respectable following and is also popular with alcoholics, perhaps because of its blandness and good value strength against price. The French (dry white) sort is popular with ladies and others who don't really like drinks at all. Chamberyzette is a French vermouth flavoured with wild strawberries, delicious to some, reminding others of whitewash.

Standing near the vermouths on the off-licence shelves are their close relatives, the so-called wine aperitifs, Dubonnet, St Raphaël, Amer Picon, Byrrh, etc. These have never really caught on in the UK, though Dubonnet itself used to be seen as part of gin and Dubonnet, a mixture that once reduced me to complete silence. Next in line comes Campari, which as everyone knows has made an immense impression on the British market in the last twenty years or so. Not my cup of tea, alas. But, hurray, an acceptable drink can be cobbled together from this and another innocuous potation. Take two parts Italian vermouth and one part Campari (or in another recipe one of each), mix them with ice and add Pellegrino or soda water and a slice of orange, and you have an Americano. Good at lunchtime and before Italian food.

If you feel that, pleasant as it is, it still lacks something, throw in a shot of gin and the result is a Negroni. This is a really fine invention. It has the power, rare with drinks and indeed with anything else, of cheering you up. This may be down to the Campari, said by its fans to have great restorative power.

Today I offer some further remarks on the interesting and neglected topic of not drinking. "Did you miss it?" is of course the question most people want to ask a temporary abstainer, though in my experience they're usually too polite to use those actual words. The answer depends on what exactly "it" is understood to mean. Did I miss the alcohol as such? No, not I, thank God, and if there ever was something to be thankful for, that's it.

Come on, didn't I ever wish I could escape from worry and boredom and tension and my accountant? Well yes, of course I did, and at such times I found myself thinking with more respectful appreciation than ever of Hoyt and Rothes.

These two great men (Americans, needless to say) conducted at some time in the sixties a tremendous survey of the effects of alcohol on Western civilization. After not sparing us endless harrowing facts about the premature deaths, wrecked careers and broken homes, they still came to the conclusion that without it—alcohol—our society would have collapsed from its own internal stresses about the year 1912. So wistful thoughts of gin and tonic at a testing time are not to be frowned upon.

Next question: did I miss having drinks in the sense of glasses of liquid? Yes indeed, or rather I certainly would have done if I hadn't made a point of being always surrounded by a huge variety of delicious soft drinks. It's quite obvious that a sizeable part of one's desire for, and pleasure in, an alcoholic drink comes from non-alcoholic benefits like quenching thirst and allaying hunger. It follows, and it's also true, that two easy ways of cutting alcoholic intake without strain are to put a bottle of mineral water on the table with the necessary glasses and to advance the time of the meal. There's more to it than just food sobering you up.

What can the well-disposed chap who's still on the booze do for his chum who's off it? Well, the first thing the chum doesn't need is a full-dress, Security Council-type discussion on why he's off it, how long for, etc., every time he asks for his Slimline on the rocks. Then, the thoughtful host at a Bloody Mary party will have a bit of straight tomato juice available. If the drinks are more general, he'll put out a fruit juice or two, including apple juice because it looks like a real drink and the non-drinking chum will appreciate that.

Also Angostura bitters: tonic or soda water with Angostura tastes pretty much like a real drink, I'm told—it doesn't sound right to me. Also Perrier, now becoming accepted as the classy all-purpose nondrink. For my money, ginger beer is the best in this department, vigorous reviving stuff with an edge to it. But, naturally, it is sweet, and what the non-drinker longs for is a dry thin-texture soft drink with a bit of flavour.

Ah, but when?

A liqueur (rhymes with secure) is a strong sweet drink flavoured with herbs, fruits or other vegetable materials. Until quite recently liqueurs were seldom drunk except alongside the brandy after dinner as part of a rather slap-up evening. Now, some of them have become popular any-time drinks in bars and elsewhere, especially in mixes. Most off-licence sales in the UK come in the Christmas season, but this too is changing.

Today I'll stick to herbal liqueurs. These probably came about because early techniques of distillation left you with a pretty rough product and the benefits of letting the stuff age in the cask hadn't been discovered. It was natural enough to try the effect of soaking a few herbs in spirits in the hope of producing something beneficial to health as well as palatable. The monasteries, with their pharmaceutical tradition, were the obvious places for this to happen. They also had an unlimited supply of another essential item—spare time. No wonder the first liqueurs came from there, including two of the most famous at the present day, Chartreuse and Benedictine.

Chartreuse is made in two varieties, green and yellow, the green being the original, the more expensive, the drier and the stronger. In fact, at nearly 55 per cent alcohol, it's likely to be the strongest drink in the house and so requires caution. Best kept out of the hands of visiting Americans, who may not have seen it before. Quite different from any other drink.

Green Chartreuse is made to a secret recipe that's said to include 130 different herbs, which sounds most unlikely. It seems, however, that the very striking colour is altogether genuine, coming from the natural flavouring ingredients and nothing else. I know of no mixed drinks based on it, but I'm told that a small quantity poured over a vanilla ice cream produces a delicious dish. Quite possibly.

Benedictine is too sweet for my taste and has about it a peculiar tang which I have never really liked, the result perhaps of the rhubarb among its flavourings. The foundation is brandy and, as always in these cases, the sweetness can be palatably and legitimately cut by adding more foundation.

In fact the company markets something called B & B which is just that, brandy and Benedictine or the other way round and extremely popular. Horrible mixtures of Benedictine and tonic water, white wine and heaven knows what are also drunk in places I hate to imagine.

The most popular liqueur in the UK is the splendid Drambuie from Scotland, a blend of fine Highland malt whiskies and honey in the proportion of two and a half to one, plus herbs. Very sweet, and though to my way of thinking not sickly, improvable by adding more malt and reducing the honey content to one fifth or less.

You can have a lot of fun establishing by experiment the formula you prefer, but remember my recent warning about the dire after-effects of all sweet drinks.

Today I conclude my remarks on the subject of being off the booze. This third instalment is actually about no longer being off it—returning, that is, to full membership of the human race. I had intended to keep a sort of diary of new first impressions of the various drinks as I came to them, but I somehow didn't, and I can't really think what I would have said if I had. "Had some Scotch (or Burgundy, or port) this evening. Excellent stuff. Tasted strongly of Scotch (Burgundy, port)." Not very helpful.

But I do remember my first drink after the break was a glass of plain Gordon's gin and water. One thing it did for me was confirm my judgement that when it comes to drinking gin, there's no other decent way. To pour sweetened fizz like tonic water into such a masterpiece of the distiller's art makes about as much sense as, well, putting tomato ketchup on caviar, I was going to say, except that that strikes me as rather a sound scheme providing you're sure you've got enough ketchup to spare. Anyway, you get the idea—leave your gin alone. Even a slice of lemon is really too aromatic to put in with it. Ice is all right, but I prefer to have chilled the bottle.

My second drink was a Carlsberg Special Brew, very cold, which I think is better than just cold. The effect was electrifying. As I drank the whole of my head seemed to become flooded with the taste and smell of beer. This was the result not so much of not having boozed for a spell as of having given up smoking.

Apart from all the other arguments, you're a fool to smoke if you like the taste of drink. It isn't the cigarette you smoke with your glass of wine or whisky that damages the taste of it, it's all the ones you smoked yesterday and the day before and last week. Your senses are chronically anaesthetized. Really, smokers could afford to consider what they're certainly missing as well as what they're in danger of getting.

After much pondering I think I understand a basic reason why a glass of something reviving is so welcome in the early evening. Partly, of course, it's just that, to revive, to relax, but it's also a convenient way of becoming a slightly different person from your daytime self, less methodical, less calculating—however you put it, somebody different, and the prospect of that has helped to make the day tolerable. And, conversely, it's not having that prospect that makes the day look grim to the poor old ex-boozer, more than missing the alcohol as such. Changing for dinner used to be another way of switching roles. Coming home from work has a touch of the same effect.

Writers haven't got that advantage—when they finish work they're at home already. So perhaps they need that glass of gin extra badly. Any excuse is better than none.

The story of liqueurs continues with a few more of the herbal type. In this context the word herb needs to be interpreted pretty broadly. Wherever drink is made, enterprising chaps will take some of the local spirit—distilled from grain, grapes, other fruit, rice or whatever it may be—and flavour it with almost anything they find growing near by. Many of these concoctions never travel from their home village, and no wonder. In the Dordogne area they produce a beverage called Salers, flavoured with the root of the yellow or mountain gentian, of which they have plenty. Well, there may be nastier drinks but I don't care to imagine them.

Other agents used in liqueurs of this general type include tea, aloes, hazelnuts, thistles, cocoa, snake root, bison grass, lavender, soya beans and nutmeg, not to speak of tangy stuff like pyrethrum and rhizomal galangae—actually the last two help to produce the pleasantly burning or "warm" taste most liqueurs have.

The distinctively clean and fresh flavour of peppermint is at the heart of one of the most popular of all liqueurs, crème de menthe, of which there are numerous brands. It comes in two versions, the white or transparent and the more familiar artificially coloured bright green. Either is best served with crushed ice and drunk through a straw. If you find it too sweet, try cutting it with an equal part of cognac. When made with the white kind this is known as the Stinger, once called for by no less a drinks pundit than James Bond.

Peppermint is supposed to help digestion; so is aniseed, used to flavour all manner of anise liqueurs and anisettes. Marie Brizard is the most famous of them. The firm recommended it as part of a long drink with ice and fresh lemon juice, topped up with plenty of soda water. There's no accounting for taste is what I always say.

Fans of Italian food, and others, will know about Sambuca, which is flavoured with a herb giving an effect very similar to aniseed. There's rather a shy-making ritual that involves floating a few coffee beans on the top of your glass and putting a match to the surface of the drink, thus singeing them slightly.

Another Italian liqueur, Galliano, has gained a good deal of ground over the last few years, not as a drink on its own but as a constituent of the famous or infamous cocktail the Harvey Wallbanger, named after some reeling idiot in California. It's basically a Screwdriver with trimmings, in other words you stir three or four parts fresh orange juice with one part vodka and some ice, then drop a teaspoonful or so of the liqueur on top.

My own favourite in this group is kümmel, flavoured with caraway seed, smooth, and best drunk slightly chilled and straight—as a liqueur, in fact.

Although Spain has more acres under the vine than any other country in the world, methods of wine production are so inefficient that its output falls well below France's or Italy's. However, the Spaniards have set themselves to do something about that, and about their wine export trade in general. Over the last few years they have had an amazing success in this country with their leading table wine, Rioja. (Pronounced approximately "Ree-*ock*a," but you get extra marks for making the second syllable sound something like the Scottish "och" noise.)

Rioja is a place, a sizeable region in northern Spain along the river Ebro. Red, white and rosé wines are made there, but it's the reds that have scored over here. Thirty-something houses export to the UK, and the Spanish vintage system is hardly a system at all—a year on a bottle means little more than that quite a lot of the wine in it may well have been made about then. The best guide, as so often, is price, starting in the £2.25-ish range and going up to about £4.50. The more expensive Riojas are considered fine wines indeed, and no pundit dare turn up his nose at them.

The wine grape doesn't respond all that well to strong sun, and hot-climate wines are often heavy and a bit rough, only tolerable at the place of origin with the local food. The Rioja vineyards are in the hills 1500 feet up and get plenty of rain, thus escaping this effect. Their products are often compared with those of Bordeaux. The two regions use similar methods of manufacture and are less than three hundred miles apart by tanker lorry, a jolly useful fact for any Bordeaux grower who finds his harvest untowardly down in quantity or body. It comes back to me that once at a blind tasting on TV, I identified a Bordeaux red as a Rioja, an earburning incident at the time but rather suggestive in retrospect in view of the connection.

Regular readers of this column will know that I have my likes and dislikes, even my weaknesses and prejudices. Nevertheless I always try to be scrupulously objective. As in the present case. Everything I've said here to the advantage of Rioja wines is true and verifiable. Now comes the moment for me to state my own opinion of them, which is that they are quite vile. I haven't tried them all—who has? but my limited experience of them suggests to me that these wines are over-flavoured. None gave me any desire to try again. Perhaps those steps the Spaniards have taken to refurbish their wine trade have been misconceived. The country, when I revisited it after some years in 1980, was as delightful as ever, but about the only refreshments you could depend on were imported tinned fruit and sherry—not even the bread was reliable. And the British have been running the sherry trade for a long, long time. Sorry, *señores*.

Fruit-flavoured liqueurs turned up in various ways. It was discovered that you could preserve fruit through the winter by bottling it in spirits. Very soon afterwards it was discovered that it was worth your while to drink the liquor that had been round the fruit.

Putting orange peel into rough brandy to make it less rough must have started about the same time. To this day it's liqueurs flavoured with the peel of the bitter orange, and sweetened, that dominate this part of the market. They are either orange-brownish in colour, often labelled Orange

Curaçao, or white-colourless, often labelled Triple Sec. The alcoholic base is usually grape brandy or in some cases neutral spirit, made from anything, in other words, but pure and tasteless.

The most famous of the Orange Curaçao types, Grand Marnier, is an exception in being based on cognac, which comes through the sweetness of the drink. The most famous Triple Sec is Cointreau, often drunk on the rocks or as part of a cocktail, such as the White Lady, which goes back at least to the 1920s, but is suddenly popular again. This consists of gin, Cointreau and fresh lemon juice in equal parts (standard recipe) or in the proportions four–two–one (Trader Vic) or whatever you fancy. The South Africans make an excellent Curaçao-type liqueur, Van der Hum, flavoured with the peel of the Cape orange and other fruits.

Cherries, apricots, peaches and blackcurrants are also used as flavouring for liqueurs, and there are more out-of-the-way ones made with bananas, pineapples, cranberries and the berries of the rowan tree or mountain ash. Blends of different fruits are common. The most widely known of all drinks of this type, Southern Comfort from the USA, is made from a mature grain spirit flavoured with peaches, oranges "and other exotic fruits and herbs"—the recipe is supposed to be over a hundred pages long. Delicious, though to my taste rather fiery, on its own, it's drunk as part of all manner of mixtures. I'll mention only two.

Champagne Comfort is not a difficult drink to imagine, or to make, or to drink. My advice is to stop after the first one unless you have the rest of the day free. Then there's a thing called a Teul, which I've never tried and which consists of equal parts of Southern Comfort and tequila heartily stirred with ice—plus, I imagine, a dash of spaceship-propellant on Saturday nights.

Sloe gin, which is ordinary London gin flavoured with
sloes and sweetened, is the only all-English liqueur. Traditionally drunk at meets, you know, before going off to hunt the
jolly old fox. I can think of nothing better to brighten up a wet
Sunday after lunch. Within reason, that is.

Until not so long ago, certainly until well into this century, the
spirit drinkers in these islands were in practice quite sharply
divided by national and social boundaries. The Irish drank
their whiskey, the Scots drank theirs, the lower classes in England drank gin and the upper classes brandy. How the Welsh
managed without a national drink I don't know. The nearest
vodka, of course, was a thousand miles away.

That class division in England lingers on to this day. Gin
retains an aura of unrespectability from the years of the Victorian gin palace and music hall—it's a toper's drink, not for
a non-drinker to fiddle with or a connoisseur to go on about.
Brandy seems the opposite of all that, with a mystique around
it like vintage port and the upper reaches of table wine. You
sip it reverently after a serious meal and wouldn't dream of diluting it with anything.

Times have changed there. To the Victorian Englishman,
brandy was a before-dinner or any-time drink with water or
mineral water in it. (The Victorian Englishwoman could only
get brandy at all either by being no lady or by saying she'd
come over faint—still true until quite recently.) You could
drink it with the meal and even pour some into your wine if
you felt like it. A very relaxed policy.

An awful lot, perhaps nearly all, of the brandy that was
treated like that must have been cognac, the best in the world.

Sure enough, Cognac is also a place, a small town and considerable area on the left-hand side of France about halfway down. There are various grades according to which part of the area the stuff comes from. The top grade is *grande champagne*, the next one down *fine champagne*. You won't see the others much in the UK, any more than you see bottles labelled "ordinary Scotch whisky." The *champagne* part just means open country or steppe, nothing to do with the bubbly or the region on the other side of France where they make it.

French law is terrifically strict on your *grande champagne, fine champagne* and the rest, but says nothing about the more familiar and apparently important grades stuck on by the manufacturer—Three Star, VSOP (Very Superior Old Pale), XO (Extra Old), etc., which aren't even standardized among the different firms. Luckily, when ordering you can forget all about *grande champagne* and VSOP too: the most expensive is likely to be the best and the not quite so expensive not quite so good, as in so many other departments of life. You won't find a bargain cognac, though a lot of people do say Hine Three Star is the best of that grade.

The other French quality brandy is Armagnac, which again is also a place, farther down on the map. Cognac is supposed to be more delicate, Armagnac earthier and more pungent. But there are other brandies, and many brandy drinks.

As I was saying, the world's quality brandies are cognac and Armagnac from France. A Frenchman quite expects you to use a three-star cognac in mixed drinks, though he'd be shocked if he caught you drinking a higher grade any other way but neat.

A great proportion of total brandy sales in the UK goes into the medicine cupboard as a life-saver. It's quite a powerful heart stimulant, a property which gives some people a restless night if they take too much of it. Anyway, no surprise that it features in a couple of morning-after recipes. There are various mixtures called a Corpse Reviver but this is the simplest—large tot brandy, fill up with sweet ginger ale, optional dash of Angostura bitters, best drunk without ice and fast. The other curative potion is supposed to alleviate the trots. I've never seen it written down or heard of a name for it, but it's widely believed in. Just mix equal parts of brandy and ruby port and drink as it is. Folklore says if you take the two parts separately it doesn't work.

To turn to pleasanter thoughts—the Alexander comes in all the cocktail books, but it isn't really a cocktail in the sense that it's good before a meal, being more of a meal in itself. Take one to four parts brandy according to taste, one part crème de cacao, which is a sweet chocolate liqueur, one part double cream plus ice, shake hard and strain. The sweetness and the cream slow down the intake of alcohol, so it may not be until after two or three that you realize, or she realizes, how strong they are. You'll actually like the Alexander if you like gooey drinks, but if not, not. It was Anthony Blanche's tipple in *Brideshead Revisited*.

There are dozens of proper cocktails based on brandy, of which the Sidecar is the most famous. Take two to eight parts brandy, one or two parts Cointreau, two parts lemon juice and ice, and shake if you feel like it, though a good stir should be enough. Named after the sidecar that used to carry the inventor of the drink to his favourite bar and, more important, home again. A sidecar is the ideal vehicle for a soak when he's been soaking—he can forget about the driver and snore away in peace.

You'd expect to find the Champagne Cocktail under "champagne" rather than here, but there wasn't room in my champagne article the other day, and brandy is involved. Saturate a lump of sugar in Angostura bitters and put it in a wineglass, add about a pub single of brandy, top up with chilled champagne. Everybody seems to think this is an overrated drink, but it keeps going all the same. If offered it at a private house, at a wedding reception, etc., sneak round behind the scenes and check that the empties really are champagne and not some questionable substitute. If in doubt, ask for a real drink.

You'll soon be needing one anyway.

The publishers Mitchell Beazley are bringing out a very useful series of pocket guides to this and that. They really do fit in the pocket, aren't bulky and have semi-stiff covers to keep them neat. Topics to date include photography, cheese, architecture and the stars and planets (Patrick Moore), not forgetting booze.

My eye fell on Michael Jackson's *Pocket Bar Book*, which covers a great deal of ground reliably and entertainingly. There's a section on travel and drink—what to go for in what sort of establishment the world over, from rum with pickled fish in a Caribbean cold-supper shop to ouzo, cheese and olives in a Greek kafenion. Next, valuable hints on serving drinks, tools of the trade and glasses. The A-to-Z of drinks lists and describes the different kinds, such as lager, Campari, Plymouth gin, mezcal, Grand Marnier, Sauternes, punch. Includes kvass, Russian near-beer made from rye bread, but not koumis, fermented liquor from mare's milk used by Tartar nomads in Central Asia—no, actually I've never tried it.

. The catalogue of cocktails is very complete and helpful, old stalwarts like the Manhattan, new horrors like the Pina Colada, though surprisingly no White Lady. Finally, a page on the hangover, which after all that you may feel is too little. A splendid handbook for the drinking man, and most enjoyable to read and dip into.

Hugh Johnson's *Pocket Wine Book* is the most practical I've ever seen on the subject and bang up to date, with the author's vast knowledge skilfully deployed. The main part is a midget encyclopedia of wine world wide, including the more farflung producing countries like Cyprus, Chile, New Zealand and, of course, England. The various entries not only give information about the kind of wine produced by a given area or vineyard, they also list recommended years with ready-to-drink vintages in bold type. A star system shows the quality to be expected, along with a box sign meaning "usually particularly good value in its class."

On the important question of what wine to drink with what dish, some wine books include a page or two of patchy general indications about Burgundy and beef and so on. This one mentions a couple of hundred eatables from artichoke vinaigrette to zabaglione and offers in most cases a full choice of accompanying wines. Not always wines. Hollands gin is suggested with pickled herrings, beer with sauerkraut and, with kippers, "a good cup of tea, preferably Ceylon."

Johnson might have taken the principle further and told us what to drink with other lowbrow dishes like sausages and mash, pork pie, etc.,—cocoa perhaps. But he could fairly retort that after all he was writing a book about wine. And jolly good it is, calculated to take the terror out of the subject and nice reading too. Revised yearly.

Other, more specialized books in the same series deal with wine tasting, Italian wines and Californian wines. Like the previous two, they sell at £3.95. All excellent value.

I bet you didn't know there was a drink called a Falkland Island Warmer. I didn't myself until the other day, when I came across it while looking through the bible of mixer drinks, Trader Vic's massive *Bartender's Guide*, in search of something else. You put an ounce of Drambuie in a mug or heated glass and add hot water and half a teaspoon of lemon juice. The recipe also calls for a dash of rock candy syrup, rock candy being what we call rock in the Blackpool sense, but stirring in a flat teaspoon of brown sugar will do as well. We might have guessed that the stalwart Scots would have been leading spirits in the settling of those remote and chilly isles, and also that they wouldn't have left their beloved Drambuie behind.

As the discerning will already have discerned, this warmer is to some extent a classy and handy version of the old Whisky Toddy, which uses Scotch and sometimes honey in place of the Drambuie. You can scatter some grated nutmeg or cinnamon across the top if you feel like it. In my youth you reckoned to knock off a cold by taking a double dose last thing with a couple of aspirins crushed up in it and putting an extra blanket on the bed. Helps you sleep, anyway.

What I was actually after in Vic's tome was his formula for Hot Buttered Rum. It's even more elaborate than I remembered. He starts by making up a dose of what he calls his batter, which is 1 lb brown sugar, ¼ lb butter, ½ teaspoon ground nutmeg, cinnamon and cloves and a pinch of salt all beaten together. Each drink is 1½ oz rum and a heaped teaspoon of the batter stirred into boiling water, with cinnamon stick added as decoration. My own simpler version, from New England, calls for rum and boiling water with a teaspoon of maple syrup and a knob of butter. If you cut out the butter and substitute milk for water you get a Hot Rum Cow. The Cow is going a bit far possibly but the Hot Buttered Rum itself seems to me a major compensation for the arrival of the cold weather.

I have to tell you however that a great authority on the subject, David A. Embury, whose book *The Fine Art of Mixing Drinks* is a standard work, can't imagine how anyone could consume it with pleasure. He goes on: "I believe that the drinking of Hot Buttered Rum should be permitted only in the Northwest Passage, and, even there, only by highly imaginative and overenthusiastic novelists." Wow. He can't have meant me—Ernest Hemingway, probably.

There remains the question whether these and other so-called warmers actually warm you. I don't think they do. They make you feel warmer all right, but that isn't the same thing. I would not recommend going out into the cold after partaking of them. To my mind they're for after you come back in—after skiing it could be, though I wouldn't know about that, thank heaven.

Booze manufacturers are a thrifty lot who hate throwing away any part of their material. Thus the ingenious brewer scoops off his surplus yeast and flogs it to the makers of extract spreads and tablets. Rather in the same way, some distillers of Scotch take the protein out of their wastes and convert it into animal food.

The vineyard proprietors must have rejoiced when, many years ago, it was discovered that you could make an alcoholic drink of sorts out of the residue of grape skins, stalks and pips left in the wine presses after the juice had been taken out for fermentation. In France, this debris is called *marc*, the "tread," and the drink is familiarly known by the same name. Pronounced "mar." (When I was a lad you were supposed to tack a guttural or choking noise on at the end in an attempt to reproduce the French "r," but nowadays they seem to let you off that.)

Marc is a white/transparent spirit, a true brandy in being a product of grapes, though nobody would speak of it in the same breath as cognac or Armagnac. In fact it's quite unlike any brandy made from wine. The books do say, however, that it's "greatly esteemed by local connoisseurs." After much varied experience I find this phrase about as reassuring as "First showing on British television" in a different context. And there are not a few who, on taking a first sip of marc, and being told it's made from wine leavings, have grunted that it smacking well tastes like it, or words to that effect. To one sage its flavour is strawlike or earthy, to another leathery yet grapy; most of them call it fiery. It can seem a little on the raw side but to my mind it's marvellous after a good dinner as a treat, a change, a jolt. You only need one.

Of all the versions they make, or used to make, in the different regions of France I've never seen more than three over here. Marc de Bourgogne is the best known. You can sometimes get hold of marc de Champagne. The rarest and, I think, the finest is marc d'Alsace, made from the famed Gewürztraminer grape, which is said to be scented, herb-like, spicy, etc.

Grappa is the Italian version of marc, though Italians mightn't like me to put it like that. It's got much more to it than the straight Italian brandies, which are perfectly all right but tend to be a bit on the sweet side. Not to take a glass of grappa after an Italian meal strikes me as the grossest folly. There are delicious brands made from the refuse of muscatel wine.

Spirits in the marc-grappa mode are produced in several other wine-growing countries, including Germany, Spain, Portugal and parts of the USA and South America. Some pisco brandy from Peru, lately fashionable here, is of this type. Inca brand, available in the UK, is strange and delicious on its own, splendid in a Pisco Sour with lemon juice, sugar and Angostura bitters.

Today we kick off with a spanking recipe of my own invention. Assemble in a wineglass a slug of Calvados apple brandy, a dash of Angostura bitters and a level teaspoon of castor sugar dissolved in the minimum of hot water, and stir vigorously. Add ice cubes and stir vigorously some more. Take out ice, top up with chilled top-quality cider, drop in an apple slice and serve.

Knowledgeable topers will have already seen that this is an apple-based version of the Champagne cocktail made from brandy and champagne. It's also a lot cheaper—Calvados is a few bob dearer than a three-star cognac, but the classiest cider is a fraction of the cost of the commonest champagne. Though I say it as shouldn't, the Normandy Cocktail—Normandy being the apple orchard of France—is a delicious concoction, deceptively mild in the mouth. But be careful how you use it.

Calvados, a strong spirit pot-distilled from a fermented

apple mash, belongs to the catalogue of fruit brandies. These are a separate family from the fruit-flavoured liqueurs I described a few weeks ago, where the alcohol derives from grape, maize, parsnips, etc. The difference is the difference between the fruit brandy Kirsch, a dry, colourless distillate of a mash of cherries, and a rich, sweet, dark, cherry-flavoured liqueur like Cherry Heering. Each is a splendid drink in its way. A bit confusingly, Calvados itself, being aged in wood, emerges pretty dark, but it's dry all right, also smooth, fragrant, full-flavoured, you name it. The Normandy cuisine is rather fatty, dripping with cream and butter, and Calvados is the ideal corrective to that sort of meal. In fact, it's an excellent out-of-the-way round-off to any serious lunch or dinner.

The same applies to the other fruit brandies. Most of them come from an area on the eastern side of France and the adjoining parts of Germany and Switzerland. Apart from Kirsch they include poire Williams (made from pears), quetsch and mirabelle (plums), prunelle (sloes), framboise and Himbeergeist (raspberries), and so on. There even used to be one made out of hollyberries, but I doubt if they can get the blokes to pick them these days, don't you?

These are very fine unusual drinks, running you into money in the £12–£15 range, but worth it for a particular treat and a wonderful Christmas present for anybody known to take a serious interest in these matters. Some care in serving is needed. Calvados you just pour straight out, but the trick with the others, in Germany at least, is to pre-freeze the glass though not the bottle. There, by the way, they're more often drunk before the meal than after.

The Balkan countries have slivovitz, made from plums. It features, heated in a saucepan and mixed with honey, as a winter warmer and cold cure known as Serbian Tea. A user says,

"Great, but after two or three you can feel the lining of your stomach wearing thin." So watch it.

It was the late, great Stephen Potter who invented one-upmanship, or rather brought the concept out into the open. You could define it roughly as the technique of getting or keeping the edge on the other fellow in any gathering or situation, probably by bluff, brass or straight lying. The field of booze, with all its snobbery and true and false expertise, is obviously a rich one from this point of view.

Potter wrote some good stuff on what he called winesmanship, in which he explains how to get away with giving your guests the vilest plonk imaginable and passing yourself off as an expert at the same time. It's partly what you do—pretend to fetch the bottle from the cellar, take for ever uncorking it, keep staring at it before you pour—and partly what you say—"Over the top now, of course, but still with a hint of former glories. Keep it in your mouth a moment . . . see what I mean?" At this, the other fellow will start thinking that the flavour of carbolic he thought he'd noticed is actually rather interesting or even pleasant.

And so on. This last bit strikes me as brilliant but dangerous. There are too many people around these days who aren't quite ignorant about the subject and, more important, aren't afraid to state their likes and dislikes. Safer to stick to neutral ground—a restaurant—wait for someone to drop a grain of knowledge, and work the old jujitsu trick of turning his strength to his disadvantage. As soon as he mentions tannin or chalky soil or the '79s coming on fast—or slowly—shush everyone else and say: "Listen, chaps, here's a chance for us all to learn something. Carry on, Percy"—the equivalent of dropping him on his head.

When he's finished, which should be pretty soon, ask a lot of questions, the more elementary the better, like: "Does that make it good or bad?" Then, having wrung him dry, say: "Fascinating! Some of these fellows are uncanny. I met one the other day who could tell which end of the vineyard the grapes that had gone into an individual bottle of something-or-other had come from because he knew they, er, harvested the place from east to west and so the western grapes got that many more hours' sun. Well, well, what? I'm eating steak, and that means, er, red, doesn't it, Percy? What's a good one? Burgundy's good, isn't it? Right, I'll have some." Don't sound sarcastic or amused or superior—play it straight. The object is to make knowing about wine seem like an accomplishment on the level of knowing about the flora and fauna of Costa Rica or the history of tattooing—well worth while, but hardly in the mainstream of serious thought.

Another time there may be someone like Percy present but not declaring his presence, so never offer an opinion yourself. If asked what you think, say breezily, "Jolly good," as though you always say that whatever it's like. This may suggest that your mind's on higher things than wine, like gin or sex.

If this goes wrong, say suddenly, "I don't suppose any of you chaps have seen last year's French government report on wine manufacture?" Which is pretty safe, since there wasn't one. Continue. "No surprises, of course, but a bit upsetting here and there. Apparently in some districts as a matter of course they just . . . oh well, never mind. Cheers." Take a hearty swig from your glass, give a worried frown and follow with an unconvincing laugh. Say finally, "Oh well, I'm sure there's nothing wrong with this. How much did you say it was?"

This is the time of year when thoughts naturally turn to hot alcoholic drinks. These are of two main sorts—basically spirits and hot water, such as Whisky Toddy and Hot Buttered Rum which I described the other week, and heated wine with spices and usually a slug of something stronger, today's subject.

I said spices, but this raises a question. Some people go to endless trouble with cinnamon sticks and grated nutmeg, even sticking cloves into an orange, roasting it in the oven and crushing it into the brew, or rubbing lemon rind off on lumps of sugar, a most exhausting business. I wonder whether it's worth it for the marginal effect on the finished product. Those shakers of ready-ground spices are quick enough, but in my experience they contribute more sediment than flavour. What I have been known to do is simmer a cinnamon stick in water for a few minutes before I start making the main drink. You'll taste it then all right, too much perhaps for some palates but worth trying. Certainly throwing in a few slices of lemon and orange only takes a moment, and they look cheerful.

Now at last to the drink itself. What I'll call simply Mulled Wine is best made as follows. Pour into a saucepan a bottle of decent red wine, nothing fancy but one you could face drinking in the ordinary way. Mix in a glass or so of French cooking brandy and add any fruit and spices. Heat the mixture slowly, stirring in castor sugar as you go until it tastes right. When it's hot but not yet bubbling pour it into pre-heated or otherwise protected glasses so that they're half full. Add half as much boiling water, stir and serve.

So much for the basic formula and method. Variations

start with substituting a sweet liqueur for the brandy and cutting back the sugar, and there's no doubt that Grand Marnier or Cherry Heering raises the whole concern to a more exalted level. Some people replace half or all of the brandy with run-of-the-mill ruby port. If based entirely on port with the wine omitted, the drink becomes Bishop or Hot Bishop—this is where the roast orange comes in, and those who enjoy messing about with drinks will probably have a go at it whatever I say.

A number of the recipes for these mulls leave out the water. The case for putting it in is that you can get the drink hotter, because you can boil water but not booze.

The punchiest of all hot punches is Glögg (rhymes roughly with berg), by origin a Swedish winter-sports beverage. No two recipes for it are more than rather similar. Mine is a Swedish one. Take first a bottle of aquavit, the Scandinavian white spirit, and ideally it should be the Swedish sort, but that's rare in the UK and the Danish sort is easier to find and will do. Take also a bottle each of port and Burgundy. Mix and mull by the standard method. Add a handful of raisins to the pot and drop a blanched almond into each glass. The almond is supposed to be a Scandinavian good-luck symbol. You'll need it.

Here are some further notes on boozemanship, the art of coming out ahead when any question of drinking expertise or experience arises. This time they come not under the heading of wine, the usual field for this kind of contest, but under spirits and beer, where less is generally known. It's strange that we in this country tend to be better informed about a foreign import, confined until recently to a tiny elite, than what have been our national drinks for nearly three hundred years.

First, a simple ploy with gin, equally effective in private house and pub. Asked what you'd like to drink, say simply, "Gin, please." Wave away tonic, lemon, even ice, and accept only a little water—bottled, naturally. Someone's sure to ask you if that's all you really want, etc. Answer, "Yes, I must say I like to be able to taste the botanicals, which just means I like the taste of gin, I suppose. Of course, a lot of people only like the effect." Any gin-and-tonic drinkers in earshot will long to hit you with a meat axe, which after all is the whole object.

Later, switch to Scotch, saying in tones of casual explanation, "I get sick of these fully rectified spirits after a bit, don't you?" That should draw a fairly blank stare. Then, "I mean I like a bit of the old pot still. Well, I just enjoy the touch of malt." If that doesn't clear things up much, say, "I'm sorry, I didn't realize," making it clear that you're adding under your breath, "that I was talking to a bunch of peasants."

These days your host might offer you a malt whisky almost any time. If he's mad enough to offer you ice or, better still, drop it in unasked, you get bonus points for the way you manage to restrain your horror at the fellow's barbarism. When you finally taste the stuff, say, "Ah, the old Glencluskie. Magnificent, but not what it was. It's this damned Canadian barley. Too much starch, not enough protein and fat. Thank heaven there's still some peat in the kilning." All very well today, but on present trends there'll soon be whisky snobs fit to compare with any wine snobs of yesteryear.

Beer is a far dodgier subject in these post-real-ale days— there are experts everywhere. Safest to adopt the generic Amis Defence Against Knowledge and treat the whole subject as an eccentric fad. If forced to drink beer say, "A glass of any old lager, please, if it's there. I'm sure all this business about top fermentation and CO_2 is quite fascinating, but life's too short."

Don't get too clever for your own good. Offered the choice of red or white wine at a stand-up party the other day, I explained that my stomach objected to the acid produced by wine without food, whereas spirits were all right. "Sorry to hear that," said the host. "I'm afraid there's nothing else in the house." My stomach took five minutes to change its mind.

Here is a mixed bag of seasonable concoctions. First and foremost and indispensable, Irish Coffee. It's a bit of a pest to make, but never was such labour more richly rewarded. To make each drink, stir thoroughly in a large pre-heated wineglass 1 teaspoon of sugar or a bit more, about a quarter of a pint of your best and freshest black coffee, and 1–2 oz Irish whiskey—no other sort will do. When the mixture is completely still, pour onto its surface over the back of a spoon about 2 oz chilled double cream. The cream must float on the other stuff, not mingle with it. If this goes wrong, take Michael Jackson's excellent advice: "Don't serve the drink to your guests— knock it back quickly yourself, and try again."

Other drinks have sprung up in imitation with the same coffee and cream content but with other spirits as a basis, like Benedictine, which gives Monks' Coffee, and Drambuie, which gives Prince Charles's Coffee—yes, that's what the UK Bartenders Guild call it. Of those I've tried, none compares with the original.

Except for being warm, the next drink could hardly be more different. This is the Raging Bull, an Amis original, though no great powers of invention were called for. Make

Bovril in a mug in the ordinary way and stir in a shot of vodka, a couple of shakes of Worcester sauce and a squeeze of lemon juice (optional). That's it. Very heartening in cold and/or hungover conditions.

Now, an unusual evening warmer, the Broken Leg. Having had a real broken leg myself earlier this year I puzzle over the significance of the name, but the drink's straightforward enough. Slowly heat about a quarter of a pint of apple juice in a saucepan with a few raisins, a cinnamon stick and a lemon slice. When it starts to bubble, strain into a preheated glass or mug. Pour a couple of ounces of bourbon whiskey into the pan, warm for a few seconds and pour into the remainder. Formula from John Doxat.

Lastly, American Milk Punch. You drink this cold, but it'll soon light a fire in you. The previous evening—this is the hard part—put milk instead of water into your refrigerator ice trays. On the day, mix thoroughly in a jug one part bourbon whiskey, one part French cooking brandy and four parts fresh milk. Pour into biggish glasses, drop in milk cubes, stir gently, dust with grated nutmeg and serve. This punch is the very thing for halfway through the morning of Boxing Day, when you may be feeling a little jaded and need a spot of encouragement before some marvellous treat like the in-laws coming over for lunch. In fact, it can be treated as a Snowy Mary, sustaining as well as uplifting, and much kinder to the digestion than the old Bloody Mary, a delicious drink, I agree, but full of acid fruit juices.

Remember the Milk Punch for the New Year as a heartener before air trips, interviews, etc.

Christmas is traditionally a time when we behave kindly to our fellow human beings and push goodwill about all over the place. Well, to get myself into any kind of shape for being nice to others, I'll have to take a lot of care of myself—and nowhere more devotedly than in the sphere of drink. I intend to see that I have ample supplies of the few key items without which my Christmas would be a mockery, leaving me with no good will to spare for anyone.

My list leads with the Macallan Highland malt whisky, my Drink of the Year (also of last year) and widely regarded in the trade as the king of malts. The flavour's rich, even powerful, but completely smooth, as smooth as that of a fine cognac, and immediately enjoyable. Over Christmas I'll be staying off it until comparatively late in the day, because the only drink you want after some of it is more of it. Macallan comes in various strengths and ages. I'll be going for the standard 40 per cent alcohol at ten years old rather than the Macallan Royal Marriage, a unique blend of whiskies from 1948 and 1961, the couple's respective birth years—wonderful stuff but a bit steep for me at £26.

I'll also need a malt of a different type for when I'm not drinking the Macallan, selected from Highland Park, Isle of Jura, Tormore, Bowmore. And a good blend, preferably Famous Grouse, both for itself and for the interesting results if you move to a malt after it.

Must check that the Dry Martini makings are in place—Gordon's gin, Martini Rossi dry vermouth, and a jar of the largest possible hard, white, acid cocktail onions, much more of a sweat to find than the gin and vermouth. Check too on basic Bloody Mary makings—vodka, Worcester sauce and expensive tomato juice.

Table wines are not my forte, but on special occasions like the appearance of the Christmas turkey and trimmings I enjoy throwing down a good strong red. The one I'd go for is a Chateauneuf-du-Pape, not too recent, say '76 or '77. Any left over will go well with the Stilton. (Perhaps a spot of port too with that, nothing fancy—somebody's Special Reserve at about £5.)

I won't be able to resist spoiling myself with some Muscat de Beaumes de Venise, a sweet white wine from the Rhône that's been tremendously successful here in the last couple of years. Made with the muscatel grape, fruity, flowery, all that, an ideal dessert wine, good with melon too.

We're now beginning to deal with luxuries and treats, rather than the sheer necessity of Scotch or gin. Among liqueurs I'd certainly favour kümmel, which with its caraway flavour does seem to take the fullness off after the plum pudding. Or a gross concession to guzzling like Bols apricot brandy or cherry brandy. But I'll probably end up with Drambuie, drinking some of it cut 50-50 with my malt whisky, if I can spare any.

Back to the realm of stark need with the question of beer. I'll be filling the refrigerator as full as I'm allowed to with large cans of Carlsberg Special Brew and about half as many of the ordinary Carlsberg Pilsner lager. Special Brew is a wonderful drink, but after a certain amount of it you do tend to fall over. Diluted with a weaker version of itself it gives you a longer run. To quaff the two of them half and half, really cold, out of a silver tankard produces as much goodwill as anything I know.

Continuing our course in boozemanship, the art or science of coming out ahead in drinking matters, we move today to the practical section. The object here is not just to give a party on the cheap, but to get away with it and even end up looking good, or good enough. The traditional strategy is notoriously to offer your guests a flat choice between (boring) red wine and (dull) white wine. Youngsters and other uncritical persons quite like this policy, but it's becoming increasingly vulnerable to the kind of old stager who doesn't mind asking loudly for a real drink. Yes, you can tell him there's none around all right, but you won't look good.

Clearly a more flexible approach is called for. Lead with the old choice of red and white, but give it a face-lift by picking a couple of those so-called country wines from southern France now to be seen in off-licences and supermarkets. They're plonk actually, but their fancy French names will prevent the fact from getting through to most of those there. Say threateningly: "Of course, they are a wee bit off the beaten track" to anyone who looks doubtful.

Follow this up with quite a large jug of Bloody Mary and another of Sangria or Wine Cup. Only the old stagers will notice that the Bloody Mary is nine tenths tomato juice and the Sangria mostly lemonade darkened with Angostura bitters— a nice touch—and they won't dare say anything, at least not with their wives around. Those wives can be very useful. Ingratiate yourself by lighting their cigarettes, complimenting them on their appearance, even seeming to listen to what they say. Your ideal, long-term objective is a quarrel between each old stager and his wife on their way home, with him going on about your meanness and her saying you were very sweet and he's nothing but a frustrated drunk.

If anybody has the pluck to ask for a gin and tonic or a whisky and soda, respond by leaving the room at once and staying away a good ten minutes. You spend them in some nook or niche or broom cupboard where you prepare all the drinks. In the present case fill a glass with ice, which is troublesome but softer on the pocket than booze, add tonic and pour in about a teaspoon of gin over the back of another spoon—it's the first sip that counts. Whiskies are trickier. Use the darkest brand you can find and put the soda in first. When that's done, hang on until you reckon you've been absent long enough to deter anyone from having a second try. Fill in the time by reading the paper and gulping your own private malt whisky.

If you're entertaining the wretched crowd to dinner, not just drinks, then of course a whole new world of short-changing opens up. And don't, by the way, imagine that this is no more than a light fantasy. Anyone who does can't have been around much yet.

Whiskey in the USA has a long, colourful history. (Note that it is indeed spelt with an "e," along with Irish whiskey—the Scotch and Canadian varieties are both plain whisky.)

One of the most illustrious early American distillers was George Washington, who manufactured the stuff commercially at his place near Mount Vernon in Virginia, and was very proud of the high reputation of his merchandise. I'm sure it was great for its time, but then and for long afterwards the general run of whiskey must have been pretty rough. I've often thought that the really amazing achievement of the Western hero wasn't his ability to shoot a pip out of a playing card at fifty paces, nor even his knack of dropping crotch first into his saddle from an upstairs window, but the way he could stride into the saloon, call for whiskey, knock it back neat and warm in one and not so much as blink, let alone burst into paroxysms of uncontrollable coughing.

All that, of course, is changed now. American whiskeys are second to none in smoothness, blandness, everything that goes to make a fine spirit. Some of them, like Washington's product and many since, are based on rye, but nearly all the brands we see in the UK belong in the bourbon category. Bourbon (rhymes with turban) gets its name from Bourbon County, Kentucky, where the first stills of this type were set up, though it's long been regularly made in several other states besides. Federal law requires bourbon whiskey to be derived from a cereal mash of at least 51 per cent corn, which is to say Indian corn, often called maize over here, though it's the identical vegetable that makes you, or me, so tremendously fat eaten off the cob.

The manufacturing process is carried out by means of large stills that operate on exactly the same principle as the patent or Coffey stills used in the production of grain whisky in Scotland. The young spirit is then drawn off to mature in specially charred oak barrels. Until recently, these were required to be new, but it seems that nowadays used casks are permitted. This is bad news for some distillers in Scotland, who formerly imported the secondhand casks to age their own whisky in.

Prominent brands of bourbon available in the UK include Jim Beam, Old Grandad, Wild Turkey, and Jack Daniel's. Wild Turkey is a newcomer, to this country at any rate, and increasingly tipped as the best. Jack Daniel's is the established quality leader. Strictly it isn't a bourbon at all, but a Tennessee whiskey, made at Lynchburg in Moore County, no less.

Don't go there, as I once did. Moore County turned out

to be dry, and all I got to drink all day was a glass of cold tea at Madame Bobo's Boarding House. I doubt if things have changed much.

Like malt Scotch and all other first-rate spirits, bourbon whiskey from the USA deserves to be taken straight, neat, or, as I prefer it, with a little water, but no ice. Probably it's at its best like that. At the same time, bourbon is, of course, a quite different drink from Scotch—comparatively sweet, lighter in body, less penetrating in flavour. This means that, whereas Scotch won't mix happily with anything, bourbon is the perfect foundation for famous and delicious concoctions like the Mint Julep and the Old-Fashioned cocktail. The Julep can wait until there's mint in the shops to put in it, but the time to run up an Old-Fashioned is now.

Some cocktails, like the Dry Martini, can be prepared in quantity beforehand—the Old-Fashioned needs to be made up in individual drinks. For each partaker, then, put into a short tumbler a teaspoon of sugar and dissolve it in a little warm water. Add a couple of dashes of Angostura bitters, a squeeze of fresh orange juice and up to 3 oz bourbon, and stir vigorously. Add ice cubes and stir again. Push a slice of orange in alongside the ice, with the option of a maraschino cherry. A teaspoon of Grand Marnier, if you have it, upgrades the mixture.

Strong drinks arouse strong feelings and, should they ever read it, some experts will soon start to twitch with fury at this recipe. One school of thought insists on rye whiskey instead of bourbon. Another regards the use of water as an intolerable dilution. Objections noted.

The Old-Fashioned is a sweet drink and that just has to be faced. More than two will probably seem excessive. It's admittedly a bit of a pest to make, but not as much as it may sound, and the result is the only cocktail to rival the Dry Martini at the other end of the taste spectrum.

You can produce something in the same range as the Old-Fashioned with less trouble by knocking out a Manhattan, once one of the great standards, now rarely seen and overdue for a revival. Mix a dash or two of Angostura bitters, 2 or 3 oz of bourbon and an ounce or so of Italian vermouth, the sweet red kind. Add ice cubes and a maraschino cherry. Sometimes called the Sweet Manhattan to distinguish it from the Dry Manhattan, which is similar with French vermouth instead of Italian, and very nasty indeed according to me.

Bourbon is popular as the base of the Whiskey Sour and the Whiskey Collins, also known as the Colonel Collins. The Sour is whiskey with fresh lemon juice, melted sugar and ice, the Collins adds soda water. If you feel you can't face toiling away with squeezer and strainer and whatnot at your time of life, there's an excellent cop-out. Pour a good shot of bourbon over ice cubes in a long tumbler. Fill up with standard bitter lemon drink. Stir. Drop in a cocktail cherry. That's it, your instant Whiskey Collins.

Southern Comfort, being a bourbon-type liqueur, is a suitable and enjoyable substitute for bourbon in, at any rate, the Old-Fashioned. Its fruitiness and sweetness mean you can go easy on the fruit and sugar in the recipe. And take it slow, man.

By common consent, Irish whiskey comes third in the league after Scotch and bourbon, with a much smaller output than either. Nowadays most Irish is made in the same basic way as most Scotch, being a blend of malt and grain products but with a malty emphasis.

This comes out strongly in the much-praised Old Bushmills Black Label ("Black Bush"), a premium blend from Northern Ireland. It's supposed to have once been sprung on a French expert, completely flooring the poor gent, who after much consideration said it could only be a fine and unusual Armagnac. I don't quite know what that story proves, but however you look at it Black Bush is a splendid drink for sipping not swilling. But Irish whiskey in general is indispensable only as the foundation of Irish coffee.

Canadian whisky is often thought and spoken of as a rye whisky, and indeed rye is used in its manufacture, though corn (maize) normally preponderates. All Canadian whiskies are made with the patent still and blended with a proportion of neutral grain spirit, so that the final result is lighter than any other type, that's to say with less body and less fullness of flavour, half a step towards vodka. It seems to be benefiting from the recent trend towards light drinks. I can't help thinking that the Canadians are a great crowd, but are perhaps the only people who could have produced a boring whisky.

Japanese whisky isn't exactly boring, or at least isn't a boring subject. They're very keen on the stuff there—they drink more of it than anyone else except the Americans. How could they resist trying to do with whisky what they were already successfully doing with their car, television, and electronics industries? The making of whisky, of fine whisky at least, is notoriously a long-term matter, one where experience and climate and all sorts of X factors play their part. The Japanese effort is a fascinating demonstration of how far adaptability, patience and boldness will take you instead. Especially boldness—it seems that, in 1973, Suntory, the principal firm, opened the largest malt distillery in the world, a structure covering three times the area of Liverpool Cathedral, if my calculations are correct.

On admittedly very small acquaintance, the product seems to me unlikely to drive anyone out of business, except makers of bad whisky everywhere. The comparison with Scotch is inevitable. It put me in mind of instant versus real coffee—very like in one way, and yet nowhere near. Never mind. What they must be looking for over there is a style of whisky as distinctive and different and striking as any other, and when they find it we can all look out.

Many other countries import malt whisky from Scotland in bulk, blend it with locally distilled grain spirit and market the combination nationally. I wouldn't mind trying, say, Zambian, Egyptian, Thai and Guyanan whiskies. Just once.

I think the nastiest drink I've ever drunk in my life was some stuff called mezcal in a Mexican market town. It's made, I find, from the same aloe-like plant that gives us tequila, of which mezcal is a kind of downmarket version, if you can imagine such a thing. When I bought my bottle at the grocer's it had a small packet tied to the neck. Inside was what looked like a shrimp in talcum powder. "What's that?" I asked my American friend. "That's the worm," he said, "the best part. You can try it without." I tried it without. My head filled with a taste of garage or repair shop—hot rubber and plastic, burnt oil and a whiff of hydrochloric-acid vapour from the charging engine. When I sold Mack the rest of the bottle he emptied in the pounded-up worm, recapped, shook, and poured himself a tumbler of greyish liquid with little pink shreds in it. Give me Tizer any day.

I haven't yet sampled Ruou Tiet De, a North Vietnamese mixture of rice alcohol and goat's blood, or Central Asian koumis, fermented from mare's and camel's milk. Sake, a sweetish rice beer from Japan, goes well with Japanese food, so if you happen to like eating raw fish and seaweed this is obviously your tipple. You drink it warm. I may say that when I heated some on the stove recently to check that it was as horrible as I remembered, it took all the deposit off the lining of the saucepan.

You needn't go as far afield as that to find a drink offensive to any person of culture and discrimination, especially if mixes are on the agenda. In South Wales you're liable to find them throwing down Guinness with Lucozade and Ribena, or Mackeson and orange squash—not in the more refined areas, true. In Scotland they put fizzy lemonade in their whisky. Yes, in respectable places in the Highlands there are quart bottles of the stuff on the bar alongside the Malvern water and the siphon. The objection is not that it's vulgar, but that, of course, it kills the Scotch and tastes frightful.

Not that we down south have any excuse for self-satisfaction while we allow the atrocity of the Pina Colada to flourish unchecked in our midst. I ask your tolerance while I explain that this disgusting concoction is made by pouring into a tumbler over ice a measure of something called Malibu, which describes itself as tropical coconut laced with light Jamaican rum, and filling up with a semblance of pineapple juice, fizzy or still according to whim. Just the thing for a little 95-IQ female, fresh from a spell on the back of the bike, to suck at while her escort plunges grunting at the fruit machine.

Mind you, he'll be no ornament to his sex either, quite likely clutching a lager and lime—an exit application from the human race if ever there was one.

Bourbon whiskey blends into cocktails. Irish whiskey gives us Irish Coffee, Canadian whisky goes well with most mixes, Mexican whisky is probably all the better for a shot of tequila—but Scotch stands apart, proudly resistant to being combined with fruit juice, bitters, vermouth, anything.

Well, almost anything. Certainly anything that goes to make a cocktail of whatever sort. So at least I've always found, but with my famous impartiality I'll describe one well-regarded drink you may care to sample. This is the Rob Roy cocktail. At its simplest it consists just of equal parts of Scotch and sweet (red Italian) vermouth poured over ice and mixed in a smallish glass. With proportions two to one, a dash of Angostura bitters and a cocktail cherry, this becomes a Scotch Manhattan, and an added teaspoon of Drambuie produces a Bobbie Burns. To my mind all versions are bearable, but quite unrewarding. Then, of course, one or other of them might turn out to be just what you've been waiting for all these years.

To turn to more serious matters, Scotch and ginger ale, with or without ice, is a reasonably invigorating beverage. If you can be bothered to cut a long strip of lemon peel and drape it over the rim of the glass, you're entitled to call it a Horse's Neck.

A 50-50 amalgamation of Scotch and ginger wine, the Whisky Mac, takes the edge off a chilly morning, or seems to. Seldom seen in the books, probably because it's a totally British article, but a favourite in some pubs.

Don't ask in the pub for Scotch and milk or everyone in earshot will gawp in bewilderment. There may be milk a yard off to pour in the coffees, but they'll still look at you as if you've called for a dram of snake venom. Not responsive to unfamiliar ideas, the British. Wait till you get home and serve yourself. This any-proportion drink, which has no name I know of, is a good answer to that sadly rather common problem, when you quite fancy a little something but aren't at all sure what view your turn will take of the project.

One unusual, enjoyable and (I should guess) ancient mixture consists of Scotch and alcoholic cordial of cloves. I'd forgotten it, and had thought the cloves had stopped being made, as many old drinks have, until it popped up the other day on the Peter Dominic list. Proportions not critical. You could call the thing a Clove Hitch if you felt inclined.

Don't forget the great Atholl Brose. English recipe— equal parts Scotch, clear honey and cream. Warm, blend and allow to cool. Scottish recipe—instead of the cream, use the liquor made by soaking two or three handfuls of oatmeal in half a pint of water for some hours and straining. Better so, with less richness and more flavour. But either is delicious, fortifying, on a chilly Sunday afternoon in lieu of tea, or late at night.

So much for infallibility just now. I stated firmly that Scotch was not a suitable foundation for any cocktail, and the echoes had hardly died away when, in a book by Clement Freud, I came across a recipe for one that overturned my decree. The eminent radio panellist and non-smoker describes something called a Godfather, consisting of one part Amaretto and three parts whisky poured over crushed ice. He doesn't specify Scotch, but I tried it with Scotch and found it was good. I also found that the crushed ice could be acceptably replaced by ice cubes and a brisk stir.

Amaretto, very popular in the States and now on the move here, is a liqueur from northern Italy consisting of a spirit flavoured with apricots and almonds. The name means "little bitter," which can't help being a joke because, of course, it isn't bitter at all, but sweet and fruity, though not cloying, a nice winder-up to a serious meal.

The Godfather is inevitably a sweet or sweetish drink, too. Some people object to any but bone-dry cocktails and aperitifs. I see nothing wrong with an occasional bit of sweetness at the pre-food stage. A cocktail, in my world at least, is a rather once-in-a-way affair, something of a treat, and if you feel quite relieved when you get back to your basic tipple, well, that's part of the idea.

Another unfamiliar Scotch mix, though no cocktail, was suggested by remembering a story about Nubar Gulbenkian. The great financier was seen astride his horse at a meet imbibing from a pocket flask when some pathetic protester wanted to know what was in it. "Scotch and fox's blood!" was the reply. Not true, I imagine, but a splendidly offensive thing to bawl at a weed of an anti-hunt demonstrator. However, I wouldn't mind betting that what the old plutocrat was actually quaffing was a combination of Scotch and cherry brandy known, according to Cyril Ray, as a Percy Special, after a hunt or pack of hounds or whatever you call it, in Northumberland, and highly thought of as a stirrup cup. Not much improvement, you may feel.

This is the time and place for a quick glance at the Scotch Toddy, just the thing for these Arctic nights. Trader Vic pours boiling water over a lump of sugar in a preheated glass, adds a good shot of whisky, stirs and drops in a lemon slice. Finally he throws some grated nutmeg on top. Good, but don't overdo it or the drink will look muddy.

When all is said, God undoubtedly made Scotch to be drunk on its own, but what does this mean in practice—ice, soda, water or not? Well, tastes differ, but with an ordinary brand, a standard-price brand, I'll take ice and soda; with an expensive "premium" blend probably water and no ice; with a malt plain water, about one to one.

But what water? Well, tap water if there's nothing else, and provided it isn't chlorinated. If it is, and there's still nothing else, try pouring some from one jug to another and back again a few times. The infusion of air seems to get rid of the chlorine.

The Soviet government recently issued one of its condemnations of public drunkenness and the usual warning about stern countermeasures. This is partly routine, like official attacks on rock music, jeans and other signs of decadence, but it's also an indication that the legal booze supply is improving after a setback. Like every other industry in the USSR, the state liquor monopoly, Prodintorg, is appallingly inefficient, the constant victim of breakdowns and shortages. At such times the authorities' attitude to illicit distilling, normally harsh in the extreme, mellows wonderfully. The bootleg stills spring up in their tens of thousands and the police look the other way until Prodintorg recovers.

Because, come what may, Soviet man has got to be given his drink. Some say the Russian Revolution of 1917 happened because the Czar had banned alcohol three years before as a wartime measure, or at least that was why it was so bloody. Certainly the Russian attitude to drink is different from ours in the West, probably always has been. Centuries ago, travellers recorded that a typical Russian meal was one where everybody got speechlessly drunk, all classes, all ages, both sexes, seven days a week, that people were always falling down dead in public through over-use, that "drinke is their whole desire," as an English diplomat wrote of his visit in 1568.

Drinking to get drunk is probably known in every country, and there are alcoholics in most places, but even the ordinary Russian drinks to be drunk with the minimum of delay—hence the down-in-one ritual, which of course also shortens the agony of getting down the local hooch. And once drunk he acts drunk. It's expected of him; indeed the regard and sympathy shown drunks in public is something almost unknown in the West outside Ireland—a suggestive comparison. From time immemorial a Russian needing to buy a bottle has gone to the head of any queue in a grocery or market, not by law but by natural right.

Nowadays, of course, there's more to get away from than the cold, the monotonous food and the frustrations of life in a backward, bureaucratic, corrupt society. Obviously you can get falling-down drunk at home, but there are no bars that serve anything stronger than beer, except in Intourist hotels, reserved for foreigners and officials. If you want to be served vodka, or any other spirit, you have to go to a restaurant and order it with your meal, which in itself can take an hour or two. So sometimes you team up with a couple of fellows at work, form a troika. (A troika can be a three-horse carriage but it's just three of anything, a threesome.) You get hold of a half litre of vodka and what's probably harder to come by in a socialist country, three paper cups. Perhaps the grocer will let you stand in his shop, anyway you find some place where the wind isn't blowing and you drink the vodka, quite fast I expect, and then you go home. And that's your night out with the lads.

In its way I find the thought of that almost as depressing as anything to do with the Gulag or mental hospitals. Remember it when the juke box in the pub is too loud or they can't do you a Harvey Wallbanger.

Despite what I may have said or implied just now the Russians make some very fine upstanding vodkas. The ones they export some of, like Stolichnaya, Moskovskaya, Krepkaya, tend to be colourless or "white," pure, straight, and are certainly well enough. But it's the vodkas they lay themselves out with at home, the flavoured ones, that fascinate me, though I know them only from descriptions. Additives are said to include ginger, cloves, vanilla, brandy, Russian port, chocolate, honey, dill and sugar, though not all at once. A cayenne-pepper version is supposed to have been a favourite with Stalin, always the man for a pungent bit of wit.

To my mind the best vodka of all is not Russian but Polish. Among the straight kinds is some stuff called Pure Polish Spirit, which is 80 *per cent*—not proof—alcohol, a drink to be tiptoed up to. They also export Zubrowka, which has a blade of special primitive grass in the bottle and I think tastes pretty ropey, but it's quite popular and you may like it. There's also a cherry or cherry juice variety which I can disrecommend without reserve. On the other hand, the Polish vodkas flavoured respectively with lemon peel and rowanberries (mountain-ash berries) are excellent and most unusual, though to my knowledge to be seen here only in specialist shops.

In comparison, an Anglo-Saxon domestic vodka such as Cossack or Smirnoff is a plain straightforward affair, unflavoured, rather dull on its own, good for stiffening punches and other mixes, but not so good, I think, in cocktails where the other ingredients smother it. For instance, I don't really like the Vodka Martini because I don't really like the taste of French vermouth, which is about all you get. But you might care to try my personal variant, which changes the odds by adding cucumber juice. Proportions: twelve vodka, one Martini Rossi dry vermouth, two juice (easily made on an ordinary glass or plastic lemon squeezer and strained). The Lucky Jim is my name for it. Well, I had to call it something.

Here's how to make another great unknown, which some nice lady described to me at a party in the sixties and I've never heard of elsewhere. It takes a bottle of British vodka, a lemon and a hell of a lot of patience. Cut all the peel off the lemon without also cutting off any of the white pith underneath. (There are clever dicks who can do this in one go, so that they end up with a single long strip of peel.) Poke the peel into the vodka and screw the cap on again. Put the bottle on a shelf and leave it for about a week, giving it a shake whenever you happen to be passing. Finally, take the peel out, chill the vodka and pour into small prechilled glasses. Tastes like the Islands of the Blest. Use carefully.

Recently my local shut itself up for several weeks to be redecorated. The first time I went back in I proceeded with caution, mindful of the assorted horrors perpetrated on our pubs over the last decade and more. My first look fetched a sigh of relief. The small room, which in days gone by was probably called the private bar, had been smartened up but not transformed, likewise the tiny snug opening off it—rather dark, quiet, unluxurious, almost dowdy. The main bar, which was bright and cheerful enough, had a sort of thirties flavour, with copper trays on display, what could have been a genuine post horn, and colourful plates that looked like earthenware but were really paper, not that it bothered me.

How I'd hated all that kind of thing in the past! How I welcomed it now! It wasn't flashy or aggressively up to date or eye-catching—though you couldn't help noticing some pictures here and there, they were small, conventional and above all not by local artists. There were plenty of comfortable places to sit. And, wonder of wonders, no music. But, alas, every so often a horrible racket was kicked up by a pair of giant fruit machines, loud fluting, piping noises like a steam organ alternating with bursts from a First World War machine gun. At those times, sitting there stopped being enjoyable and became no better than bearable.

All the same, the place is a paradise compared to the common run of London pubs where bawling music from the Bottom Twenty hinders conversation and even thought, or where, in the middle of the day at least, you often can't put your glass down for the pepperpots and bottles of sauce, and you find yourself discussing the SDP across someone else's steak pie and chips, all of it on a tabletop the size of a dartboard. Food is the curse of the drinking classes, at any rate in pubs—in the one I've described they just do cheese rolls and such, which is about right.

I know that these days a lot of pub food is good, beating the local bistro and trattoria on value for money and speed of service, though not on amenity. But the pub should segregate the eaters and the drinkers at least into separate rooms, preferably separate establishments. Pubs that are also lunch counters, and often coffee bars and soft-drinks stands as well, too easily become places for all the family. And that's an en-croachment, an attack on the pub's time-honoured function as a male refuge.

I said the last bit nearly a year ago on this page. Nobody wrote to me then to correct me, or even to agree with me. Per-haps someone will this time. On the various points, am I prej-udiced, out of date, generalizing from too little data, just wrong, or devastatingly right? Letters c/o *Daily Express* by 25 March, please. State your age, sex, favourite drink, etc.

I can't go on evading the wine problem—it won't go away. Just coming out against the tyranny of wine, as I've done, isn't enough. Mind you, I stand by everything I've said on the sub-ject. Let me recap, with additions. Most of us would agree that wine is at its best with food, and can perhaps only be ap-preciated like that. Not all of us, it seems—it's odd that when experts choose and grade wine, they do so with nothing to eat but the occasional palate-cleansing dry biscuit, and spit out the wine too instead of swallowing it, which I doubt if they usually do at dinner. But let that go.

Under normal conditions then, wine goes with food, though obviously not any wine with any food. No wine at all goes with eggs however prepared, most salads, strong or ripe cheeses and almost any highly seasoned dish, let alone with kippers, fish and chips, bacon and tomatoes, sausages and mash and a whole range of staple unsmart British dishes. Beer or stout goes with them.

Quite a few people, true, will drink a good red wine with roast beef, lamb or pork, and why not, if they enjoy it? Fine, but they won't enjoy it so much if they also take on board our traditional condiments, like English mustard, horseradish, mint sauce, red currant jelly or apple sauce, the last of which, as I know from bitter experience, can ruin an expensive claret. Similarly, roast chicken can be agreeably washed down with either red or white wine, only much the more so if bread sauce and sage-and-onion stuffing aren't let into the act. And I need hardly say, keep the parsley sauce off the cod and the poached egg off the haddock. Wine of any merit is too delicate for that kind of thing.

In fact, it follows that the nearer you can get to reproducing a dish from the Burgundy region, say, with all the right herbs and other trimmings, and if possible a stove from there to cook it on, the better your bottle of Burgundy will taste with it. Outside a few specialist restaurants, imitating someone else's food to go with someone else's drink seems an absurd proceeding, especially given the quality of British meat and cooking vegetables. This is not a wine-producing country, and our national cuisine evolved without it.

Unfortunately the matter can't be left there. It doesn't touch the wine problem. Haven't I said what that is? It's simply that people expect wine, confound them. When they come to dinner or just drop in, they require it. No use telling them how much better off they'd be with Guinness. What to do?

It's some years since a Cambridge don of my acquaintance served his guests tea to wash down their Chinese-style dinner, on the reasoning that with any given food the correct drink was the local drink, and tea was Chinese and wine clearly not. I should imagine—needless to say I wasn't there myself—he only just got away with it then. Nowadays he wouldn't dare. But offering beer wouldn't be much more popular, I feel, even alongside Chinese food, which it's not at all bad with, better than wine in my view. Such is the infatuation with wine that people will throw it away on serious Indian-restaurant curries, which surely call aloud for beer, cold beer and plenty of it. Or water. One day, though, I must follow an ingenious friend's suggestion and drink a sweet white wine with curry, something pretty atrocious from Cyprus or Bulgaria, on the reasoning this time that I'm only following in the track of the mango chutney.

An under-regarded but surely powerful argument against wine is that very few of us can afford to drink quality wine with any regularity, whereas a fair number can afford reasonable amounts of the best beer available most nights of the week. It's hard to prefer somebody's Light Fruity red to a well-chilled can of export lager, let alone a glass of pub plonk to almost any real ale.

And yet the blighters keep insisting on wine, not just with food but before meals, after meals, any time. "Dry Martini?" you say politely to your guest, even rather proudly, having sweated at getting the proportions just right and the cocktail really cold. "Or gin and tonic? Or Scotch? There's the Glenlivet and Long John, or dry sherry if you'd rather. Or Perrier, of course." Pause for consideration. Then: "Could I have a glass of white wine?" he asks.

Actually it's she who asks, more often than not. To some kinds of female, white wine is the ideal thing to ask for in another fellow's house. First, it's fashionable—light-coloured drinks are in, and drinks light in alcohol are in. Then, to choose wine rather than spirits shows superiority to that horrible lot, men most of them, who drink to get drunk, or at least to have a good time. Above all, white wine is the only drink the host is dead certain not to have by him on his tray or trolley—it'll be in his fridge in the kitchen. To ask for a glass of it an hour before dinner sends him belting satisfyingly out of the room, looking for, finding, and plying the corkscrew while new arrivals stack up. Well, there we are, what?

We reached the point where a female visitor or guest of yours has asked for a glass of white wine as a pre-meal drink. Sometimes she'll specify a small glass, sounding as if she thought she was considerately saving you the burdensome extra work involved in pouring and carrying a large glass. But in any case the stuff had better be there in the refrigerator, preferably with the cork pulled and stuck back in to improve your quickness on the draw.

What sort of stuff had it better be? First, the stuff it isn't going to be when I'm doing the buying. By pretty rough rules, which are all you need at this stage: nothing Spanish, because too horrible; nothing Yugoslav, because too boring; nothing French, because too expensive, and often too horrible as well. The last part deserves some expansion.

Be clear that we're talking about dry white wines. I know well enough that overall the French produce the best wines in the world, including the sweet wines of Bordeaux, which are often called incomparable and can have uncommon prices. But the dry ones are mostly too dry to suit me, whether with food or solo. That's if dry is the right word. I mean more than absence of sweetness—I mean the quality that makes the saliva spurt into my mouth as soon as the wine arrives there. Perhaps I mean what wine experts call crispness or flintiness or even acidity, which for some mysterious reason they think is a good thing in a wine. But whatever you call it, I don't want it. Chablis, the average white Mâcon, Muscadet, Sancerre, Pouilly-Fumé—not today, thank you. Unless, of course, you're ready to throw your money about like a man with three arms: a very tolerable little Montrachet can be yours for £35 or so. The French wine growers are mighty clever fellows, but I think they overcharge, also overproduce, tarnishing some of their great names in the last ten years or so.

Italian wines, both red and white, are better value for money. That bottle of dry white in my fridge is most likely to contain Frascati, a famous wine from the hills near Rome, where I can claim to have consumed it in quantity. To me it's free of all sweetness, but also totally free of the mouth-pursing component I've tried to describe, a wine you don't have to get to know, or talk about for half an hour before you drink it in order to like it. Romans apparently drink it with everything. I've found it good with fish, good with roast pork, good on its own. You should get away at about £2.35 a bottle.

Last month I asked for readers' views of my complaints about present-day pubs. Today I present the first half of my report. The response wasn't overwhelming exactly, but it was a good deal larger than I'd expected, also more favourable. Only one reader, by her own account a hotelier and Tory activist who's also been a probation officer, took serious issue with me. "Your writing," she stated, "is getting more and more biased and entrenched in reactionary fuddy-duddyism." An excellent summing-up, I thought, of my contribution to the eighties' cultural scene.

To those many in broad agreement with me, the most detested feature of the modern pub was clearly noise, whether in the form of music or row from machines or both. The general and strong feeling was that noise was destroying or had already destroyed "the conversation and conviviality that has made the British pub the envy of the world," to quote a lady from Cumbria, not in my view overstating the case. Of course, it's the youngsters, many said. Affluent yobbos is what a reactionary fuddy-duddy might call them.

Food was next on the hate list, for getting morally and physically in the way, for using up staff time that should be spent serving drinks, above all for raising unwanted cooking smells, a point I'd overlooked. Certainly if you're not eating or going to eat, you don't need great clouds of vapour from chips or curry under your nose. The eaters on their side could do without cigarette smoke at equally short range. The case for returning to a two-room system in pubs seems strong, if not to segregate eaters then to install a yobbos' beargarden or a crèche. Children underfoot displeased a third of those writing. Minor aversions included nasty decor, necking teenagers, TV and unobliging staff, but on the whole staff came off pretty well.

At some point like now, I have to reveal what will come as no great surprise, that the average age of my correspondents was, well, on the high side—though one sterling lad of twenty from North Wales reassured me that I wasn't out of touch. There have to be changes, we're told. But do we know that? I wish I felt that at any rate the public were getting what they want, instead of what some "expert" thinks they want. Brewers please note.

I was struck, and now and then greatly touched, by the pleasant, friendly tone nearly everybody took. Even the fuddy-duddy charge came in such a good natured letter that I couldn't possibly resent it.

Second half of report will quote quotes, name names and announce the winner. Oh yes, there's a winner, and a prize. Guess what sort.

"Let's go back to the spit and sawdust and start again." So says Mr. E. Quested of Peacehaven, neatly summing up the view of many who kindly wrote to me in answer to my call for readers' reactions to present-day pubs. A lot of them would also agree with Mr. R. P. Taylor, of Leamington Spa, who mentions "one certain sign of a good pub . . . at least as many old people use it as young."

I was greatly taken with a suggestion from Mr. C. S. Lowther, of Blaydon—the forming of a club to fight juke boxes, etc., Peace in Pubs (PIP). "A lapel badge or tie could be sold to finance printed attacks on the offending breweries," he writes.

Not impossible. I have dreams of an organization of pub-users that would emulate that dazzling success of CAMRA, the Campaign for Real Ale, which forced the brewers into an about-turn. But this one's unlikely. I don't think there's enough strong feeling on the subject. As we see all too often, hordes of people just put up with the noise and the intrusive food and the kids underfoot. At least they, the hordes, have somewhere to go, unlike poor Miss or Mrs. M. J. Boyd, of Arundel, whose local has shut for good after four hundred years of service.

An expert summing-up of good and bad in pubs came from Mrs. Madge Dawkes, of Spalding, Lincs, who grew up in the business. She knows the giveaways—tables sticky *underneath*, stale flower-water and dead flowers, stingy ice in drinks, lighting you can't see your change by, miserable bar staff. The last one, of course, points straight to the landlord, who is the heart of any good pub.

On the other side of the bar, words of wisdom come from Mr. Al Hix, in London, needless to say an American, but one who knows us well, and our pubs. "I want my pubs to look like pubs," he said. "I want them to function as a place where I can drink and talk with friends or read. My local is my club." And what decent club has a juke box?

The most informative and best letter was written by Mr. A. Gurr, of Evenley in Northants, for many years a tenant landlord. He puts all the postwar changes down to economics— falling beer sales, the gap left by the disappearance of Lyons and other tea shops, the publican's handy share of fruit-machine profits, the working wife who wants to come to the pub and brings the kids. "One can't stop it," Mr. Gurr concludes sadly. But cheer up, sir—a rare three-litre bottle of twelve-year-old malt Scotch whisky is on its way to you. Thank you all for your letters. Answers coming.

In discussing the wine problem a couple of weeks back, I let fall the information that myself can sometimes be seen drinking the stuff. This may strike some readers as a base betrayal of my crusade against wine. And maybe it is—but the distressing fact remains that there are occasions when not to drink it becomes virtually impossible. For the moment I'm referring not to mealtimes, but to before, after and between— especially before—and even more especially to those situations where, for one reason or another, the gap between starting to drink and starting to eat is going to be unusually wide. A long session, that's to say, quite likely with rounds being bought and the speed of intake thereby hotted up.

Now of course there's always gin, and always a lot of other things like that as well, but I personally find that after half a dozen large Dry Martinis and a proper lunch my customary skill with the commas and semicolons becomes a little eroded. Whereas if it's the evening, let me just say that I like to make my way to my carriage unassisted.

Well, there's always beer too, but here again the way is far from easy. In the pub, almost any decent brew is almost equally shattering on the timescale we're talking about, and quite a number of topers past their first youth probably find with me that the sheer bulk of beer of any strength gets too much, well within an hour of the start.

The various objections to sherry, vermouth, wine aperitifs, etc., can wait for the moment. Wine remains the practicable alternative—if conditions are right.

In the pub, in the average pub, wine is a dodgy option, a really boring drink if not positively harmful—especially the red—and nearly always overpriced. So find a pub where these matters are properly seen to, or go elsewhere, go to a wine bar, go on to the restaurant, stay at home. Assuming you have control over your choice of tipple, my advice for a pre-meal wine would first of all be to avoid red. Red wine, to most stomachs, is more closely associated with food than white, and even a single glass can set off internal expectations. Keeping these unsatisfied for an hour and a half or so does no good to the digestion and general wellbeing. Nibbling away at nuts or dry biscuits doesn't do much either, except make sure that if you ever do get to the table, you won't feel like eating anything else.

White wine steers you clear of the difficulty. Frascati, as

mentioned before, is an obvious choice, but there are others no less worthy.

As anybody who goes there will soon see, the national drink of Germany is beer—1364 breweries in the Federal Republic at the last count known to me, as against fewer than two hundred in Britain. Germany's wine-growing districts are confined to the southwestern corner of the country, and their production is only about one seventh of that of France. Nevertheless Germany is often thought to have the edge in quality and to make the finest white wines in the world. (No reds to speak of.) The thing is that they don't go all that well with food, very much not, it might be thought, with the generally rich German food. In the past few years the manufacturers have made strenuous efforts to deal with this situation, partly by denying it exists.

Some time ago I attended an admittedly most enjoyable session, masterminded by a gigantic and voluble German count, at which a specially cooked meal was accompanied by specially chosen hocks and moselles, with the object of establishing that they at least went with that food. They didn't go at all badly, but what was established was how much better French wines would have gone, also that at some stage in an elaborate meal like that you get fed up with white wines, however good, and long for a red. At the same time the makers have been pushing their drier wines, those supposedly more suited to the table. An untoward result of their campaign in Germany has been that the public there, urged to drink wine with their food, have in many cases fastened on imports from

France. Others have gone on drinking beer with their meals and sweet or sweetish German wine after and between, and no doubt before as well. That's where I come in.

A few glasses of hock (rather than moselle, which can be a bit subtle for me) are just the thing to get me relatively un-damaged through a heavy session as described last time. As to which hock, this is a question I leave to menial persons. A German wine label is one of the things life's too short for, a daunting testimony to that peculiar nation's love of detail and organization. If I don't want a too-sweet wine, I say so, and if that doesn't work where I am, I go somewhere else.

Any way it turns out, those few glasses I mentioned will hit the pocket of whoever's paying—the fellows surely know how to charge. When you tax them with it, they moan about their unreliable weather and the high cost of labour. And, of course, their production methods are very expensive. Of course I sometimes wonder about those production methods. Or rather I don't wonder at all.

Years ago an old friend, a wine merchant, was in Bordeaux buying for his London firm. "How much of this can you let me have?" he asked his supplier about an item he'd fancied. "I can't say yet," he was told. "I don't know for sure how much I'll be getting from Algeria." Noticing the horrified stare this earned him, the fellow added quickly: "Don't worry, Christopher, whatever you get will be the real thing—I just have to meet my orders from Paris, and, er, elsewhere."

I repeated this mini-story to another London shipper, who seemed a bit puzzled that I'd bothered. I ended with a hopeful smile: "But I dare say the German wines are genuine enough," and got the reply: "Let me ask you a question. Who are the greatest chemists in the world?"

That one comes back to mind whenever I sniff and sip a glass of hock or moselle and find everything absolutely right, impeccably balanced, in perfect condition, just on the point of being too good to be true, in fact. There's nothing new about this—a writer of sixty years ago went off moselle because it had "a horrible suspicion of the laboratory." I don't think he meant he could taste chemicals, which would be the sign of failure. No, the stuff's a great success on the nose, on the palate, in the throat, in the stomach. It's in the head that it bothers you.

Five minutes' investigation is enough to start coming across tales like these. It's been known long since that after a poor summer in Burgundy the manufacturers get on the blower to their friends in the Rhône—further south, warmer, sunnier—and in no time the tankers are thundering up the autoroute with millions of litres of stronger, tastier reinforcement. The same thing happens in Bordeaux with Rioja across the Spanish border, not to mention places further afield, further than Algeria now that output there has been almost halved in ten years.

The practice of silently topping up a wine with the output of another, usually inferior, vineyard is sometimes known as "stretching." Unless the end-product is labelled something like French Red Wine, the word is "fraud." But cynics would call it nothing more than part of the normal run of manufacture.

At some point on the price scale you presumably start getting what you're paying for, but nobody knows, or is saying. Certainly cheaper wines are all too apt to be adulterated, or at least treated. Even one of my favourite Italian wines is mostly pasteurized now, as a colleague remarked the other day. Still, if a glass of wine tastes reasonably pleasant, doesn't hurt the digestion and has some cheering effect, who cares? I do, but not much.

The adulteration of wine is not a popular subject with wine drinkers, and especially not with wine writers. In all my vast library I can find only a brief encyclopedia entry: "Adulterated wine . . . wine which has been treated with unauthorized material or excessive amounts of permitted substance." I like that "unauthorized material." Perhaps the writer was thinking of the products of figs, tea, banana skins and other vegetable elements, along with whole racks of chemicals, periodically found in wines of high repute and detonating one of those breathtaking scandals that set the wine world reeling—but somehow never bring anyone to book or provide any assurance for the future.

Such "treatment" must be less widespread than the practice of topping up the local vintage with other wines, sometimes from a neighbouring but inferior region, often from a thousand miles away. Algeria was the French wine manufacturer's friend in need for many years, but now she produces less and sends most of it to the Russians to cheer up their plonk, he must look further, to Eastern Europe, especially Greece. So along the length of the Mediterranean chug the tankers, bearing wine not good enough to be offered Greeks as it stands, but okay for the French blenders. And this while the law sternly forbids Greek wine to be sold in France in bottle unless clearly marked "Greek wine."

Nobody knows, or is saying, how much of it goes on.

What is known is that a great deal of wine is more or less openly tampered with by the maker, subjected to "treatment" without being actually adulterated. The process of chaptalization consists of adding sugar to the grape juice before fermentation. The added sugar will all be turned to alcohol, so you're out to make the wine stronger, not sweeter. Very useful in thin years, illegal in California, semi-legal in France, which means in practice you're only allowed to do it when you need to. Many wines, including some Italians and young Burgundies, are pasteurized, boiled to kill off all the organisms and render them stable.

Now I don't mind this kind of thing much, as I said, so long as the result is palatable, harmless and alcoholic. But it makes me doubly uncomfortable with wine chatter. When I find someone I respect writing about an edgy, nervous wine that dithered in the glass, I cringe. When I hear someone I don't respect talking about an austere, unforgiving wine, I turn a bit austere and unforgiving myself. When I come across stuff like that and remember about the figs and bananas, I want to snigger uneasily. You can call a wine red, and dry, and strong, and pleasant. After that, watch out. . . .

To some people, a taste for dry drinks is a sign of sophistication. This is so firmly entrenched that it often goes against personal preference. In such cases it's the idea of dryness that's attractive, whereas the old tastebuds actually prefer a touch of sweetness. This little peculiarity, which the Americans go in for at least as doggedly as we do ourselves, is well enough understood and allowed for by the makers of drinks.

You can see the tendency in the labelling of sherry and champagne, where "dry" can be far from bone dry and "medium dry" or "demi-sec" will almost always be distinctly sweet.

Saying and perhaps thinking you like dry drinks, when, in fact, you prefer sweet or sweetish ones, is probably the result of a confused feeling that sweet drinks are ladies' drinks, perhaps even old ladies' drinks. Permit me to say that this is rubbish. More important, those who believe it, or act on it, are missing something substantial. One of the good things about the literature of wine, and you may well think that there aren't that many, is that sweet wines, dessert wines, after-dinner wines are always given their due there as an outstanding part of the drinks scene.

Port, of course, has never needed much in the way of defence, and all I'll say of it for now is that while vintage port is the really marvellous and singular thing, the variety called late-bottled vintage port, or just late-bottled port, is by no means bad in comparison, and can be poured straight from bottle to glass, saving you the fuss of decanting as well as a good deal of cash.

As for what to drink with puddings and sweets and such, the white wines of Bordeaux and from Germany are the greatest, also the cruellest on the pocket—you can pay £35 a bottle if you feel like it. The best value in this department will be stuff labelled simply Barsac, the name of a village in the Sauternes area and of a fine fruity drink.

Possibly the most delicious of all sweet French wines, and one that has had a tremendous success over here in the last couple of years, is Muscat de Beaumes de Venise from the Rhône, buffed up with grape spirit to a formidable 21.5 per cent alcohol, stronger than port, splendid with a fruit course, also with a melon starter, also on its own.

For something that's still unusual in this country even

after three centuries of importation, go for Tokay from Hungary, not so strong, golden brown, sweet as hell, supposedly tasting of the volcanic soil it's grown in. If you want a wine to talk about, this might as well be it.

The world of booze is rent by little controversies that are never settled—the rights and wrongs of putting ice in dry sherry, the stirrers of the Dry Martini versus the shakers, and so on. One of the fiercest of these differences of opinion concerns what you should do with the mint in making a Mint Julep. I'd better give my ruling fast, because the Julep is the very thing for a sunny day, and we might be getting one of those any month now. But first the preliminaries.

Get a bottle of bourbon whiskey, the only suitable sort; Scotch is hopeless for this job. Put into a highball glass—a long tumbler—half a dozen or more fresh mint leaves, the small ones from the top of the sprig. All are agreed so far—no one recommends old, slug-nibbled mint leaves. Add a dessertspoon or more of sugar and about as much water. Right. Crush the mint, sugar and water together, says the UK Bartenders Guild. Don't crush the mint, says Trader Vic, or you'll get the bitter taste as well as the pleasant, and he goes on to allege that he claps the leaves between his hands to "loosen" the oils in them. There you have the stark choice—to crush or not to crush?

Don't crush, say I. But I also say, dissolve the sugar in warm water, stir the mint up in the result and leave the whole thing to infuse for an hour or so; that's if you want to taste the mint. Then add a generous slug of bourbon, like a pub double or treble, stir vigorously, take out the mint leaves, which will be bedraggled by this time, add a lot of crushed ice, or ordinary ice if you can't face the crushing, stir again, garnish with fresh mint leaves and serve with straws. It's a bit of trouble, sure, but, as I always say, a non-professional who wants to make a good mixed drink has to take trouble.

Now, yet another Amis original, the Antiquato, easy to make for a change and (though I say it) delicious. Pour over ice cubes four parts Scotch or other whisky and one part Amaretto liqueur from Italy. Add a couple of dashes of Angostura bitters, stir thoroughly and there you have it. Those who notice such things will have noticed that the whisky-plus-sweet-plus-bitter combination recalls the Old-Fashioned cocktail, and of course *"antiquato"* is Italian for "old-fashioned." Dead cunning, what?

This is the last of the present series of drinking columns. They've been great fun to do. Hearty thanks and good wishes to all who kindly took the trouble to write in with questions or information. Cheers!

How's Your Glass?

INTRODUCTION

ALTHOUGH DRINK IS a contentious subject—I have seen grown men close to blows over whether you should or should not bruise the mint in a Mint Julep—there are a lot of facts connected with it, some well known, some less so, and some on the fringes which may have their own appeal. (What would you probably have been offered to drink at the court of Attila the Hun? Mascara—where might you find yourself drinking some? How is Freddie Fudpucker remembered?) And although tastes differ here at least as widely as in any other field, there is consensus too—you and I may well not see eye to eye over which Tuscan red is our favourite, but we would have to agree with everybody else that the finest brandy in the world is Cognac.

All in all there is a great deal of ground to cover, even if the enterprise makes no claim to be comprehensive and limits itself to giving samples of A and interesting bits of B. To reel such things off one after another on the "Did You Know?" principle would be boring for the writer and indigestible for the reader. An obvious answer was a series of quizzes. I love trying to answer such things myself if the subject is right, in the hope of scoring points of course, and impressing the other fellows with my genius, but at least as much to acquire information offered in a teasing way. I may turn out not to know the year of Schumann's birth—it was 1810, I find—but I would be quite tickled to learn it from the answer to somebody's question 17 (b). So I have been prodigal of information, some of it not specially useful information, quite a lot of it historical, vaguely literary, and concerned with the origins of words. This last, I think, appeals to a fair number of those who speak our extraordinary language.

Besides information there is inevitably opinion, sometimes others', more often mine. Drink, as I have said, is not a field where all agree, and an objective essay on it, even in such a form as this book, would be a poor thing. At the same time I have tried not to let those opinions of mine affect the nub of question or answer. I praise or query or am rude parenthetically, from the sidelines.

Whether or not readers will feel the same, compiling this questionnaire suited me down to the ground. It put together in a unique and pleasurable way my abiding partiality for the subject, the attraction of a kind of writing new to me and an outlet for my starved didactic instinct, and was great fun to assemble.

There are a few trick questions and other dodges in what follows, but it would spoil things to be more specific.

LIST OF ABBREVIATIONS

COD—Concise Oxford Dictionary
OED—Oxford English Dictionary
Q—quiz
q—question
a—answer

QUIZZES

WINE—ELEMENTARY
Short of demanding to know why red wine is called by that name or what champagne is, I have made this quiz as easy as possible. But I advise you to deign to answer it and pile up marks for what may be thin times ahead. So straight to business without lingering over explanations that wine is often kept in bottles, drunk out of glasses, etc.

1. Wines vary in many ways, of which perhaps the most important is the amount of alcohol they contain. What percentage of alcohol would you expect to find in:
   (*a*) a light wine
   (*b*) a strong wine?

2. When a wine is said to lack body an adverse criticism is obviously being made, and everyone knows what is meant without necessarily being able to explain just what "body" is. Can you?

3. Some wines can be told apart by the bottles they come in. Describe briefly the characteristic shape of

(*a*) the Burgundy bottle
(*b*) the claret bottle (by the way, what exactly is claret?)
(*c*) the Chianti bottle?

4. A fluid ounce (UK) is one-twentieth of an Imperial pint. State:
    (*a*) the number of fluid ounces in a standard wine-bottle
    (*b*) the metric equivalent of that amount in terms of litres.
    For good measure (ha ha ha) explain
    (*c*) what an American means by a fifth of liquor.

5. What is meant when a bottle of wine is said to be corked?

6. The following are all types of—what?
    Cabernet   Sauvignon   Muscat
    Riesling   Gamay   Sylvaner.

7. Three well-known French wines. Briefly describe each (e.g. "a dry white wine") and name the region where it is made; extra marks for further precision. In this and the following two questions the main or usual product is meant, so if a lot of red and a little white is made the answer is "red."
    (*a*) Barsac
    (*b*) Sancerre
    (*c*) Beaune.

8. Three Italians. Proceed as before, but naming the places will probably be harder, so double any marks you get in this way.
    (*a*) Asti Spumante
    (*b*) Valpolicella
    (*c*) Frascati.

9. Three from—elsewhere. Double bonuses again.
   (a) Rioja
   (b) retsina
   (c) *vinho verde*.

10. It has been said (no doubt untruly) that some show-off Japanese businessmen buy the most expensive bottle of claret they can find, take it home and stand it on the mantelpiece. Apart from the showing-off, what is ill-advised about this practice?

WINE—INTERMEDIATE

Here is a further selection of miscellaneous questions about wine, some historical or literary, some modestly technical. I excluded with reluctance several that appeared in my first draft, such as the one asking for a definition of a wine-table—a semi-circular or horse-shoe-shaped table with metal wells for bottles and ice and sometimes a revolving wine-carriage. The drinkers sat round the longer edge. Good to know, perhaps, but unenlivening to be asked about.

1. Which famous poet referred repeatedly to the "wine-dark sea," and what is the significance of that?

2. Can you give a date for the first mention of wine in (a sort of) English?

3. What was the revolutionary seventeenth-century discovery that made possible wine as we know it today?

4. In the 1860s and later a new species of aphis or aphid or plant-louse attacked and laid waste many European vine-

yards. Give its name and say how the situation was (partly) retrieved.

5. Climate, weather and soil are all obviously important in the first stage of wine-making. Describe a fourth factor.

6. Is *vin rosé* given its colour by leaving the (black) grape-skins in the must (fermenting juice) a shorter time than for red wine, or by just mixing red and white wine?

7. When the wine-grower has got his grape-juice ready for fermentation, how does he cause that process to start?

8. Nearly all sweet white wines are made by checking fermentation, so that some of the sugar stays as sugar instead of becoming alcohol. How does the wine-maker do that?

9. Red wine goes with red meat, white with fish and white meat. True or false?

10. What was the precious trade secret bequeathed by the dying wine-maker to his assembled family?

WINE — ADVANCED

It is impossible that, among the many thousands trying to solve these quizzes, there should not be some few who know more than I do about one or other of the topics covered. Nowhere is this more likely to be so than in the field of wine. For reasons too boring to go into, my expertise there has never been of a very high order. In the present quiz particularly, some questions may appear too easy, others too difficult to offer a sporting chance of a solution. Well, there we are.

1. Let us imagine a wine-tasting, nothing elaborate, just someone out to try an unfamiliar wine. What information can he gain by noting the appearance of the wine in the glass before him?

2. I will not ask you what the taster might notice when sniffing at the wine in his glass, because you cannot be trusted not to start using words like flinty or forthcoming or dumb to describe various smells, so just stick to mentioning a couple of olfactory signs that all is not well.

3. You are undoubtedly aware that acids are most important in the production of wine, being essential to fermentation, also required in the finished article to impart bite or crispness. But can you name the principal acids naturally found in grapes?

4. You know no less well that the presence of sufficient tannin is equally necessary, in red wines at least. (Some writers refer to tannin as "tannic acid," how properly I have no idea.) What is its contribution?

5. Identify:
   (a) Chablais
   (b) Misket
   (c) Muskat-Ottonel.

6. Identify:
   (a) Inferno
   (b) Rust
   (c) Buzbag.

7. Assign the following to their countries:

(*a*) Tassenberg

(*b*) Schramsberg

(*c*) Brauneberg

(*d*) Kahlenberg

(*e*) Steinberg.

8. Assign the following to their countries:

(*a*) Quincy

(*b*) Malmesbury

(*c*) Worcester

(*d*) Bellingham

(*e*) Llanarth.

9. Assign the following to their regions or districts:

(*a*) Chiroubles

(*b*) Coulé de Serrant

(*c*) Domaine de Mont-Redon

(*d*) Scharzhofberger

(*e*) Frecciarossa.

10. Assign the following to their villages within the Bordeaux region:

(*a*) Château Branaire-Ducru

(*b*) Château Durfort-Vivens

(*c*) Château Pedesclaux

(*d*) Château Cos-d'Estournel

(*e*) Château Marquis-d'Alesme.

WINE — FRANCE

To find a generalization about French wines that should be both true and unhackneyed would take a very long time. Their pre-eminence continues, though not as before. Thirty years ago, the wine drunk at any kind of serious meal had to be, in the UK at least, a French wine—Chianti was okay at Luigi's. Now, half a dozen other countries are competing at the lower and middle levels, where French performance seems to have fallen off. But at the heights no doubt they still lead. If Australia or California ever catch up, we shall have to go there to find out. Can you see them sending us their best stuff?

1. Some wine is produced in almost every part of France, but certain regions are regarded as outstanding. List the top six—not in order of merit, which would be a hopeless undertaking.

2. What do these letters stand for and what is their significance?
    (a) AOC or AC
    (b) VDQS.

3. Recently the French have been pushing products called *vins de pays* in the UK. What is the significance of this name?

4. Perhaps unwillingly, the wine-drinker finds himself picking up small bits of French. For an easy five marks, translate the following:
    (a) *brut*
    (b) *frais*
    (c) *pétillant*
    (d) *mousseux*
    (e) *blanc de noirs*.

5. In certain humid conditions, white wine-grapes are attacked by a disease that causes them to concentrate their sugar and eventually produce the marvellous sweet wines

of Sauternes. What is the disease called, and what brings it about?

6. The traditional champagne-glass is rather like a small saucer on a stem. Experts dislike them, moaning that they make the bubbles escape too fast. Whatever view you take, say how the thing is supposed to have been given its shape.

7. How did the bubbles get into the champagne in the first place?

8. Has all champagne got bubbles in it?

9. Some champagne is put into freakishly large bottles, larger than the magnum or double bottle, though the practice is probably on its last legs. Give the names and respective contents of these monster bottles.

10. It would be hard to think of a wine-producing country that did not make at least one wine from the Muscatel grape. They are all of course sweet dessert wines. Or are they?

WINE—GERMANY

German wines are highly respected for their quality, the average of which must be unequalled elsewhere. They are so good that it seems a pity to spoil them with food. Despite strenuous efforts by the trade, this remains the German view. Outside and largely inside the small wine-growing region in the south-west of the country, what washes down the pig's knuckles and dumplings is beer, from one or other of the 1,400-odd breweries in the Federal Republic. The time for a hock or moselle is mid-morning or after dinner, here no less than there.

1. What do these letters, seen on wine-labels and elsewhere, stand for and what is their significance?
    (*a*) QmP
    (*b*) QbA.

2. The German vineyards are often said to be the northern-most in continental Europe. This cannot really be so, as Holland is said to produce some wine, though I cannot discover (or imagine) where the Dutch vineyards are. Anyway, if you drew a latitudinal line westwards from the northern tip of the German ones, where would it hit England? Or would it miss altogether? Hands off the atlas.

3. Until the seventeenth century, just after Shakespeare's time, Englishmen called wine from the Rhineland "Rhen-ish." Then they started switching to "hock." Where did the new name come from?

4. German wines are grouped today as hocks and moselles or mosels. I undertake to tell them apart before they are even poured out. Am I vainly boasting?

5. There is a variety of wine called *Eiswein*, not often seen even in Germany and very expensive. Explain what it is.

6. The sweet dessert wines of Germany are very highly es-teemed and are thought to be surpassed only, if at all, by those of Sauternes. The same disease of grapes is at work in both cases. Give its German name.

7. Now an easy one. Name the odd man out:
   Rheinhessen   Rheingold   Nahe
   Rheingau   Rheinpfalz.

8. Define the following:
   (*a*) *schaumwein*
   (*b*) *sekt*
   (*c*) *liebfraumilch*
   (*d*) Riesling
   (*e*) *tafelwein*.

9. If *Trockenbeerenauslese* signifies the sweetest wines of Germany, and it does, how can *Trocken* alone indicate a dry wine, as it does?

10. There is a vineyard and a wine in the Rhineland named after one of our monarchs and another in the moselle country whose name commemorates the fact that the personal physician of another strongly recommended it. Can you identify them, i.e. the vineyards/wines? Clue: the two monarchs were related.

WINE—ITALY, SPAIN, PORTUGAL

Although wines from these three countries are drunk in the UK in fair quantities, those from Spain and Portugal increasingly so, not a great deal is generally known about them. In the case of Italy, lack of knowledge may be something to do with the amiable semi-chaos of its labelling habits. As regards Spanish wines, to me what may need explaining is less the prevailing ignorance about them than the prevailing readiness to drink them. Wines from Portugal, on the other hand, quite different from those of Spain, have long struck me as mysteriously underestimated for their merit and variety.

   Answers on p. 258

1. Nobody deserves a mark for knowing that *"vino secco"* is Italian for "dry wine." It may be a little harder to arrange the following in ascending order of sweetness, starting with a word meaning "bone-dry."
   amabile   asciutto   abboccato   dolce   pastoso.

2. What do the letters DOC, seen on a wine-label, stand for and what is their significance?

3. Some Italian wines have the term *"classico"* attached to their name, as Chianti Classico. Does this mean anything substantial?

4. What about *"riserva"* similarly used?

5. Name the odd man out:
   Verdicchio   Vermentino   Frascati   Barolo

6. Few of those reading this will be unaware that *"viño blanco"* is Spanish for "white wine." The following are used to indicate other kinds of wine. Name them.
   (*a*) *Espumoso*
   (*b*) *rosado*
   (*c*) *corriente*
   (*d*) *tinto*
   (*e*) *de mesa.*

7. The Spaniards like ageing their best wines, especially the reds, in oak barrels. What is the most noticeable effect of this on the flavour?

8. A lot of Spanish red wine perhaps understandably finds its way into Sangria, the cold punch. Give its essential ingredients; quantities not required.

Answers on pp. 258–259

9. There are some very decent table wines, both red and white, made in a region of north Portugal. Can you say their collective very brief name?

10. What is the wine speciality of the town and region of Setúbal not far from Lisbon?

WINES—OTHERS

"Others" is not a very sonorous or evocative term for anything, certainly not wine. But some such expression is hard to avoid when the produce of five continents is under discussion. No disparagement is intended. Strange to think that one or other of the "others" will sooner or later be producing the first wines in the world to give Lafite and Yquem a run for their money.

1. You probably know a lot about Tokay or Tokaji, the famous dessert wine of Hungary, its amber colour, the volcanic soil it comes from, all that, but can you define the following?
  (*a*) Tokay Aszu
  (*b*) Tokay Eszencia
  (*c*) Tokay Szamorodni.

2. Another wine from Hungary is probably more widely known today than Tokay, namely Egri Bikavér. What sort of wine is it, and what is it called in the UK?

3. What is Schluck?

4. Cyprus has been rapidly improving its wines of late. Its best-so-far dry red has a name most inappropriate to an export to the UK. What is that name?

5. The wines of the USA are expanding their overseas markets by leaps and bounds, but they are not yet well enough known in this country for a detailed question on them to be fair. So just name a few states of the Union at present making wine of some quality.

6. Which South American country produces the most wine, more than all the others put together?

7. Distinguish between English and British wine.

8. Australian wines have had a great and deserved success over here in recent years, but are individually known only to a small circle as yet. So have a go at the date of the first wine-harvest there. As a special concession you may look up the date of the first settlement, or alternatively allow yourself ten years' leeway.

9. The South Africans have also been doing well in the UK, but the same applies. If you want to find out more, whom do you ask? (Not much of a quiz question, perhaps, but you might like to know the answer.)

10. Name the odd man out:
    Japan   China   Afghanistan   India   Canada.

BEER IN GENERAL
Until about ten years ago nobody in this country seemed to know anything about beer. The drinks it was proper to know about came down pretty much to wine, fortified wine and brandy. Now all that is changed, and beer has become a field not

just of knowledge but of aggressive knowledgeability too. I suppose this has its good side, and certainly a decent glass of draught beer is not the rarity it was in many places. The trouble is that there are so few pubs where one can endure to stay long enough to drink it.

1. In most contexts, "ale" and "beer" are names for the same thing, but the terms were far from interchangeable in previous ages. Can you say what the difference was?

2. What is or was porter as applied to beer?

3. What was the original meaning of the term "stout" as applied to beer? What gives it its distinctive dark colour?

4. The brewing process begins with the malting of barley. Explain this and say what it does.

5. A later stage in the brewing process involves wort. What do you understand by this term?

6. Hops were probably first used in brewing as a preservative, and they clarify the beer too. But they also have an important effect on the flavour. Describe it.

7. We all know, assuming that we can take in what we read, that yeast is used in the making of beer (and wine), but what exactly is yeast and what is its function?

8. What does sediment in a bottle of beer normally indicate?

Answers on pp. 261–262

9. We sometimes see on a pub beer-pull an announcement that the stuff is "cask-conditioned draught beer." Give the shorter and more usual expression.

10. What are the advantages of pasteurizing beer?

BEER IN PARTICULAR

This is likely to be a difficult quiz for uncommitted beer drinkers. What is still our national drink draws less attention and interest than wine, a foreign importation. A man who will be able to tell you unhesitatingly that Margaux is in the Médoc is more than likely to look quite blank if asked where Ruddles Bitter comes from. [Rutland, in fact Oakham, once the county town, now said to be part of Leicestershire.] But general knowledge should be of some service here.

1. About 30 per cent of the beer sold in GB nowadays is lager. Everybody knows this blanket term for vaguely continental-style lively beer, but what is the significance of the name?

2. Pilsener beer or Pilsener lager is a popular type of beer in many countries. Where does the name come from?

3. Diät Pils from the Holsten brewery in Hamburg has been very successful in GB. Although plenty of British drinkers believe it to be a weight-watcher's beer, it is actually rather more fattening than the average brew. True or false?

4. Where can you:
   (a) legally get a Fix
   (b) find Time for a Tiger?

5. Which famous expedition ended up in the wrong place for lack of beer?

6. Various lagers originating abroad are brewed under licence in GB. Name the parent country of:
  (*a*) Stella Artois
  (*b*) Kronenbourg
  (*c*) Carlsberg
  (*d*) Heineken
  (*e*) Vaux.

7. Name the Big Six brewers in GB.

8. Here are five outstanding English beers. Give the home town of each.
  (*a*) Greene King Abbot
  (*b*) Gale's Prize Old Ale
  (*c*) Brakspear's Pale Ale
  (*d*) Adnam's Bitter
  (*e*) Fuller's ESB.

9. Identify:
  (*a*) bock
  (*b*) kvass
  (*c*) saké
  (*d*) erdbeer
  (*e*) lambic.
  One is odd man out.

10. Four London pubs have given their names to districts, reputedly, at least. Can you name them?

VODKA

It was in the early 1950s that vodka began its amazing progress to popularity in the Western world, doubly amazing when you consider what a dull drink it is, no good neat, unsuitable for cocktails. Its only respectable role is as a kick-provider in what would otherwise be soft drinks; I once recommended its sparing use as a stiffener for the cold punch at a Darby and Joan Club party. These remarks of course apply only to Anglo-American vodka. Many Eastern ones are flavoured, often with what may seem bizarre substances like cayenne pepper or chocolate, but even the straight ones have some character.

1. What does the word "vodka" mean literally?

2. What is the drink made from?

3. When and where was vodka first made? Approximate answers permitted.

4. Name the leading firm of vodka-producers in Imperial Russia. Not an unfair question, as you will see.

5. Name the Polish vodka of which every bottle contains a blade of so-called bison grass, supposedly brought from the forests of east Poland where the surviving beasts are said to roam.

6. There are Russian and Polish vodkas distilled out at 96 *per cent* alcohol, and legally too. What is the reason (or excuse) for this?

7. Most people know the delicious (but rather indigestible) Bloody Mary with its tomato-juice, Worcester sauce and

other juices and spices stirred up in vodka, but can you describe:

(*a*) a Bullshot
(*b*) a Hotshot
(*c*) a Bloodshot?

8. How can you tell a White Russian from a Black Russian?

9. One of the least offensive drinks made with vodka is the Moscow Mule—vodka, ginger beer and lemon-juice traditionally served in a copper mug. In what circumstances did it come into being, and what is the historical significance of its arrival?

10. Name the famous Russian who, while on a visit to Paris, wrote home to his wife, "There's only one bottle of vodka left; I don't know what to do."

APERITIFS AND SUCH

A disagreeable word, aperitif, but eighty years or so after its introduction into English it can surely be considered naturalized and lose its French pronunciation and accent. No native word will do its job; taking its anglicization a stage further and talking and writing about an aperitive is quite inoffensive, indeed admirable as far as it goes, but seems unlikely to catch on. And now, on to the quiz, lest I fritter away what information I have about this, to me, less than wildly exciting province of alcohology.

1. When a waiter or a host mentions an aperitif he means one thing; a man in the drinks trade means another, more specific. Give:

Answers on pp. 265–266

(a) the broad and
(b) the narrow senses of the term.

2. Apart from wormwood and many other herbs and spices and such, what are the main constituents of vermouth?

3. Wormwood and vermouth. Are the two similar-sounding words related?

4. French vermouth is dry, Italian sweet. True or false?

5. What is:
   (a) Chambéry
   (b) Chambéryzette?

6. (a) What is the name of the popular mixed drink made from Campari and red vermouth?
   (b) What does it become if you add gin?

7. Campari is named after the ancient Roman town of Camparum, where a supposedly health-giving drink was made in classical times. True or false?

8. Angostura is another famous bitters in a completely different style from Campari. The name comes from the place of origin, but it is now made somewhere else. Can you say where? One mark for the general area, an extra one for the precise location.

9. Some brands of bitters are used as pick-me-ups or remedies. Can you name:
   (a) an Italian and
   (b) a German version?

10. What is the main ingredient that imparts bitterness to bitters and to some other drinks?

GIN

"Drunk for 1d, dead drunk for 2d, clean straw for nothing." It is apparently compulsory to give that quotation, supposed without any evidence to have come from a notice displayed outside eighteenth-century gin-shops in London, in every book about drink and article on gin. However, it does serve to make the point that gin had for many years a thoroughly unrespectable "image," not quite lost even today. Like Scotch whisky, and unlike vodka and white rum, gin is associated with people who like drink.

1. Give the derivation of the word "gin."

2. Gin has always had a pretty bad press. The very first citation in OED, dated 1714, refers to it as an "infamous Liquor" and "intoxicating"—not just inebriating but fatally poisonous. A later writer called it "liquid Madness sold at tenpence the quartern" (gill or quarter-pint) in 1839. Can you say who?

3. Not all writers have taken such a harsh view. Which famous poet, asked where he got his inspiration from, replied, "Gin and drugs, dear lady, gin and drugs"?

4. What is unusual about the flavour of gin compared with that of brandy, whisky and most other spirits?

5. Where and when was gin (probably) first made, and what was its first use?

6. What are the basic materials from which gin is distilled?

7. Apart from the advantages of its being the capital, what was it about London that made it an excellent place to set about making gin?

8. What is pink gin? Be specific.

9. How long must newly-distilled London gin be matured in cask or vat before it is ready for bottling?

10. A drink based on gin was drunk by Sir Horatio (later Lord) Kitchener's officers during the campaign in the Sudan in 1898. What was it, or what is it now called?

LIQUEURS

This is a wide, vague term embracing drinks made by radically different processes (see q 1). A few years ago one could safely have drawn the generalization that liqueurs were used for drinking after meals. They still are, but what must be a greater quantity finds its way into mixed drinks. Southern Comfort from the US is the example here, allegedly to be seen in company with white wine or even tequila.

The word itself is a useful shibboleth, separating the good Joes who make it rhyme with "secure" from the affected persons who frenchify it as "lee-*cur*."

1. The Danish drink familiarly known as Cherry Heering and the almost equally famous Kirsch from the upper Rhine region both taste of cherries, but there is a basic difference in their modes of manufacture. State it briefly.

2. Not many liqueurs are based on gin, but Sloe Gin is. I can reveal that it is obtained by steeping sloes (small

wild plums) in gin. What is the traditional occasion for serving it?

3. What was the most important result of the battle of Culloden?

4. Name the odd man out:
    Grand Marnier   Orange Curaçao
    Yellow Chartreuse   Strega   Benedictine.

5. Why should a liqueur made from Armagnac, honey and herbs remind me of pelota?

6. What are you supposed to do when a glass of Sambuca, an Italian liqueur made with witch elder-brush (eh?) and liquorice, is served to you with three coffee-beans floating in it?

7. Name liqueurs made with:
    (*a*) mint
    (*b*) apples
    (*c*) blackcurrants
    (*d*) caraway seeds
    (*e*) plums.
    Easy. An extra mark for naming the country of origin.

8. Name liqueurs made with:
    (*a*) lemon-tree leaves
    (*b*) arbutus berries
    (*c*) walnuts
    (*d*) naartjies
    (*e*) shaddocks.
    Not so easy. Country of origin as before.

9. Liqueurs are often used in cocktails, of which the best-known is probably the White Lady. Give its main ingredients.

10. Who is supposed to have introduced liqueurs into France? (Clue: she came to marry the Dauphin of the day.)

RUM

Rum started in the Caribbean, where the Royal Navy took it up in the early eighteenth century because it kept better than beer and, presumably, made life just bearable. The daily rum ration, to which the seamen's rights were carefully protected, continued until 1970. It—the ration—had been strong and large enough to put the consumer well over the limit permitted to car-drivers, and their lordships no doubt felt that this was unsuitable in the days of guided missiles. The vogue for white and pale rums was getting into its stride at about the same time.

1. Give the derivation of the word "rum."

2. Rum is made from various products of the sugar-cane.
   (a) What is sugar-cane botanically, i.e. what type of plant is it?
   (b) On which islands was it first seen by Europeans?

3. Grog was traditionally a drink of rum and water introduced into the RN in 1740. Whence the name?

4. The rums made in the various islands and in Guyana differ widely, being made by different methods, but all are

Answers on pp. 270–271

the same colour when they leave the still. What is this colour?

5. Rum is or was reputedly known as Nelson's Blood. Is there more to this than affectionate metaphor?

6. A Cuba Libre is a drink nowadays made of white rum, Coca Cola and lime-juice (rum 'n coke to unworthy persons), the name meaning "Free Cuba." Free from what or whom?

7. White rum, lime-juice and sugar produce a delicious cocktail which could legitimately be called a Rum Sour, but is usually given a more particular name. What is that name, and whence is it derived?

8. Planters' Punch is traditionally made from dark Jamaica rum, lime-juice, sugar and water or soda-water. Can you recite the doggerel rhyme that states the recommended proportions?

9. Apart from the British and Americans, rum-drinking nations include the Australians and the Mexicans, who make their own, and the French, who import theirs—from where?

10. Rum is indeed made in many countries, islands, regions. Which of them is the top producer in quantity?

COGNAC AND ARMAGNAC

These two are by common consent the finest brandies in the world. To a lot of people they are rather similar, but then a lot of people never get the chance, or just possibly cannot be

 Answers on p. 271

bothered, to move about among the many and various brands and grades of each and make comparisons. Connoisseurs seem to think Cognac is quite different from Armagnac, and in trying to describe the difference excel even themselves in high-flown writing. The excellent Pamela Vandyke Price admits to having written that the appeal of Armagnac is emotional whereas that of Cognac is intellectual. If you have to go to such heights, or lengths, to distinguish the two, well, perhaps a lot of people are not so wrong after all.

1. As well as being the names of drinks, Cognac and Armagnac are names of places, regions of France. Roughly where are those regions?

2. Again by consent, the product of Cognac is the finer of the two. Name the area within it that produces the best Cognac of all.

3. When do we first hear of something like brandy being made:
   (a) in Cognac
   (b) in Armagnac?
   Roughly.

4. Arrange in ascending order of quality:
   VSOP   VSTO   VO   Three Star   XO
   Cordon Bleu.

5. Which of the following substances may legally be added to Cognac during manufacture?
   Neutral spirit   Sugar   Burnt sugar or caramel
   Martinique rum   Infusion of oak-chips.

Answers on p. 272

6. Name the odd man out:
Otard   Hine   Delamain   Delaforce   Camus.

7. What kind of still is used in the making of:
(*a*) Cognac
(*b*) Armagnac?

8. How long on average should a high-grade Cognac or Armagnac be allowed to mature in bottle before drinking?

9. Is there such a thing as Napoleon brandy?

10. What part of Cognac is said locally to be consumed by the angels?

BRANDY (ONE STEP DOWN)

Nowadays most brandy in this country is drunk either after full-dress meals or for medicinal purposes, and a brandy and soda or brandy and water before or between meals is rarely seen. In the past, however, these diluted versions were very popular and were often served at table alongside wine. On the other hand, some early brandies may well not have been brandies at all, but primitive and no doubt quite vile forms of whisky. The restriction of the term "brandy" to mean "distillate of wine" is comparatively recent. Fruit brandies, as plum brandy, pear brandy, distillates from the fruit specified, are considered in Q Liqueurs.

1. What is the derivation of the word "brandy"?

2. Since, as noted above, "brandy" used by itself means a spirit made from grapes, one might think that the phrase "grape brandy" was a tautology. But not so; it has a precise meaning. State it.

Answers on pp. 272–273

3. What do they give you in France if you ask in a bar or restaurant for a *fine à l'eau*?

4. The taste and particularly the aroma of brandy come out in full only if the glass is slightly warmed. What is the approved method of bringing this about?

5. As Dr. Johnson famously said, "Claret is for boys; port for men; but . . ." But what? Exact words, please.

6. "Brandy will do soonest for a man what drink *can* do for him." Who said that?

7. Of which country can brandy be said to be the national drink?

8. Identify the following:
    (*a*) marc
    (*b*) grappa
    (*c*) weinbrand
    (*d*) bagaceira
    (*e*) pisco.
    One of the five is an odd man out.

9. An Alexander Cocktail is obviously made with brandy or it would not be here. Best made with a decent but not first-rate one. What are the other ingredients, and why is it often called an after-dinner cocktail?

10. Which mode of transport would be most useful to a tax official out to identify the brandy warehouses in a brandy-making centre?

DISTILLATION

The process that gives us spirits or strong drink is very old, but it has been only very recently in comparative terms, from about the time of the first railway systems, that the distiller has had any but the vaguest and most general control over his product. Nowadays distillation is a branch of technology, and yet essential parts of the procedure continue to defy measurement. There is no substitute so far for the stillman's skill and experience.

1. Give a short definition of distillation. (Remember, water can be distilled.)

2. What is the physical property of alcohol that is so useful, indeed indispensable, to the distiller?

3. To obtain a spirit or spirits, the distiller needs as raw material some substance containing alcohol. By what process will this have been produced?

4. It is safe to say that the invention of the still is the sort of thing that happens independently in more than one place. Nevertheless, give the conventional account of the historical beginnings of distillation. (Clue: It may be helpful to read the next question before starting to answer this one.)

5. Proponents of this view often cite linguistic evidence in its support. State it, and evaluate it if you can.

6. Outline a more up-to-date proposal about the provenance of distillation. (NB: We are of course interested in distillation less as a technological process than as the source of whisky, gin, etc.)

7. Stills of a type that has not changed in principle since the earliest times continue in use for the production of Cognac, malt whisky, tequila and other spirits. Name this type and indicate its three basic parts.

8. When a spirit emerges from the type of still just mentioned, it retains a content of substances called congeners or congenerics. What are these, and what are their effects?

9. Many spirits on leaving the still are blended with another liquid which may itself have been distilled. What is it, and what is the purpose of introducing it?

10. Some potable spirits, such as gin and vodka, are said to have been rectified. What is meant?

MINOR SPIRITS

Somebody once said it must be depressing for God to notice that, all over the world he created, his children were drinking spirits in an effort to get away from it, and if I could remember who it was I would have set a question asking who. But the unknown sage was certainly right about the near-universality of the hard stuff, and no one needs to be told about the enthusiasm with which spirits have been taken up by those few races that, like the American Indians, were too backward to have developed them off their own bat.

The description "minor" refers to geographical distribution and volume, not quality. Akvavit, in particular, is a drink fit for a king, and Aalborg brand is the worthy holder of a warrant to the Danish court.

Quizzes

1. Akvavit or aquavit is the staple spirit of Scandinavia, a very pure distillation from grain or potatoes made like gin and usually flavoured with—what?

2. How are you supposed to serve and drink akvavit?

3. What is Linie Aquavit?

4. Swedish Punsch is not a punch in the ordinary sense of an on-the-spot mixture but a ready-bottled blended drink to be served hot or cold. What is the principal ingredient?

5. Pernod and Ricard, respectively brands of anis and pastis, are two very popular French drinks said to resemble the long-exiled absinthe whose drinkers were portrayed by Degas and Toulouse-Lautrec. What are the two (drinks) made from?

6. Both these drinks are traditionally taken with water in the proportion 5:1. Can you say why, from being clear though coloured liquids, they turn cloudy when the water is added?

7. Elsewhere in Europe there is another popular drink with a strong family resemblance to Pernod and Ricard, in that it too clouds with water. Say where and what.

8. Mezcal and tequila are both made in Mexico from the fermented sap of a plant related to the American aloe—not a cactus after all, it seems, in spite of what is often said. What is the relation between the two?

9. The best-known tequila cocktail is the Margarita. I know few more delicious, nor any as productive of aggro. What does it consist of?

10. This quiz is supposed to range widely, so I ask you finally to name the spirit the Tartars of central Asia distil from fermented mare's milk.

SCOTCH WHISKY I

In about a century Scotch has been transformed from a purely local restorative, designed to get a poorly-fed, badly-housed populace through hard days and cold nights, to a major export of the UK, the most widely distributed of all quality drinks and, at its best, the equal of any spirit in the world. Recently its prosperity has been hindered by economic depression and a trend, in the UK and elsewhere, against strong, dark-coloured drinks, but there is still no competitor in sight.

1. The Finance Act of 1969 embodies a necessarily complicated definition of whisky, but its subsequent definition of Scotch whisky is straightforward enough. What is it?

2. The Act also specifies a minimum time the spirit must spend being "matured in wooden casks in a warehouse" before it is sold. What is that time? Choose from:
Ninety days   One year   Thirty months
Three years   Five years.

3. Give the derivation of the word "whisky."

4. Most Scotch sold is a blend of malt whisky, made in a pot still, and grain whisky, made in a patent still. In what way is the patent still greatly superior to the pot still?

5. Malt whisky is made from malt, i.e. malted barley. What is grain whisky made from?

6. Some malt whiskies are said to have a peaty taste and aroma. Where do these qualities come from?

7. Many factors influence the character of a malt whisky. Perhaps the best known of these is the water, also important in determining the flavour of beer. Name three others known to affect malt whisky.

8. A malt whisky is often listed and labelled as a single malt. What is the significance of this?

9. Most of the malt whisky distilleries of Scotland are in the Highlands. There are, however, three other named areas producing their own types of malt whisky. Enumerate them.

10. Dr. Johnson said he had only tasted whisky once in his life, "for experiment," and added: "It was strong but not pungent. What was the process I had no opportunity of inquiring, nor do I wish to improve the art of making poison pleasant." True or false?

SCOTCH WHISKY II

Professor R. J. S. McDowall, the great authority on Scotch whisky, wrote that whiskies "are almost as numerous and varied as the wines of France," and the more one explores the truer his remark proves to be. Yet all Scotch has one thing in common—it goes badly with anything but water and more of itself, in short it is a bad mixer, a fact that makes its worldwide success surprising as well as splendid.

1. Name the odd man out:

Chivas Regal   Glen Grant   Glenfiddich
Glenlivet   Glenmorangie.

   Answers on p. 278

2. In what important way does the chemical composition of a mature whisky, aged in cask for ten or fifteen years, differ from that of a whisky at the end of manufacture but before casking?

3. Blended whisky was well into its stride in Scotland by 1865 or so. The distillers began to cast their eyes on England, where whisky was all but unknown except as the stuff you drank on grouse-moors. What historical accident greatly helped their sales drive?

4. About how many brands of blended Scotch whisky are made?

    90   250   800   1,200   3,000

5. What is Atholl Brose?

6. What sort of casks are used for the maturing of malt whisky? ("Wooden" is not a sufficient answer.)

7. Which royal personage is said to have been partial to a half-glass of claret topped up with Scotch? Not impossible to guess.

8. In a blended Scotch, what are the proportions of malt whisky and grain whisky likely to be?

9. From what does Scotch receive its colour?

10. Where is the largest distillery of malt whisky in the world? A precise location is not required. But something of an imaginative leap is.

WHISKIES AND WHISKEYS

Only Ireland, the US and Canada dare put themselves forward as producers of whisky fit to be compared to Scotland. (The first two customarily spell their wares "whiskey.") There is a fifth land, however, thousands of miles away from the nearest of the other four, that almost any moment will be pronounced worthy to be put in their league. Irish resembles Scotch in its intractability, not going well as part of any orthodox mixed drink.

1. One of the Irish whiskey distilleries is said to be the oldest in the world. Which and where is it, and what is its most famous product?

2. Irish coffee is a delicious exception to the rule about Irish whiskey's unsuitability for mixtures. Its preparation is not very troublesome, but it becomes virtually impossible in the absence of one commonplace implement. What is it?

3. There are many varieties of whiskey made in the US, of which bourbon is the most popular and best-known and the one usually seen in the UK. Where does it get its name from?

4. What is bourbon:
   (*a*) made from
   (*b*) matured in?

5. A few American whiskeys are known as "sour mash" whiskeys. What does this signify?

6. The Old-Fashioned Cocktail is the most famous of all those made with whiskey. List its ingredients.

Answers on p. 280

7. Which of the following were whiskey-distillers as well as pursuing other activities?
   George Washington   Thomas Jefferson
   Walt Whitman   Glenn Miller   John Wayne.

8. Name the odd man out:
   Old Grandad   John Jameson   Jim Beam
   Old Forester   Wild Turkey.

9. Canadian whisky has been very successful in recent years outside as well as inside its own country. Which of its characteristics is usually thought to be responsible for this?
   Strength   Weakness   Purity
   Lack of after-effects   Aroma

10. Whisky, so called, is made in dozens of countries, including Argentina, Iran, Tanzania and India. What do these drinks usually consist of, and can any of them properly be called whisky?

PORT
The trade in port grew up to meet English demand, and its general character was designed to meet the centuries-old English taste for sweet wines. To this day, many of its great names are English or Scottish—Sandeman, Cockburn, Dow, Croft, Taylor, Graham. The UK no longer holds the position of the world's biggest customer for port, having yielded it to France, where they make no bones about drinking sweet wines before meals. Nevertheless port has held up best in the national drift away from drinks in this category.

1. Port not only comes from Portugal, it comes only from there, in the sense that under our law no wine from any other country may use the name. More precisely it comes from Oporto in north Portugal, whence it gets its name. But where are the vineyards where the wine is grown?

2. Nearly all port is sweet and all of it is appreciably stronger than ordinary table wine. These are the results of a single process in the manufacture. What is that process?

3. Some months after being made, the immature port is moved to a convenient point for ageing, blending and bottling at the shippers' lodges or warehouses. Where are these?

4. Of the various styles of port the most ambitious is vintage port, invented by the British and still drunk by them almost exclusively, though there is a small market in the US. Define vintage port.

5. What happens to a vintage port:
   (*a*) before and
   (*b*) after bottling?

6. Vintage port is traditionally drunk at the end of a meal, either on its own or with cheese. Which cheese or cheeses does it go best with?

7. In recent years the shippers have been drawing our attention to styles of port that lack the "mystique" of (and are cheaper than) vintage port, but are a cut above the standard rubies and tawnies. Describe:

 Answers on pp. 281–282

(*a*) Late Bottled Vintage Port
(*b*) Late Bottled Port
(*c*) Vintage Character Port.

8. Some white port is made and, especially in France, drunk as an aperitif. How is it made? You can be very brief.

9. Port and lemon (fizzy lemonade) is an old charladies' drink, and very good it is on a hot summer's afternoon, but few mixed drinks include port. However, there is one, also known of old, that is intended for nothing more dashing than the relief of diarrhoea. What does it consist of?

10. What was the reaction of the so-called three-bottle men to the arrival of port-as-we-know-it (more or less) in the early eighteenth century?

SHERRY

Like port, sherry was developed for the English market. In former times its different varieties were drunk as a table wine, before meals, after meals, at mid-morning with a biscuit. Now no longer universally seen at the dinner-tables of the well-off, it often appears in its drier forms as a prelude to a serious meal and as an accompaniment to first courses like smoked salmon, avocado and consommé.

1. Where do sherry the wine, and "sherry" the word, come from?

2. "A good sherris-sack hath a two-fold operation in it. It ascends me into the brain; dries me there all the foolish and dull and crudy vapours which environ it; makes it appre-

hensive, quick, forgetive, full of nimble, fiery and delec-
table shapes; which, delivered o'er to the voice, the tongue,
which is the birth, becomes excellent wit. The second
property of your excellent sherris is, the warming of the
blood; which, before cold and settled, left the liver white
and pale, which is the badge of pusillanimity and cow-
ardice: but the sherris warms it and makes it course from
the innards to the parts extreme." Who said so?

3. There are plenty of references to sherris-sack, or just sack,
   at the period of the above. What does "sack" mean in this
   context?

4. "Sherry is dull, naturally dull," said Dr. Johnson, normally
   quite tolerant of alcoholic drinks (except at the times when he
   was off them altogether). What had he got against sherry?

5. Sherry is traditionally made by the solera system. Describe
   this briefly.

6. While sherry is developing in the barrel a thick white layer
   of yeast forms on its surface. Give its name.

7. Sherry is naturally a dry wine, but some types are sweetened to varying degrees. Arrange in ascending order of
   sweetness:
   Oloroso   Amontillado   Manzanilla   Fino   Cream.

8. Quite a lot of Fino sherry gets drunk at its place of origin,
   mostly in half-bottles. Is this thrift, temperance or what?

9. Montilla is a type of wine made about 100 miles from
   Jerez, very enjoyable and rather like sherry in taste, but
   with one big difference in its composition. What is it?

   Answers on p. 283

10. What is:

(*a*) a sherry-cobbler

(*b*) a sherryvalley?

MADEIRA, MARSALA AND OTHERS

The fortification—"making strong"—of wines by adding spirit during or after fermentation is a widespread practice, originally intended as a preservative measure or to cheer up thin wine rather than in pursuit of any kind of quality. But a number of such wines have been highly regarded for many years, though in general the demand for them has fallen off more recently.

1. Madeira, a fortified wine once in the same league as sherry and port, comes from an island of that name in the east Atlantic. What does the name mean, and with what common English words is it connected?

2. Four main types of Madeira are made. The most obvious difference between them is in their degree of sweetness. Arrange in ascending order:

   Sercial   Verdelho   Bual   Malmsey.

3. You come across a satisfactorily old-looking bottle labelled Verdelho 1810. Would it have to be a fake? If not, could the wine possibly be drinkable?

4. Who accused who of selling his soul to the devil on Good Friday last for a cup of Madeira and a cold capon's leg?

5. The best-known Italian fortified wine is Marsala. Can you say where it is made, and name either or both of the famous historical characters who took it up and popularized it?

6. If you frequent Italian restaurants at all, you have probably tasted Marsala without knowing it. How?

7. Name a third fortified wine beginning with M.

8. The great dessert wine from the Rhône, Muscat de Beaumes de Venise, is classified as a *vin doux naturel*. What does this mean?

9. It is common for wine-producing countries to make a sweet red wine comparable with port, in general style as a rule, not merit. A French effort comes from the extreme south of France by the Spanish border. What is it?

10. What is Yalumba Brandivino and where does it come from?

COCKTAILS AND MIXED DRINKS

The revival of interest in cocktails is very recent, so much so that that close observer, Cyril Ray, could write in 1977 of "the passing of the cocktail craze." Some specialized bars in our large cities had kept them going ever since the 1920s, but the only one to survive throughout in anything approaching general circulation was the Dry Martini. And now, in trendy pubs, blackboards invite you to sample the Harvey Wallbanger, the Tequila Sunrise and other exotica our fathers never knew. For those many who like going or being taken to pubs but dislike the taste of drink, a cocktail may be just the thing.

1. Can you give the true, authentic origin of the word "cocktail"?

2. Defining a cocktail is something else again, and not easy. Try for a form of words that admits all the examples you can think of—or most of them.

3. Cocktails became very popular in the 1920s, particularly in the US. Can you suggest a reason why this should have happened at that time?

4. The Manhattan is a type of cocktail usually but not always made with bourbon whiskey. Name the other ingredients. (There is more than one answer.)

5. A cocktail is preferably served in a cocktail glass, a medium-sized affair with a stem. The Old-Fashioned Cocktail (see Q Whiskies and Whiskeys, q 6), however, is properly served in an Old-Fashioned glass. Describe this, and give the practical reason for its particular shape.

6. A Collins is a popular mixed drink, especially in the US. It consists of gin (John Collins, sometimes Tom Collins), whisky or another spirit and what else?

7. What is:
    (a) Buck's Fizz
    (b) Black Velvet?
    And can you name and describe two other potations, (c) and (d), that also possess the feature shared by the first two?

8. It is no secret that Irish Coffee (see Q Whiskies and Whiskeys, q 2) is made with Irish whiskey. But similar drinks with other alcoholic bases may not be so easy to identify. State what the bases are in:

Answers on pp. 285–286   240

(*a*) Caribbean Coffee

(*b*) Italian Coffee

(*c*) Monks' Coffee

(*d*) Prince Charles's Coffee

(*e*) Roman Coffee.

9. Five traditional mixes. Give the chief ingredients of the following (you may skip the fruit-slices, etc.):

(*a*) the Gimlet

(*b*) the Sidecar

(*c*) the Screwdriver

(*d*) the Stinger

(*e*) the Singapore Sling.

10. And five trendy ones:

(*a*) the Freddie Fudpucker

(*b*) the Harvey Wallbanger

(*c*) the Blue Hawaiian

(*d*) the Piña Colada

(*e*) the Godfather.

INVENTORS AND INVENTIONS

The really important discoveries in the making of alcoholic drinks, such as the ability to induce and control fermentation, are lost in the mists of antiquity. That particular one was probably made several times over in different places, like the making of fire, another important step in human development. But as soon as technology began to enter into the manufacture of drinks, names and dates start appearing. The first five questions here contain the names of five people who invented or devised or for some other reason are associated with something alcoholic. Say what it was or is in each case.

One or two clues are given, but no really helpful ones.

1. Johan Siegert, a German army surgeon who served in the Napoleonic wars and later with Simón Bolívar the Liberator in South America.

2. Aeneas Coffey, an Irishman, once an excise official, in 1831.

3. Robert Stein.

4. The late Felix Kir.

5. Dr. Pierre Ordinaire, in Switzerland, about 1790.

Now five questions from the other side of the fence. Say who invented or otherwise had to do with the following:

6. Chaptalization, the practice of adding sugar to grape-must to boost the alcoholic strength of a wine. Very popular with wine-makers in thin years.

7. The *cuve close* (sealed vat) method of making sparkling wine. The manufacturer induces his refermentation in a large vat instead of individual bottles. Widely used outside the Champagne region.

8. The traditional British system of calculating the strength or proof of alcoholic drinks, whereby standard spirits are 70 degrees proof or 70°.

9. Champagne. Not as easy as it may look.

10. The Dry Martini Cocktail. There is no certainty here, but it was *probably* one of the following:

Answers on pp. 287–288   242

Jerry Thomas   Martini Rossi   Martini di Arma di
Taggia   Martini-Henry   John Doxat

POUSSE-CAFÉ 1

My French dictionary says a *pousse-café* is a liqueur, my English one says much the same, helpfully adding "[F, = push-
coffee]," but the UK Bartenders Guild explains that it
consists of liqueurs of different densities poured into a glass
one after the other in such a way that they remain separate
bands of fluid, and gives a recipe involving Grenadine,
Crème de Menthe, Galliano, Kümmel and brandy. I use it as
the heading of this quiz to indicate fancifully that the questions here involve different sorts of drink, this one wine, that
one spirits, a third something else again. Here and there I
hope the question will not directly reveal the category concerned.

1. What, apart from its availability, is the characteristic of the
   human foot that fits it so well for the making of wine?

2. What is twice a chota peg?

3. If you were to ask for "a beer" in English at a French café,
   especially in Paris, what might you very well be given?

4. No substantial authority has ever found drinkable any of
   the so-called "cotton gins" of Mississippi and Texas. True
   or false?

5. In what circumstances might you find yourself drinking
   Mascara?

6. There is a fearful drink called a Snowball which combines Advocaat, lime-juice and fizzy lemonade or even 7-Up. But Advocaat itself is not bad as a between-meals drink. What is it?

7. Distinguish between Ay and Ahr.

8. The neck label on a bottle of Hungarian Tokay wine may carry the legend *"Aszu 2 puttonyos"* or some other number. What is the significance of this?

9. Every serious drinker in this country owes a small debt of gratitude to the French physicist Joseph Gay-Lussac (1778–1850). Why?

10. "People may say what they like about the decline of Christianity; the religious system that produced Green Chartreuse can never die." Who wrote that?

POUSSE-CAFÉ II

Here is another miscellany quiz. Whatever answerers may feel about them, setters like the freedom of manoeuvre such arrangements give them. The answer to a wine-quiz question, say, is already partly indicated by its presence there. But here, some legitimate mystification is possible.

1. Name the odd man out:
   Beaujolais Villages   Beaujolais Primeur   Beaujolais
   Gamay Beaujolais   Beaujolais Nouveau

2. What is the largest alcoholic product of Jerez de la Frontera in Spain?

3. It is safe to say that wherever spirits are made, a proportion will be illicitly made. Some of the slang terms for these are widely known. Give three:

    (*a*) orginating in UK
    (*b*) in US
    (*c*) in Ireland.

    (You may well think that (*a*) too has US origin.) For bonus marks, guess dates of first recorded use; twenty-five years' leeway allowed.

4. Soda-water was first made as a substitute for naturally gassy spa waters thought to be beneficial to health. But something called Spa water, in bottle, is to be seen today. Where does it come from?

5. What is meant by saying that a bottle of wine is *chambré*?

6. In the production of alcoholic drinks, which country leads in quantity in:

    (*a*) spirits
    (*b*) wine
    (*c*) beer?

7. What soft drink, still very popular as a mixer, was enforced in the Royal Navy in the mid-nineteenth century, and for what purpose?

8. Vintage port and other wines that throw a sediment are traditionally decanted, but in recent years people have been taking more and more to decanting light, clear wines, even whites. What is the purpose of this?

9. Define negus.

 Answers on pp. 291–291

10. "It is WRONG to do what everyone else does—namely, to hold the wine list just out of sight, look for the second cheapest claret on the list, and say, 'Number 22, please.'" Who wrote that?

POUSSE-CAFÉ III

1. Name the Roman god of wine, and his Greek counterpart.

2. You still occasionally see mead, which may well be the oldest of all fermented drinks and certainly goes back to the beginnings of the English language, about AD 700. What is it made from?

3. And what is metheglin, once supposedly the national drink of Wales?

4. Wine and spirits are often matured in wooden casks. Which wood has proved to be best for this purpose?

5. Give:
   (a) the approximate date when and the probable place where wine was first made.
   Also the approximate dates of its introduction to:
   (b) Greece
   (c) France
   (d) England.

6. On average, by and large, etc., how many bottles of wine are made from the fruit of a single vine—or how many vines are needed to produce a bottle?

7. A certain stage in the making of wine and beer involves what is known as racking. Define this process.

Answers on pp. 291–292

8. Every good host, perhaps every civilized person, ought by rights to have a bottle of sparkling water in his refrigerator. While you may assent to the general proposition, do you consider it true or false?

9. Name the odd man out:
(*a*) whisky-jack
(*b*) brandy-snaps
(*c*) Scotch snaps
(*d*) Danish snaps
(*e*) gin-wheel.

10. "No animal ever invented anything so bad as drunkenness—or so good as drink." Who wrote that?

ALCOHOL AND YOUR INTERIOR

There can be few subjects of general interest more ridden with folk-lore and superstition than the physical effects of alcohol and the measures taken to limit and alleviate them. We have all met the man who says he actually drives better after a few drinks than when cold sober. Many people believe that black coffee—why *black* coffee?—sobers you up, whereas all it does is keep you awake. On the other hand, the consensus that liqueurs are tricky has good sense in it.

Remember that doctors disagree on these matters quite as much as on any others, so some of the answers here must fall some way short of total scientific objectivity. There is no way to measure drunkenness, after all, nor, thank heaven, a hangover.

1. Winter warmers' are a recognized category of drink, but does alcohol warm you?—it certainly makes you *feel* warm. Elucidate.

 Answers on p. 292

2. We are often warned against mixing our drinks, especially "grape and grain," i.e. wine/brandy and beer/whisky. Doing so supposedly:

    (*a*) makes you drunk

    (*b*) gives you a hangover.

    How much truth is there in these assertions?

3. Quantity of intake is an obvious factor in drunkenness. So is food, or rather lack of it. Can you suggest others?

4. Apart from a large alcoholic intake, what else seems to cause or aggravate hangovers?

5. Most of us have learnt better by now than to call alcohol a stimulant; it is, we keep hearing, a depressant. Does it inevitably cause a state of depression?

6. Excessive drinking is a cause of cirrhosis of the liver. True or false?

7. Excessive drinking, especially of port, is a cause of gout. True or false?

8. Apart from the unthinkable resort of drinking less, is there any stratagem that will limit the intoxicating ravages of alcohol?

9. What is and what is not good for a hangover is such a personal matter, and so much influenced by suggestion, that any ruling must be tentative, but try to give a balanced, educated view of:

    (*a*) two beneficial things

    (*b*) two useless or harmful things.

Answers on pp. 293–294

10. Although a small amount of alcohol daily is beneficial to health, there will always be some support for teetotalism—a terrible word, many will think. What is its origin?

 Answer on p. 294

ANSWERS

1. (a) *8–10 per cent* (b) *13–15 per cent.*

2. The proportion of grape-products as opposed to water-content. A wine of good body is a thick wine in this sense.

3. (a) Cylindrical, with sloping shoulders.
   (b) Cylindrical, with squarer shoulders. Claret, traditional UK term for red wine from Bordeaux region. Now used also for other wines of the same general type.
   (c) Traditionally, long neck, rounded body, straw jacket and base. An extra mark for noting that a lot, an increasing amount, of Chianti turns up nowadays in a bottle similar to (b).

4. (a) *26⅔*. Not an obvious quantity but it seems about right.
   (b) Three-quarters of a litre or *75 cl*. The French and others must have thought it was about right too.
   (c) (A bottle containing) a fifth of a US gallon, smaller than the Imperial at *128 fl. oz.* compared with *160*. When a tiny difference in the size of the US *fl. oz.* is taken into

*account, the fifth emerges at 46.5432 cu. in. as against
the standard wine-bottle's 46.2458. So the Americans
must also have thought it was about right.*

5. That it has acquired an unpleasant smell and taste from a
mould in the cork. Very rare today.

6. Wine-grapes. There are at least 1,000 different varieties.
Many wines, from Alsace, California, Australia, etc., are
known by the type of grape used. They are called varietal
wines.

7. (a) Sweet white from Bordeaux. In Sauternes district.
(b) Dry white from Loire valley. Central France.
(c) Dry red, (district of) Burgundy. East-central France.

8. (a) Sweet white sparkling Muscatel from Piemonte in the
north west.
(b) Dry red from Veneto, north-central, near Verona.
(c) White, usually dry, some semi-sweet and sweet, Latium,
near Rome.

9. (a) (Chiefly) dry red, from Rioja region in north Spain.
(b) Dry white flavoured with pine resin, from Greece (At-
tica).
(c) "Green wine," i.e. young, immature wine, red and
white but usually white in UK, dry, with a slight
sparkle, from north Portugal.

10. The cork of an upright bottle will eventually dry out and
admit air, rapid fluctuations of temperature will injure the
contents and daylight will, in the case of a red wine, turn it
brown. But not drinking it is worse than any of that. One

such offender, father of a daring and ingenious son, is supposed to have decided eventually to drink his 1959 Château Haut-Brion after all and found his mouth full of red ink.

WINE—INTERMEDIATE

1. Homer. His use of the phrase suggests that wine had become a familiar part of eastern Mediterranean life by 700 BC at latest.

2. About AD 700, in the Old English epic poem "Beowulf."

3. The cork. Wine could now be kept and matured in the bottle instead of sitting (and frequently going off) in the barrel.

4. "Phylloxera vastatrix"—"dry-leaf devastator." Retrieved by grafting European vines on to relatively immune rootstocks from the eastern US. But e.g. in 1981 one-third of German vineyards were still affected.

5. The type of grape used or principally used, given increasing emphasis in recent years. Crosses are becoming common.

6. Both, naturally; e.g. Tavel rosé by the first method, some pink champagne and some cheap still wines by the second. Then, of course, there is the "vin rosé" your host has created half an hour before your arrival by mixing the undrunk red and white from yesterday.

7. Years ago he just hung about and let the natural ambient yeasts do it, but nowadays he usually kills them off and puts in his own pure strain, perhaps with a little added heat for encouragement.

8. *He can chill the must or add brandy or sulphur dioxide to deaden the yeast, or strain the must to get the yeast out.*

9. *True! Which does not mean to say that red will not go with chicken or pork, or that individual preferences are somehow bad.*

10. *"Wine can also be made from grapes." You may specify a French, Spanish, etc., wine-grower according to where your last lousy bottle came from.*

WINE—ADVANCED

1. *Having satisfied himself that the wine is not cloudy—a sign of trouble—he studies the colour. With reds, a purple tinge indicates a young wine, brick-red a more mature one. With whites, lightness, perhaps with a greenish tinge, indicates youth, straw colour is standard, yellow may well mean age, but depth of colour also indicates degree of sweetness. Any hint of brown in red or white may foreshow bad quality.*

2. *A woody or metallic smell suggests a fault in the cask. A vinegary smell calls for no great powers of reasoning. But other acid smells are harmless, and chemical smells from disinfectant agents often go away after a few minutes. All the same, I would avoid (where socially possible) any wine with an unexpected smell, not to speak of a disagreeable one.*

3. *Tartaric and malic. There may be traces of citric and more than a dozen other acids.*

4. *It may sharpen the flavour, though not everyone cares for its bitterness or famed "mouth-puckering" effect. "Plenty of* *tannin" is a fashionable commendation. Also a preservative, lengthening the period of improvement in bottle. Often artificially introduced into poor wine.*

5. (a) *Mostly dry white wine—some red—from the district of Chablais near Lake Geneva (Switzerland).*
   (b) *Bulgarian Muscat. You hardly need telling that this is the generic name for sweet white wines made from the Muscat or Muscatel grape.*
   (c) *The same, from Romania, Yugoslavia, etc., named after the variety of Muscat grape.*

6. (a) *Red wine from an area so named in northern Italy. (Paradiso is next door.)*
   (b) *White wine, dry and sweet, some red, from the Rust area in east Austria.*
   (c) *The standard red produced by the Turkish state wine industry.*

7. (a) *South Africa*
   (b) *US (California)*
   (c) *Germany*
   (d) *Austria*
   (e) *Germany.*

8. (a) *France*
   (b) *South Africa*
   (c) *South Africa*
   (d) *South Africa*
   (e) *Wales (Dyfed).*

9. (a) *Burgundy (Beaujolais)*
   (b) *Loire*

    (c) Rhône

    (d) Mosel (Saar)

    (e) Lombardy.

10. *(a) Saint-Julien*

    (b) Margaux

    (c) Pauillac

    (d) Saint-Estèphe

    (e) Margaux.

    All of these four names are within Haut Médoc.

WINE—FRANCE

1. *In alphabetical order:*

    Alsace   **Bordeaux**   **Burgundy**   **Champagne**
    The Loire   **The Rhône**

2. *(a) "Appellation (d'Origine) Contrôlée," Means that the wine comes from where the label says it comes from. Also some assurance that it has been properly made and is up to strength.*

    (b) Similar, but not so strict about area and other things.

3. *A "country" or local wine coming from a general region. Inferior to the other two, with nothing especially authentic or esoteric to them. Worth trying for curiosity's sake, says Hugh Johnson. Well yes.*

4. *(a) Completely dry, unsweetened (of champagne). But very little wine so marked is in fact totally without added syrup.*

    (b) Cool, chilled, not ice-cold.

    (c) Slightly sparkling, with a "prickle."

(d) (Fully) sparkling, but never applied to champagne. One of the minor airs that overpriced stuff gives itself.

(e) White wine made from black grapes. This is theoretically possible if you whip the skins out the moment the juice is removed, but in practice such wines are pale pink.

5. *"Pourriture noble" or noble rot, the result of attentions of the fungus "Botrytis cinerea."*

6. *From the shape, but surely not the size, of Marie Antoinette's breasts. I find this story tempting but implausible.*

7. *Well, because after a few months in store each bottle has yeast and sugar added, causing the famous second fermentation with resultant bubbles.*

8. *By no means. Some of the wine, not worth giving the expensive treatment described above, is marketed in its original still form. I have met people who say they like it. There are still reds too, of which the best is supposed to be Bouzy.*

9. *Jeroboam* — *4 bottles*
Rehoboam — *6 bottles*
Methuselah — *8 bottles*
Sennacherib — *10 bottles*
Salmanazar — *12 bottles*
Balthazar — *16 bottles*
Nebuchadnezzar — *20 bottles*

10. *There is one French exception, Muscat d'Alsace, bone dry but with all the rest of the grape still there, a remarkable experience. Sadly, André Simon found it underbred. Oh well.*

*There is an intruder in the answers above, a fact of-
fered as a plain fact that is not a fact at all. You will find
the solution on page 294.*

WINE—GERMANY

1. (a) *"Qualitätswein mit Prädikat," quality's-wine with title
   or mark. Official designation for top-grade wine that
   must not be chaptalized (have sugar added to boost the
   alcohol).*
   (b) *"Qualitätswein eines bestimmten Anbaugebietes," actually, or quality's-wine of a definite cultivation-territory,
   in other words of a named wine-growing region. Good
   wine, but may be chaptalized.*

2. *Like much else, not easily discoverable from a modern atlas, but the line from Bonn, which is about right for the
   northernmost German vineyard, passes through or near
   Bournemouth and Exeter, which incidentally is north of at
   least four modern English vineyards.*

3. *From the name of the local port of Hochheim on the river
   Main, whence most or some of it was presumably shipped.*

4. *Not this time. Hocks come in brown bottles, moselles in
   green.*

5. *Ice-wine, made from frozen grapes with the ice, i.e. water
   content, taken out, and so very heavy and sweet, also good,
   though not the best Germany can do, it appears.*

6. *"Edelfäule," the exact translation of noble rot or "pourriture noble." A less regular visitor to the Rhineland than to
   Sauternes.*

7. *"Das Rheingold" is of course the preludial opera of Wagner's "Ring" cycle, and the Rheingold also is or was an early-morning express train from the Hook of Holland to Milan. The other four are denominated wine-producing regions of the Rhineland.*

8. (a) *Foam-wine, i.e. sparkling wine, lower grade.*
   (b) *Sparkling wine, higher grade, or "Qualitätsschaumwein" if you prefer.*
   (c) *Almost meaningless term for all-right, nothing-special hock. Well defined by COD as "mild white Rhine wine." Legally a QbA, which says something about QbAS.*
   (d) *The best and commonest German grape. Also used for wines from Alsace, Austria, California, Australia, etc.*
   (e) *Table wine. Equivalent to "vin ordinaire." A blend of German wines and those of other EEC countries. "Deutscher Tafelwein" indicates a blend of German wines only.*

9. *Quite easily. "Trocken," like "dry," can mean at least two things. "Trockenbeeren" are dry, i.e. withered, nobly-rotten, sugar-concentrating grapes. "Trocken" on its own equals "sec."*

10. *Königin Viktoriaberg (Queen Victoria-hill) and Bernkasteler Doktor, the doctor in question being Edward VII's.*

WINE—ITALY, SPAIN, PORTUGAL

1. *"Asciutto" (bone-dry), "pastoso" (off-dry), "abboccato" (lightly sweet), "amabile" ("amiable," a touch sweeter), "dolce" (sweet).*

2. *"Denominazione di origine controllata," controlled designation of origin. Result of belated (1963) Italian attempt to*

follow the French AOC *example and regulate descriptions and methods. No assurance of quality as such. A higher category is supposedly on the way.*

3. Yes, something. It means the wine comes from a reputed best area within the larger area indicated by a DOC.

4. This refers to age. Barolo Riserva and others are three years old, but many named wines have no such grade.

5. Barolo is a red wine, one of Italy's best, from Piemonte in the north west. The others are whites.

6. (a) *sparkling*
  (b) *rosy, pink*
  (c) *"current," ordinary, like "vin ordinaire"*
  (d) *red*
  (e) *"of table," denoting a table wine. (A mesa in Arizona etc. is a table-land.)*

7. A flavour of vanilla is imparted to the wine. Some people like this; I find it intolerable.

8. Ice, fresh fruit, sweetness, a kick, bubbles—you can do sweetness and kick together by using a sweet liqueur, or sweetness and bubbles together with fizzy lemonade. Oh, and wine, which after all need not be Spanish.

9. Dāo, rhyming with "cow" but nasalized by the conscientious.

10. Moscatel de Setubal, a fortified dark-white dessert wine made from the muscat grape and redolent of

Victorian elevenses. They do a nice red table wine round there too.

WINES—OTHERS

1. (a) *Standard Tokay, with added "aszu" syrup from "nobly rotten" grapes.*
   (b) *Even sweeter version, low in alcohol, supposedly life-saving "essence," very rare today. Hugh Johnson persuaded them to give him a swig out of the barrel in the State cellars at a place called Tállya.*
   (c) *The heavy natural wine minus the "aszu."*

2. *A good full-bodied red table wine that goes down well with pizzas, stews, oxtail, shepherd's pie, chili con carne, etc. Bull's Blood is the name.*

3. *An Austrian wine for swilling, reputedly enjoyable. Not to be confused with schlock, Yiddish American for "rubbish."*

4. *Othello. Well, Shakespeare's Othello had a horrible time in Cyprus. Iago's deadly plot against him started with a drinking-session, at which Cypriot wines were presumably on offer.*

5. *California (of course), New York, Oregon, Washington, Idaho, Ohio. Take note that vineyards have been planted in Texas.*

6. *Argentina. But Chile probably leads in quality.*

7. *English wine is made from grapes by proper methods and is perfectly serious, though a bit marginal. British wine is*

imported as grape concentrate from nameless places, rehydrated and fermented, finally blended and given a brand-
name. In some cases, raisins are probably the nearest
things to grapes it has ever seen.

8. 1790/91, which does sound a bit soon after the founding of
the first settlement in 1788. They brought vine cuttings
from Rio de Janeiro and the Cape—where they had had
wine for 100 years before that.

9. The South African Wine Farmers' Association. Tel: 01-734
9251.

10. Canada is in North America. The others are in Asia. (All
five produce some wine.)

BEER IN GENERAL

1. Ale was made from fermented barley without added
flavour, beer was treated with hops. In the UK beer was a
novelty of the fifteenth century.

2. A type of dark beer apparently first brewed for, or popular
with, London porters. Recently revived after long abeyance.
Also see next answer.

3. Strong. "Stout porter" was the full expression, and what
was once called an extra stout porter still flourishes. The
colour of stout comes from the roasted barley used.

4. Steeping the barley in water causes it to germinate and convert its insoluble starch into soluble starch.

5. *The infusion of malt which is boiled, hopped, and fermented into beer. The word rhymes with Bert.*

6. *Hops confer bitterness on the brew to balance the inherent slight sweetness of the malt content.*

7. *The Latin name, "Saccharomyces," "sugar-mushroom," tells the story. Yeast is a substance consisting of minute fungous organisms that produce fermentation, in the present case converting the sugars in the wort into alcohol and carbon dioxide.*

8. *That the beer is still fermenting, is a "natural" beer, unpasteurized.*

9. *Real Ale. "Cask-conditioned" is the jargon of brewers, who are nervous of the term Real Ale because they probably make unreal ale, i.e. keg, as well.*

10. *Beer is pasteurized by heating it and so killing yeasts and bacteria. It will now not change any further. The advantages of a consistent, stable product are obvious. The process is of course—by definition—frowned on by Real Ale lovers, but bottled and canned lagers as we know them would be impossible without it.*

BEER IN PARTICULAR

1. *"Lager" is German for warehouse or store. A lager beer is kept in store for up to three months to settle and mature.*

2. *From the town of Pilsen (Plzen) in West Czechoslovakia, where the first light-coloured lager was made in the last*

*century. Pilsener Urquell is made there and exported to GB
and elsewhere ("Urquell"=original source).*

3. True. It has quite high alcohol and therefore calories. Not
for dieters in the slimming sense but for those on a diabetic
diet. And for beer-drinkers.

4. (a) Greece. From the brewery called that, a fair shot at the
name of the German brewer, Füchs.
(b) Malaysia and Singapore, a Pilsener lager. The phrase is
the title of a novel by Anthony Burgess.

5. That of the Pilgrim Fathers, who were bound for Virginia,
but landed at Plymouth Rock, "our victuals being spent, especially our beer."

6. (a) Belgium
(b) France (Strasbourg)
(c) Denmark
(d) Holland
(e) England—Vaux Breweries, Sunderland. Sorry, but the
name was irresistible.

7. Allied Breweries, Bass, Courage, Scottish and Newcastle,
Watney, Whitbread.

8. (a) Biggleswade and Bury
(b) Portsmouth
(c) Henley-on-Thames
(d) Southwold
(e) London.

9. (a) In Germany, a strong type of beer, in France, a weak one.

(b) A type of Russian drink made from bread, beer of a sort.

(c) Japanese rice beer. So describable from the mode of manufacture, not the end result.

(d) Odd man out—German for "strawberry."

(e) A type of Belgian beer made from wheat.

10. The Angel, the Royal Oak, the Swiss Cottage and the Elephant and Castle. The last name, by the way, is not a corruption of "Infanta of Castile." The inn-sign obviously showed an elephant carrying a castle, which was the regular fifteenth-century term for a small wooden fighting-tower fitted to an elephant's back.

VODKA

1. "Little water" or "waterlet," from Polish/Russian "voda," water. No doubt a Slavic jest. But note that Russians particularly are prone to the use of diminutives, and in practice will ask for "vodochka," "waterletkins."

2. It varies. Theoretically, vodka is a type of uncoloured grain whisky or pure spirit of grain, and it regularly is that in the US and officially in the USSR. In the UK, often a molasses spirit filtered through "activated" charcoal, and unofficially in the USSR anything available—potatoes, beetroots, nuts, sawdust, etc.

3. Eighth-century Poland, they say, but this was probably a distillation of wine, and so a form of brandy. For what would nowadays be called a vodka, eleventh- or twelfth-century Poland, more likely.

4. Smirnoff. *The modern Western product derives from a member of the original family, who originated in the Polish city of Lvov, now incorporated in the USSR.*

5. Zubrowka. *Horrible muck according to me, though other Polish vodkas are first-rate.*

6. *They are designed for winter drinking in extreme northern latitudes, where anything weaker would freeze. (Does that mean you are supposed to drink them out of doors?)*

7. (a) *Vodka, beef consommé, lemon-juice, Worcester sauce, lightly iced, a warmer or reviver.*
   (b) *The same, gently heated.*
   (c) *As (a), but featuring tomato-juice half-and-half with the consommé.*
   (d) *An invention of my own for a bonus, the Raging Bull— vodka, lemon-juice and Worcester sauce in a mug of Bovril.*

8. *By the colour. A White Russian Cocktail has vodka and Kahlua Mexican coffee liqueur mixed with cream floating on top, the Black Russian omits the cream. But either is to be avoided by sensitive persons.*

9. *In 1946 in a place called the Cock 'n Bull (a suitable name, you may feel) in Los Angeles a man with a lot of unsold vodka met a man with a lot of unsold ginger beer. A third man, brought in later, had a lot of unsold copper mugs. The success of their joint venture was the beginning of the success of vodka, first in the US, later the UK and elsewhere.*

10. *Peter the Great, in 1716. He took a close personal interest in these matters and invented an improved still.*

APERITIFS AND SUCH

1. (a) *A pre-prandial drink supposed by convention to stimulate the appetite, such as white wine, dry sherry and most of the drinks in this quiz.*
   (b) *A branded drink, also called a wine aperitif, in the vermouth style, such as Dubonnet and Punt e Mes.*

2. *Inferior white wine, a little grape spirit or sugar syrup, artificial colouring (red, rosé and sweet white vermouths).*

3. *Our word "vermouth" comes from the French word "vermout" which is a frenchifying of the German word "wermut" which is cousin to the medieval English word "wermod" which got changed to "wormwood" because the herb was formerly used in medicine to get rid of intestinal worms, or quite possibly "wermod" got changed to "wormwood" because it sounded better and they used it for worming merely because it was called that. So yes, but distantly.*

4. *Once a valid distinction, showing healthy disrespect for the literal fact that the famous Martini Rossi dry vermouth was made in Italy. Now, pedantry on one side and ignorance on the other have rendered it unsafe. False, then.*

5. (a) *A classy white vermouth from the French Alps.*
   (b) *The same, coloured pink and flavoured with wild strawberries (and therefore with a whiff of whitewash to my taste).*

6. *(a)* An Americano
   (b) Negroni.

7. *False: it was invented about 1870 by a Milan café-proprietor called Gaspare Campari.*

8. *The Caribbean—Port of Spain, Trinidad.*

9. *(a)* Fernet Branca
   (b) Underberg.

10. *Quinine. Such drinks were and often still are thought to have tonic and prophylactic virtues.*

GIN

1. *Perhaps an abbreviation of "geneva" from Dutch "genever"="gin," following Old French "genèvre" after Latin "juniperus"="juniper," the shrub or low tree whose berries are used in flavouring gin. The form "geneva" arose from confusion with the name of the Swiss city. I think it more likely that "gin" is an abbreviation of the English word, of which "giniper" and "ginnuper" are early spellings.*

2. *Thomas Carlyle. That Germanic capital should have given it away.*

3. *T. S. Eliot, at a women's luncheon club in the US in the 1950s. He may have been thinking of Byron's remark, "Gin and water is the source of all my inspiration," another playful allusion to gin's disreputability.*

4. *The flavour comes from flavourings, substances added to a pure spirit, principally juniper but also coriander and usually* *cassia bark and orris root, whatever they are. In contrast, the flavour of brandy and whisky comes ultimately from the grape and grain they are made from.*

5. *At Leiden in Holland in the seventeenth century, for medicinal purposes—like every other tipple in the book. Gin was supposed to be beneficial to the urinary system, and English gin is perhaps still taken in moderate quantities to alleviate gout.*

6. *Dutch or Hollands gin is made from malted barley, maize and rye. The English distillers are rather evasive. Grain, they helpfully say, also "vegetable matter," also, less often, molasses. But all the original flavour is taken out anyway.*

7. *Because of the excellence of its springs or wells, such as Clerkenwell and Goswell. Water is a most important constituent of alcoholic drinks. Or was—the statement is less true today, with the distiller or brewer in control of the chemistry of his water-supply.*

8. *Gin and Angostura bitters—score a quarter of a mark. For specifying Plymouth gin—half a mark. For confining the bitters to just a few drops—three-quarters. For leaving it to the drinker's taste—a full mark.*

9. *No time at all. "You can make gin in the morning and drink it in the afternoon," as they used to say.*

10. *Pimm's No. 1.*

LIQUEURS

1. Briefly, and broadly, Heering is a sweetened spirit flavoured with cherries, Kirsch is an unsweetened fruit brandy or "white alcohol" distilled from a mash of cherries.

2. At the meet before a fox-hunt, where it forms the stirrup-cup.

3. Well, the defeat of the Stuart cause, but the next most important was probably that after it Bonnie Prince Charlie is supposed to have given the recipe for Drambuie to one of his supporters as a gesture of gratitude before departing into exile.

4. Orange Curaçao, the generic name for a liqueur flavoured with orange-peel and orange in colour; the others are brands, in fact Grand Marnier is a brand of Orange Curaçao.

5. Because both Izarra liqueur (green and yellow varieties) and the game of pelota belong to the Basque country.

6. Set light to it, apparently. There will not be much combustion and the result, which chars the coffee-beans slightly, is quite drinkable (and crunchable).

7. (a) Crème de menthe (France).
   (b) Calvados (France). Only half a mark for Applejack (US).
   (c) Cassis (France).
   (d) Kümmel (Holland, Germany).
   (e) Mirabelle (France), Quetsch (Germany), Slivovitz (Yugoslavia, Czechoslovakia).
   The above is not a complete list.

8. (a) *Kitró (the Greek islands of Naxos and Ios).*

(b) *Medronho (Portugal).*

(c) *Eau de Noix (France).*

(d) *Van der Hum (South Africa). The naartjie is related to the mandarin and tangerine.*

(e) *Forbidden Fruit (US). The shaddock is related to the grapefruit.*

The above is not necessarily a complete list.

9. *Cointreau, gin, lemon-juice. White of egg too if you want a fizz.*

10. *Catherine de Medici of Florence.*

R U M

1. *Not certain. Once thought to be an abbreviation of the word "rumbullion," which might have meant "uproar," but there seems to be no real evidence of this. Some derive it from Latin "saccharum"=sugar, but again no written record shows it happening.*

2. (a) *A type of giant grass.*

(b) *The Azores. Columbus brought cuttings to the West Indies on his second voyage.*

3. *"Old Grog" was the nickname of Admiral Edward Vernon (from his waterproof grogram boat-cloak). To limit drunkenness he ordered the men's rum ration to be watered and issued in half-portions of a gill each twice a day. The equivalent of three pub doubles of 90° spirits at eleven o'clock in the morning is still not a small drink.*

4. *"White" or transparent. The darker rums gain their colour from the oak they mature in or from caramel, flavourless burnt sugar. Rum seems to have been artificially coloured in the first place to suit the Navy, which could not afford to risk having on board a strong spirit which the eye could mistake for water.*

5. *Possibly. They say that after Trafalgar the Admiral's body was brought back to England in a cask of rum.*

6. *Imperial Spanish rule, after the Spanish-American war of 1898. With the US occupying forces came Coca Cola, then a comparatively new drink (first sold 1886).*

7. *The Daiquiri. From the place in Cuba where US marines landed in 1898 (see last answer). A duller story gets it from a tin or nickel mine whose manager's butler thought up the drink.*

8. *One of sour, two of sweet, three of strong, four of weak, i.e. water or soda. The so-called American formula reverses one and two, three and four.*

9. *From the Caribbean, principally the island of Martinique. Saint James rum, or rather "rhum," is very fine, offered alongside Cognac in Paris restaurants.*

10. *Puerto Rico. Bacardi set up its base there when Castro confiscated its Cuban property and now outsells all other brands of spirits in the US.*

COGNAC AND ARMAGNAC

1. Cognac, half-way down the Atlantic coast; Armagnac, further down and further in, not far from the Pyrenees.

2. Grande Champagne. Nothing to do with the bubbly-producing part of east France, though that is the same word, meaning "grassy plain" or "open country" (obsolete English "champaign").

3. (a) Early seventeenth century
(b) Early fifteenth century.

4. These are just manufacturers' labels, but Three Star is the basic grade, which even connoisseurs will not mind you putting soda or other mixers in. Next come VO (Very Old) and VSOP (Very Superior Old Pale), with XO (Extra Old) and Cordon Bleu somewhere in front. The initials of these English words appear throughout the trade, indeed chalked on the barrels in the blending-houses in Cognac itself, a satisfying reminder of our long grip on the trade.

A VSTO gives a different kind of lift. The Very Short Take-Off aircraft was the ancestor of the jump jet.

5. Sugar, up to 2 per cent.
Burnt sugar or caramel, up to 2 per cent.
Infusion of oak-chips, no limit, but not a thing you do much. Or talk about much.

6. Delaforce is a firm of port shippers. The others are Cognac houses.

7. (a) A pot still, used for two successive distillations.
(b) A unique type of continuous still.

8. *Five minutes is plenty. No spirit improves in bottle.*

9. *Yes and no. A few bottles may survive from that period, would presumably fetch high prices as relics, but the contents would probably be off (and see last answer). Some firms use the term today merely to indicate a high grade, along with such phrases as "Grand Réserve."*

10. *That which evaporates while the spirit is in cask, the equivalent of several million bottles a year. No way of controlling this has been found which does not damage the brandy.*

BRANDY (ONE STEP DOWN)

1. *Formerly brandwine, brandy-wine, from Dutch "brandewijn"=burnt, i.e. fired, i.e. distilled, wine. The Dutch had a lot of influence on the early Cognac trade.*

2. *Unsatisfactory, illogical, and firmly established trade term in UK and US for French brandy made outside the Cognac and Armagnac regions.*

3. *Quite likely a stare of pretended incomprehension, but on a good day a glass of the above with water. In a classy place you might get Cognac.*

4. *In the hand or hands. Experts get very cross about the use of spirit-lamps and such.*

5. *". . . he who aspires to be a hero must drink brandy."*

6. *Dr. Johnson, immediately after the above. On another occasion he said, "He who drinks until he becomes a beast gets* *away from the pain of being a man," which is hardly funny at all.*

7. *South Africa. Something like half the national spirit production and consumption is brandy. But cane, a pure spirit made from molasses, is catching up.*

8. *The odd man out is (c). Weinbrand is a type of German spirit made from wine, the equivalent of French grape brandy. The others are all made by distilling the debris of skins, stalks and pips left in the presses after making wine.*
   (a) is the French version, properly "eau de vie de marc." The debris itself is the "marc," or tread (from the verb marcher).
   (b) Italian. The word means "clamp" or "vice." Also the name of California spirits of this type.
   (d) Portuguese. The word means "rope-wax." Humorous deprecation, no doubt.
   (e) Peruvian. Sometimes the debris is that of Muscatel wine. Pisco brandy dates back to the early seventeenth century.

9. *Brown Crème de Cacao and cream. Well, it would obviously take away your appetite, if you had one.*

10. *A helicopter. A black fungus forms on the roofs, encouraged by the fumes coming up from below.*

DISTILLATION

1. *The COD defines "distil" as "turn to vapour by heat, condense by cold, and re-collect (liquid)." These are the three essential stages.*

2. *It vaporizes at a lower temperature than water, permitting the separation of the two in the still.*

3. *By fermentation, the product of which will have been the wine used to make brandy, the beery mixture that issues in whisky, etc.*

4. *It was discovered by Arabs, brought into Spain by Moors some time after AD 100 and thence diffused over Europe.*

5. *Two key words are derived from Arabic: "alcohol" ("al kuhl," the essence) and "alembic" ("al inbik," the still—"alambic" is modern French for "still"). But Moorish alcohol may quite well have been nothing but a distillation of flowers for scent, not drinking-alcohol. And of course Islam forbids the latter.*

6. *Distillation as such could well be Arab, though the Alexandrian Greeks of (say) the first century AD are more likely. Distillation for drink, probably north Italy after 1200.*

7. *The pot still. The parts are a kettle in which to boil the distilland (substance to be distilled), a condenser and a receptacle for the distillate, corresponding to the stages of a 1.*

8. *Impurities, consisting of trace alcohols and other substances, that impart flavour and also cause hangovers. The more interesting the drink, the more uncomfortable the sequel.*

9. *Water. There being no chemical reason why the spirit should be diluted, and a sound economic reason against bottling and transporting water, perhaps some dim puritanical motive is at work.*

10. *A rectified spirit is one repeatedly or continuously distilled to a high degree of purity.*

MINOR SPIRITS

1. *Caraway seed. Dill and coriander are sometimes used. Individual Danes flavour their akvavit with elder, cranberry and many other plants.*

2. *Ice-cold, neat, in small glasses holding no more than 1–1½ oz., down in one, with a lager chaser and accompanied by suitable food. Until recently there was a toasting ritual, especially in Sweden, but it seems that this no longer holds.*

3. *A Norwegian brand that, following a long tradition, has journeyed to the Antipodes and back in a ship's hold, crossing the line or equator a couple of times in doing so. It is supposed to pick up something from the motion and the temperature-changes.*

4. *Arrak or rum from Java. Also aquavit and miscellaneous wines.*

5. *A neutral spirit made from grapes or sugar-beet and flavoured with a herbal infusion, anise (aniseed) preponderating in Pernod's case, liquorice in Ricard's.*

6. *The herbal infusion (see previous answer) is made in alcohol. The herbal substances are thus perfectly soluble in alcohol, but they are insoluble in water and become suspended.*

7. *Greece and Cyprus. Ouzo. Flavoured with anise.*

8. *All tequila is mezcal, but not all mezcal is tequila. Mezcal is the generic drink, like brandy. Tequila is a place, a small town in mid-Mexico and the region round it, giving its name to the superior mezcal made there, like Cognac.*

9. *Tequila, Cointreau and lime-juice in a cocktail-glass with sea-salt round the rim. Lock your flick-knife away first.*

10. *Koumiss. Camel's milk will do at a pinch. Chig-Ge is the Mongolian version.*

SCOTCH WHISKY 1

1. *Whisky that has been distilled in Scotland. Not all these questions require deviousness or subtlety in the respondent.*

2. *Three years. In practice the time is usually longer.*

3. *From Irish and Scottish Gaelic "uisge beatha," lit. "water of life" (cf. eau de vie, aquavit). Later usquebaugh, whisky-bae. The modern form is not recorded until 1746.*

4. *In efficiency, therefore economically. The patent still is continuous, turning out spirit as long as alcoholic wash is piped in. The pot still must be cleaned out and refilled after each run. In flavour, of course, the superiority is the other way round.*

5. *Unmalted maize (Indian corn, corn as seen on the cob) as well as malted barley.*

6. *If not from the drinker's imagination, then from the smoke of the peat fire, or often just peat-smoke and hot air, used to dry the malt before it is ground and fed into the mash tun to have its sugar extracted.*

7. *The method of malting the barley, the shape of the still and the method of heating it, the distilling temperature, the wood of the cask, the length of time in cask, etc.*

8. *It means that, like most malts on the market, the one concerned is the product of a single distillery. A blend of malts is a vatted malt, of which there are a couple of dozen on the market but none very highly regarded.*

9. *Lowland, Islay, Campbeltown (at the end of the Kintyre peninsula).*

10. *True. An easy mark all round to dissipate any rancour over q 1.*

SCOTCH WHISKY II

1. *Chivas Regal is a blend. The others are single malts.*

2. *None. There may be a little more or a little less water, but everything else is there in the same proportions as before. Nobody really knows what happens in the cask.*

3. *In the 1880s the vineyards of Cognac were devastated by the vine-aphid (see Q Wine—Intermediate, q 4) and production of brandy, the prosperous Englishman's standard spirit, fell off disastrously. Scotch moved into the vacuum, though naturally not overnight.*

4. *3,000. Many go straight for export and are never seen in the UK.*

5. *A dessert drink or alcoholic dish made from Scotch whisky, runny honey and a liquor produced by soaking oatmeal or porage oats in water. Sassenach recipes substitute cream for the oatmeal liquor. A partial exception to the statement in the headnote that Scotch will not mix. Atholl is a Scottish dukedom and "brose" is connected with "broth."*

6. *Traditionally, oak casks that have held sherry. Of recent years the supply of these has fallen off and distillers have taken to importing casks used to age bourbon whiskey in the US.*

7. *Queen Victoria, probably under the influence of John Brown, her Highland retainer. Her choice of tipple is said to have startled Gladstone, probably because of the violence it did the whisky. He was a good friend to Scotch, legalizing its importation into England in bottle in 1860.*

8. *The more malt, the better the blend. Good blends, not much more than 50 per cent grain. Inferior blends, up to 80 per cent. Blending is a secret process.*

9. *Whisky out of the still is colourless. The colour comes from the cask and from additives such as caramel, sherry and molasses.*

10. *Japan; precisely, the Suntory distillery in Hakushu. It produces nearly 100 million gallons of malt whisky a year, more than the whole of Scotland.*

WHISKIES AND WHISKEYS

1. *Old Bushmills in the north of Northern Ireland, licensed in 1608. Its premium Black Label blend, "Black Bush," has an unusually high proportion of malt whiskey in it.*

2. *A teaspoon (a true coffee-spoon is too small), over the back of which to pour the chilled cream on to the surface of the mixture of Irish whiskey, hot black coffee and (if wanted) sugar.*

3. *From Bourbon County in Kentucky Territory, as it then was, where the first stills were set up in the 1780s. For many years bourbon has been made in other parts of Kentucky and in other states, but Kentucky remains the Bordeaux, so to speak, of the trade.*

4. *(a) Corn (maize) principally, with some rye and barley. (b) Casks of oak charred on the inside.*

5. *An American whiskey produced as the result of a fermentation partly set off by the residue of a previous fermentation. The best known is Jack Daniel's Tennessee whiskey, often inaccurately referred to as a bourbon, though it is indeed similar to bourbon in style.*

6. *Bourbon, Angostura bitters, sugar (plus a slice of orange and ice).*

7. *Washington and Jefferson, the first and third presidents. In each case the product was rye whiskey, and pretty rough too, it may safely be inferred.*

8. *John Jameson is an Irish whiskey, the others are American.*

9. *Purity, and consequent lack of any persistent flavour, therefore a readiness to be swamped in various mixtures. "Dullness" would be my word. Of course, lack of after-effects is associated with purity.*

10. *Malt whisky imported from Scotland and blended with a local grain spirit. And yes, quite properly so called; blended Scotch is malt and local grain. The advisability of drinking such whiskies is another matter.*

PORT

1. *Along the upper valley of the river Douro to the east.*

2. *In the middle of the fermenting process, before all the sugar has turned into alcohol, grape spirit is added to the wine, stopping fermentation and increasing the overall content of alcohol.*

3. *Not in Oporto itself but across the river in Vila Nova de Gaia. (Once called Portus Cale, whence "Portugal.")*

4. *A blend of wines from the best vineyards and of one exceptional year. It accounts for only about 2 per cent of total production, but is apparently the most profitable part of the trade. In other words the poor old consumer pays through the nose and no option, since no competing product exists.*

5. *(a) It is aged in an oak cask for two years only.*
   (b) It slowly improves, becoming ready to drink after ten to fifteen years but continuing to improve thereafter. It also accumulates a crust or sediment.

6. *Stilton is the traditional answer, but some people think it and other English cheeses smother the port and prefer something milder, like unhung Brie or Camembert. This school would accompany Stilton with one of the types of port mentioned in the next question. (The practice of pouring any kind of port into a hole in a Stilton is regarded as being on about the level of brightening up caviar with a few dashes of vinegar.)*

7. *(a) A blend of wines from a single good but not necessarily vintage year aged in wood for about five years, bottled and ready to drink at once.*
(b) The same, made with wines of different years.
(c) A blend of wines from good but not necessarily all vintage years, to be laid down like vintage port, but cheaper.

8. *Just like all the other port, but with white grapes.*

9. *Equal parts of any old port and brandy. Supposed to be ineffective if the two are drunk successively. Many old stagers swear by it.*

10. *Dying like flies was the most noticeable. To drink at a sitting three bottles of old-style port, a light table wine, is one thing; to drink the same amount of the brandified article is quite another.*

SHERRY

1. *From a small area in Andalusia in south Spain to the west of the town of Jerez de la Frontera, formerly Xeres, the X denoting a "sh" sound.*

2. *Falstaff, of course, in "King Henry IV Part II." The usual mark for getting it right, but five off for not knowing. Did the last bit inspire a famous beer ad?*

3. *"Dry," from "seco," is the usual answer. But "vino seco" was not a Spanish phrase at that time, and "canary sack," also contemporary, was certainly a sweet wine, as wine normally was then. So there.*

4. *Nothing as far as I know. He was referring to R. B. Sheridan the dramatist, of whom he went on to say famously, "Such an excess of stupidity, Sir, is not in nature."*

5. *Barrels are ranked in tiers holding wines of different ages. When wine is taken for bottling from the oldest tier, that tier is topped up from the next oldest, and so on back. There are thus no "years" in sherry.*

6. *"Flor" ("flower"). Native to Jerez and still an unexplained phenomenon.*

7. *Roughly: Manzanilla, Fino, Amontillado, Oloroso, Cream. Roughly because there are occasional exceptions like sweetish Amontillados and dry Olorosos.*

8. *Both, plus the drinker's concern for the state of his drink. Half a bottle is considered about right for one man and one session, and fino deteriorates very fast when the air gets to it.*

9. *Montilla is quite a strong wine but unfortified; sherry has brandy added to it.*

10. *(a)* A drink of sherry, sugar or sweet liqueur (unless the sherry itself is sweet), lemon and pounded ice.

    (b) A kind of overtrouser once worn by horsemen in the US. From the Polish "szarawary."

MADEIRA, MARSALA AND OTHERS

1. Wood. English "material," "matter." When the Portuguese discovered the island in 1419 it was so thickly forested that a clearance fire is supposed to have burned for seven years.

2. That is the correct order. Malmsey is supposed to be the finest. However, when the Duke of Clarence was drowned in a butt of it in 1478 it was just another sweet white wine.

3. The label can hardly be contemporary, but it still might be telling the truth. If so, the wine would probably be marvellous. Madeira seems never to go over the top.

4. Prince Hal to Falstaff in "King Henry IV Part I." Another anachronism of Shakespeare's: Henry was all over before the island was even discovered. But it seems hard to care.

5. In west Sicily, the invention of an Englishman (of course). When based at Palermo in 1798 Nelson got to like it so much that he made it the official RN tipple for a time. Garibaldi called it "a strong and generous wine, like the men who fight with me for freedom."

6. In zabaglione, the delicious sweet of egg-yolks and sugar.

7. Málaga.

8. *Well, natural sweet wine, and if you think that pouring spirit into an already strong wine is a natural proceeding, no doubt the name will strike you as admirably appropri ate. But still a great drink.*

9. *Banyuls, a "vin doux naturel" (see above).*

10. *No, not Nigeria—Australia. A dessert drink and mixer made from sweet white wine and brandy. Yalumba comes from an Aboriginal word meaning "all the land around." But Yalumba table wines, some of which are now available in the UK, are perfectly serious.*

COCKTAILS AND MIXED DRINKS

1. *If you can, you have solved a mystery going back to 1806, when the word first reached print. No one has overturned the OED's verdict, itself nearly a century old: "A slang name, of which the real origin appears to be lost," And yet any day now . . .*

2. *My own shot: A short strong mixed drink served cold. So for instance the Collins (see q 6), being long, fails to qualify, whereas the Sour, the same thing minus soda, gets in.*

3. *In 1920 Prohibition stopped the legal production of alcoholic drinks in the US and all sorts of semi-potables were run up and passed off as gin and other spirits, so raw and foul that they had to be smothered with fruit, sugar, bitters, anything to hand.*

4. *All Manhattans contain a dash or two of Angostura bitters. The Sweet Manhattan (the usual variety) has sweet vermouth, the Dry dry, and the Medium a bit of both.*

5. *A short broad vertical-sided tumbler, preferably heavy. The Old-Fashioned is served with ice-cubes, and the breadth of the glass enables you to put enough in without piling them up above the surface of the drink and numbing your nose on them when you sip. Useful for any drink on the rocks.*

6. *Sugar and lemon-juice with ice, topped up with soda-water.*

7. *Champagne is the common denominator. The other ingredients are as follows:*
   (a) Fresh orange-juice. From Buck's Club.
   (b) Guinness. The mixture is also known as Bismarck.
   (c) Fresh peach-juice—the Bellini.
   (d) Angostura bitters, sugar, brandy—the (vile) Champagne Cocktail.
   (e) Even worse, and so not asked for, gin—the French 75.

8. *(a) Rum*
   (b) Strega
   (c) Benedictine
   (d) Drambuie
   (e) Galliano.

9. *(a) Gin, lime-juice, sugar.*
   (b) Brandy, Cointreau, lemon-juice.
   (c) Vodka, orange-juice.
   (d) Brandy, white Crème de menthe. A favourite of James Bond's.
   (e) Gin, cherry brandy, lemon-juice, sugar. But there are a dozen different recipes.

10. *(a) Tequila, Galliano, orange-juice.*

(b) *Vodka, Galliano, orange-juice.*

(c) *White rum, Blue Curaçao, pineapple-juice, coconut cream.*

(d) *As (c), omitting Curaçao.*

(e) *Scotch or bourbon, Amaretto.*

INVENTORS AND INVENTIONS

1. *Angostura bitters. Siegert worked in the hospital at the river-port of Angostura (which is Spanish for "narrows"), not long afterwards renamed Ciudad Bolívar. His bitters were intended as a tonic and digestive remedy. See Aperitifs and Such, q 8.*

2. *The continuous or patent or Coffey still. Coffey showed his invention to the Irish distillers, who didn't want to know, then to Scottish or Scotch ones, who did. The Coffey still, not much modified, is used to this day for the making of grain whisky, gin, vodka and other spirits.*

3. *The continuous still. Stein came up with his invention five years before Coffey, but was superseded. His name may sound German to some people, but there have been Steins in England and Scotland literally as far back as 1066.*

4. *The Kir (rhymes with "beer"), an aperitif of Cassis black-currant liqueur topped up with white Burgundy. Félix—to give him his accent—was a mayor of Dijon, where Cassis comes from.*

5. *Absinthe, an infusion of wormwood ("Artemisia absinthia") and other herbs in alcohol. Not specially more harmful than other strong drinks, but thought to be, and banned in*

many places for many years. Once thought to be an aphrodisiac. The most successful brand was Pernod. Present-day Pernod is flavoured with aniseed.

6. *Jean-Antoine Chaptal, Napoleon's Minister of Agriculture, authorized and encouraged it. He was faced with a glut of sugar-beet and a rash of under-strength wines.*

7. *Eugène Charmat, a Bordeaux chemist, in the last century. Sometimes called the Charmat process or method.*

8. *Bartholomew Sikes, an English excise officer, in 1816. The Sikes system is in process of being replaced by the percentage-of-alcohol-by-volume system, whereby 70° = 40 per cent. See Pousse-Café I, q 9.*

9. *Dom Perignon, cellarer of an abbey near Epernay, certainly had champagne-as-we-know-it going in France by 1700, but there is evidence to show that English importers had anticipated him in the 1660s. See Patrick Forbes, "Champagne," 1977.*

10. *Martini di Arma di Taggia, barman of the Knickerbocker Hotel (where it was also or earlier known as the Knickerbocker Cocktail), NYC, 1910. Jerry Thomas, a California barman, invented the Martinez Cocktail, a different drink. Martini Rossi Ltd make vermouth. The Martini-Henry gives a different kind of kick, being a nineteenth-century rifle. John Doxat, in his "Stirred, Not Shaken" (1976), puts the case for di Taggia most persuasively. Yet I cannot feel we have found out all there is to be found out of the matter.*

POUSSE-CAFÉ 1

1. *It crushes the grapes without also crushing the pips and releasing their unpalatable oils. Devising a machine to do the same proved not to be easy.*

2. *A burra peg. A "peg" is nineteenth-century, mainly Anglo-Indian, slang for a drink of spirits, usually brandy and water. "Chota" and "burra" are Hindustani words for "small" and "large."*

3. *A glass of Byrrh, a vermouthy brand of wine aperitif. Paris, because a waiter or barman there would be more likely to pretend wittily that he thought that that was what you wanted.*

4. *True. A cotton-gin is a machine for separating cotton from its seeds. But a gin-mill is punningly a drinking-saloon (US nineteenth century).*

5. *If you were there. Mascara (a different word from the cosmetic) is a wine-producing district of Algeria—but they probably export it all to Russia for blending.*

6. *A Dutch mixture of brandy, egg-yolks, sugar and flavouring. Improved when thinned by stirring in more brandy.*

7. *Ay is a village in the Champagne country whose produce is given the highest rating, and Ahr is the name of a small river in Germany round which they make red wine. So now you know.*

8. *Without going into Magyar grammar it can be said that the higher the number the sweeter the wine. The reference is to* *the number of baskets of overripe grapes added to the cask. Five is the maximum.*

9. *He devised the logical system of calculating alcoholic strength by volume. We in the UK are now going over to it, abandoning our own illogical one: 40 per cent G–L = 70° Br. proof. (I said it was a small debt.)*

10. *"Saki," H. H. Munro (1870–1916).*

POUSSE-CAFÉ 11

1. *Gamay Beaujolais is not from Beaujolais; it is a California varietal (named after the variety of grape) wine. Confusingly, the grape concerned is not in fact the Gamay as used in Beaujolais but a sub-variety of Pinot Noir.*

2. *Brandy. Though it produces a lot of sherry too.*

3. *(a) Moonshine. UK 1785, US 1875.*
   (b) Hooch. US 1877, UK 1927.
   (c) Poteen, potheen, 1812.

4. *From the town of Spa in Belgium, that gave its name to all the other "spas."*

5. *"Roomed," allowed (not artificially encouraged) to reach room temperature, in practice 63°–68° F. Most red wines do not release their full flavour when colder.*

6. *(a) USSR (UK and US jostling for second).*
   (b) Italy.
   (c) US.

7. *Lime-juice, to prevent scurvy, a prostrating disease caused by lack of vitamin C, result of a shipboard diet that lacked fresh fruit and vegetables. Hence "lime-juicer" or "limey," derogatory term for British person, sailor or ship.*

8. *Ostentation, yes, and keeping a down-market label out of sight of the guests, very much so, but also to aerate the wine, let it "breathe" more than it can in the bottle and improve both bouquet and flavour. Fanatics say decanting even improves a fine malt whisky.*

9. *A kind of mull made with port, sugar and hot water. Attributed to Col. Franctics Negus in the reign of Queen Anne.*

10. *Stephen Potter, founder of Winesmanship.*

POUSSE-CAFÉ III

1. *Bacchus, Dionysus. Strictly, "Bacchus" began life as another name of Dionysus. Dionysus was one of those gods that periodically die and come to life again. Could this be a symbolic reference to the hangover?*

2. *A solution of honey in water. Mead was popular at the court of Attila the Hun about AD 450 and centuries earlier.*

3. *A spiced or medicated mead, said to be good with curries. Not I think commercially made nowadays, but popular with amateurs.*

4. *Oak, which is strong but porous and "gives" the liquor something. This is not to say much, perhaps, there being several hundred different species of oak.*

5. (a) *6000 BC, round the Caspian Sea*
  (b) *1000 BC*
  (c) *500 BC*
  (d) *AD 100.*

6. *One vine to one bottle is the rough rule.*

7. *Removing the liquid from the solid matter left after fermentation. Nothing to do with racking brains or tenants, but from a Provençal word meaning "dregs."*

8. *False, really. If the bottle is there at all it should be on top of or beside the refrigerator, waiting to be drunk on the rocks. Chilling the bottle locks up the sparkle. (Imparted to me years ago by the head of Perrier.)*

9. *Only (d) is a drink, the colloquial name of akvavit (from a word meaning a "mouthful").*
  (a) is the Canadian jay,
  (b) are rolled gingerbread wafers, as you know,
  (c) are collectively a feature of Scottish musical style, a short accented note followed by a longer unaccented one,
  (e) is a wheel in a cotton-gin (see Pousse-Café 1, a 4).

10. *G. K. Chesterton.*

ALCOHOL AND YOUR INTERIOR
1. *A dodgy question. Alcohol draws the blood to the skin, giving a "glow" but accelerating bodily loss of heat, so overall it cools you. Anyway, avoid serious drinking before going out into the cold. Have a couple when you come back in.*

2. *(a) None. For a proof of the contrary, try spending a whole evening on vintage port.*

(b) None, but see a 4.

3. *Speed—a short sharp alcoholic shock is very drunk-making. Unfamiliar drinks—the body learns to tolerate ones it knows. Then vague things like your mood, state of health, etc.*

4. *All sweet drinks are bad. (People will usually have drunk them with a pudding or after a large meal, anyway having mixed their drinks earlier by switching from gin to sherry to table wine (say) and going on doing so with whisky or beer. Hence the (b) superstition above.) Also smoking, bad ventilation, exertion such as dancing, fatigue from staying up late, rich food.*

5. *No, not at all. Alcohol "depresses," reduces activity of, the nervous system, i.e. is a sedative, a relaxant. Nothing to do with psychological depression.*

6. *True. Some heavy drinkers eat little or no protein, thus starving the liver. You can get the same result by drinking no alcohol but eating nothing but boiled sweets, say.*

7. *False. The affliction is mainly hereditary. Gin notoriously relieves it (see Gin, a 5).*

8. *A glass of milk or tablespoon of olive oil will delay absorption and effectively slow your intake.*

9. *(a) Rest, a warm bath, fresh air, a mild alkaline like Vichy water, bread and honey (to raise blood sugar).*

(b) *Fruit-juice especially if chilled, a cold shower, coffee, a hair of the dog, anything like a Prairie Oyster (brandy, tabasco, raw egg-yolk), any rich, greasy or spicy food, aspirin (hard on the stomach).*

10. *From an emphatic form of "total" current at the time (1830s) of the first such movement. A teetotal abstainer was pledged to take no alcohol at all, not merely to eschew spirits.*

Solution to question on page 257: You will find the intruder at the foot of the answers to q 9 (page 256). No Sennacherib. He was King of Assyria in the seventh century BC and is mentioned in the Bible and a poem by Byron, but never had a bottle named after him.

INDEX